THE PSYCHOLOGY OF NATIONS

First published 1919
This edition published by Lector House in 2024

ISBN: 978-93-6138-956-6

Lector House LLP
Registered Office: H. No. 96, Block C, Tomar Colony,
Burari, Delhi – 110084, India
info@lectorhouse.com
www.lectorhouse.com

THE PSYCHOLOGY OF NATIONS

GEORGE EVERETT PARTRIDGE

2024

LECTOR HOUSE LLP

THE PSYCHOLOGY OF NATIONS

A CONTRIBUTION TO THE PHILOSOPHY OF HISTORY

BY

G.E. PARTRIDGE

PREFACE

This book contains two closely related studies of the consciousness of nations. It has been written during the closing months of the war and in the days that have followed, and is completed while the Peace Conference is still in session, holding in the balance, as many believe, the fate of many hopes, and perhaps the whole future of the world. We see focussed there in Paris all the motives that have ever entered into human history and all the ideals that have influenced human affairs. The question must have arisen in all minds in, some form as to what the place of these motives and ideals and dramatic moments is in the progress of the world. Is the world governed after all by the laws of nature in all its progress? Do ideals and motives govern the world, but only as these ideals and motives are themselves produced according to biological or psychological principles? Or, again, does progress depend upon historical moments, upon conscious purposes which may divert the course of nature and in a real sense create the future? It is with the whole problem of history that we are confronted in these practical hours. At heart our problem is that of the place of man in nature as a conscious factor of progress. This is a problem, finally, of the philosophy of history, but it is rather in a more concrete way and upon a different level that it is to be considered here,—and somewhat incidentally to other more specific questions. But this is the problem that is always before us, and the one to which this study aims to make some contribution, however small.

The first part of the book is a study of the motives of war. It is an analysis of the motives of war in the light of the general principles of the development of society. We wish to see what the causes of past wars have been, but we wish also to know what these motives are as they may exist as forces in the present state of society. In such a study, practical questions can never be far away. We can no longer study war as an abstract psychological problem, since war has brought us to a horrifying and humiliating situation. We have discovered that our modern world, with all its boasted morality and civilization, is actuated, at least in its relations among nations, by very unsocial motives. We live in a world in which nations thus far have been for the most part dominated by a theory of States as absolutely sovereign and independent of one another. Now it becomes evident that a logical consequence of that theory of States is absolute war. A prospect of a future of absolute war in a world in which industrial advances have placed in the hands of men such terrible forces of destruction, an absolute warfare that can now be carried into the air and under the sea is what makes any investigation of the motives of war now a very practical problem.

If the urgency of our situation drives us to such studies and makes us hasten to apply even an immature sociology and psychology, it ought not to prejudice our minds and make us, for example, fall into the error of wanting peace at any price—an ideal which, as a practical national philosophy, might be even worse than a spirit of militarism. What we need to know, finally, in order to avoid these errors which at least we may imagine, is what, in the most fundamental way, progress may be conceived to be. If we could discover that, and set our minds to the task of making the social life progressive, we might be willing to let wars take care of themselves, so to speak, without any radical philosophy of good and evil. We ought at least to examine war fairly, and to see what, in the waging of war, man has really desired. A study of war ought to help us to decide whether we must accept our future, with its possibility of wars, as a kind of fate, or whether we must now begin, with a new idea of conscious evolution, to apply our science and our philosophy and our practical wisdom seriously for the first time to the work of creating history, and no longer be content merely to live it.

As to the details of the study of war—we first of all consider the origin and the biological aspects of war; then war as related to the development, in the social life and in the life of the individual, of the motive of power. The instincts that are most concerned in the development of this motive of power are then considered, and also the relations of war to the æsthetic impulses and to art. Nationalism, national honor and patriotism are studied as causes of war. The various "causes" that are brought forward as the principles fought for are examined; also the philosophical influences, the moral and religious motives and the institutional factors among the motives of war. Finally the economic and political motives and the historical causes are considered. The conclusion is reached that the motive of power, as the fundamental principle of behavior at the higher levels, is the principle of war, but that in so general a form it goes but a little way toward being an explanation of war. We find the real causes of war by tracing out the development of this motive of power as it appears in what we call the "intoxication impulse," and in the idea of national honor and in the political motives of war. It is in these aspects of national life that we find the motives of war as they may be considered as a practical problem. But we find no separate causes, and we do not find a chain of causes that might be broken somewhere and thus war be once for all eliminated. Wars are products of the whole character of nations, so to speak, and it is national character that must be considered in any practical study of war. It is by the development of the character of nations in a natural process, or by the education of national character, that war will be made to give way to perpetual peace, if such a state ever comes, rather than by a political readjustment or by legal enactments, however necessary as beginnings or makeshifts these legal and political changes may be.

The second part of the book is a study of our present situation as an educational problem, in which we have for the first time a problem of educating national consciousness as a whole, or the individuals of a nation with reference to a world-consciousness. The study has reference especially to the conditions in our own country, but it also has general significance. The war has brought many changes, and in every phase of life we see new problems. These may seem at the moment to be separate and detached conditions which must be dealt with, each by itself, but this is not so; they are all aspects of fundamental changes and new conditions, the main feature of which is the new world-consciousness of which we speak. Whatever one's occupation, one cannot remain unaffected by these changes, or escape entirely the stress that the need of adjustment to new ideas and new conditions compels. What we may think about the future—about what can be done and what ought to be done, is in part, and perhaps largely, a matter of temperament. At least we see men, presumably having access to the same facts, drawing from them very different conclusions. Some are keyed to high expectations; they look for revolutions, mutations, a new era in politics and everywhere in the social life. For them, after the war, the world is to be a new world. Fate will make a new deal. Others appear to believe that after the flurry is over we shall settle down to something very much like the old order. These are conservative people, who neither desire nor expect great changes. Others take a more moderate course. While improvement is their great word, they are inclined to believe that the new order will grow step by step out of the old, and that good will come out of the evil only in so far as we strive to make it. We shall advance along the old lines of progress, but faster, perhaps, and with life attuned to a higher note.

The writer of this book must confess that he belongs in a general way to the third species of these prophets. There is a natural order of progress, but the good must, we may suppose, also be worked for step by step. The war will have placed in our hands no golden gift of a new society; both the ways and the direction of progress must be sought and determined by ideals. The point of view in regard to progress, at least as a working hypothesis, becomes an educational one, in a broad sense. Our future we must make. We shall not make it by politics. The institutions with which politics deals are dangerous cards to play. There is too much convention clinging to them, and they are too closely related to all the supports of the social order. The industrial system, the laws, the institutions of property and rights, the form of government, we change at our own risk. Naturally many radical minds look to the abrupt alteration of these fundamental institutions for the cure of existing evils, and others look there furtively for the signs of coming revolution, and the destruction of all we have gained thus far by civilization. But at a different level, where life is more plastic—in the lives of the young, and in the vast unshaped forms of the common life everywhere, all this is different. We do not expect abrupt changes here nor quick and visible results. Experimentation is still possible and comparatively safe. There is no one institution of this common and unformed life, not even the school itself, that supports the existing structures, so that if we move it in the wrong way, everything else will fall. When we see we are wrong, there is still time to correct our mistakes.

Our task, then, is to see what the forces are that have brought us to where we stand now, and to what influences they are to be subjected, if they are to carry us onward and upward in our course. Precisely what the changes in government or anywhere in the social order should be is not the chief interest, from this point of view. The details of the constitution of an international league, the practical adjustments to be made in the fields of labor, and in the commerce of nations, belong to a different order of problems. We wish rather to see what the main currents of life, especially in our own national life, are, and what in the most general way we are to think and do, if the present generation is to make the most of its opportunities as a factor in the work of conscious evolution.

The bibliography shows the main sources of the facts and the theories that have been drawn upon in writing the book. Some of the chapters have been read in a little different form as lectures before President G. Stanley Hall's seminar at Clark University. More or less of repetition, made necessary in order to make these papers, which were read at considerable intervals, independent of one another, has been allowed to remain. Perhaps in the printed form this reiteration will help to emphasize the general psychological basis of the study.

CONTENTS

PART I
NATIONAL CONSCIOUSNESS AND THE MOTIVES OF WAR

CHAPTER I

ORIGINS AND BIOLOGICAL CONSIDERATIONS

The simplest possible interpretation of the causes of war that might be offered is that war is a natural relation between original herds or groups of men, inspired by the predatory instinct or by some other instinct of the herd. To explain war, then, one need only refer to this instinct as final, or at most account for the origin and genesis of the instinct in question in the animal world. Some writers express this very view, calling war an expression of an instinct or of several instincts; others find different or more complex beginnings of war.

Nusbaum (86) says that both offense and defense are based upon an *expansion impulse*. Nicolai (79) sees the beginning of war in individual predatory acts, involving violence and the need of defense. Again we find the migratory instinct, the instinct that has led groups of men to move and thus to interfere with one another, regarded as the cause of war, or as an important factor in the causes. Sometimes a purely physiological or growth impulse is invoked, or vaguely the inability of primitive groups to adapt themselves to conditions, or to gain access to the necessities of life. Le Bon (42) speaks of the hunger and the desire that led Germanic forces as ancient hordes to turn themselves loose upon the world.

Leaving aside for the moment the question of the nature of the impulses or instincts which actuated the conduct of men originally and brought them into opposition, as groups, to one another, we do find at least some suggestion of a working hypothesis in these simple explanations of war. Granted the existence of groups formed by the accident of birth and based upon the most primitive protective and economic associations, and assuming the presence of the emotions of anger and fear or any instinct which is expressed as an impulse or habit of the group, we might say that the conditions and factors for the beginning of warfare are all present. When groups have desires that can best and most simply be satisfied by the exertion of force upon other groups, something equivalent to war has begun.

If we take the group (as herd or pack) and the instinct as the original factors or data of society, however, we probably simplify the situation too much. The question arises whether the motives are not more complex, even from the beginning, and whether both the tendencies or impulses by which the group was formed or held together and the motives behind aggressive conduct against other groups have not been produced or developed in the course of social relations, rather than have been brought up from animal life, or at any point introduced as instincts. We notice at least that animals living in groups do not in general become aggressive within the species. Possibly it was by some peculiarity of man's social existence, or his superior endowment of intelligence or some unusual quality of his instincts, perhaps very far back in animal life, that has in the end made him a warlike creature. Man does seem to be a creature of *feelings* rather than of instincts as far back as we find much account of him, and to be characterized rather by the weakness and variability of his instincts than by their definiteness. It is quite likely, too, that man never was at any stage a herd animal; in fact it seems certain that he was not, and that his instincts were formed long before he began to live in large groups at all. So he never acquired the mechanisms either for aggression or defense that some creatures have. Apparently he inherited neither the physical powers nor the warlike spirit nor the aggressive and predatory instincts that would have been necessary to make of him a natural fighting animal; but rather, perhaps, he has acquired his warlike habits, so to speak, since arriving at man's estate. Endowed with certain tendencies which express themselves with considerable variability in the processes by which the functions of sex and nutrition are carried out, man never acquired the definiteness of character and conduct that some animals have. He learned more from animals, it may be, than he inherited from them, and it is quite likely that far back in his animal ancestry he had greater flexibility or adaptability than other animals. The aggressive instinct, the herd instinct, the predatory instinct, the social instinct, the migratory instinct, may never have been carried very far in the stock from which man came. All this, however, at this point is only a suggestion of two somewhat divergent points of view in regarding the primitive activities of man from which his long history of war-making has taken rise.

The view is widely held and continually referred to by many writers on war and politics, that the most fundamental of all causes of war, or the most general principle of it, is the principle of selection—that war is a natural struggle between groups, especially between races, the fittest in this struggle tending to survive. This view needs to be examined sharply, as indeed it has been by several writers, in connection with the present war. This biological theory or apology of war appears in several forms, as applied to-day. They say that racial stocks contend with one another for existence, and with this goes the belief that nations fight for life, and that defeat in war tends towards the extermination of nations. The Germans, we often hear, were fighting for national existence, and the issue was to be a judgment upon the fitness of their race to survive. This view is very often expressed. O'Ryan and Anderson (5), military writers, for example, say that the same aggressive motives prevail as always in warfare: nations struggle for survival, and this struggle for survival must now and again break out into war. Powers (75) says that nations seldom fight for anything less than existence. Again (15) we read that conflicts have their roots in history, in the lives of peoples, and the sounder, and better, emerge as victors. There is a selective process on the part of nature that applies to nations; they say that especially increase of population forces upon groups an endless conflict, so that absolute hostility is a law of nature in the world.

These views contain at least two very doubtful assumptions. One is that nations do actually fight for existence,—that warfare is thus selective to the point of eliminating races. The other is that in warlike conflicts the victors are the superior peoples, the better fitted for survival. Confusion arises and the discussion is complicated by the fact that conflicts of men as groups of individuals within the same species are somewhat anomalous among biological forms of struggle. Commonly, struggle takes place among individuals, organisms having definite characteristics and but slightly variable each from its own kind contending with one another, by direct competition or through adaptation, in the first case individuals striving to obtain actually the same objects. Or, again, species having the same relations to one another that individuals have, contend in a similar manner.

Primitive groups of men, however, are not so definite; they are not biological entities in any such sense as individuals and species are. They are not definitely brought into conflict with one another, in general, as contending for the same objects, and it is difficult to see how, in the beginning, at least, economic pressure has been a factor at all in their relations. Whatever may have been the motive that for the most part was at work in primitive warfare, it is not at all evident that *superior* groups had any survival value. The groups that contended with one another presumably differed most conspicuously in the size of the group, and this was determined largely by chance conditions. Other differences must have been quite subordinate to this, and have had little selective value. The conclusion is that the struggle of these groups with one another is not essentially a *biological* phenomenon.

The fact is that peace rather than war, taking the history of the human race as a whole, is the condition in which selection of the fittest is most active, for it is the power of adaptation to the conditions of stable life, which are fairly uniform for different groups over wide areas, that tests vitality and survival values, so far as these values are biological. It may be claimed that war is very often, if not generally, a means of interrupting favorable selective processes, the unfit tending to prevail temporarily by force of numbers, or even because of qualities that antagonize biological progress. Viewing war in its later aspects, we can see that it is often when nations are failing in natural competition that they resort to the expedient of war to compensate for this loss, although they do not usually succeed thereby in improving their economic condition as they hope, or increase their chance of survival, or even demonstrate their survival value. It is notorious that nations that conquer tend to spend their vitality in conquest and introduce various factors of deterioration into their lives. The inference is that a much more complex relation exists among groups than the biological hypothesis allows. Survival value indeed, as applied to men in groups, is not a very clear concept. There may be several different criteria of survival value, not comparable in any quantitative way among themselves.

Scheler (77) says that we cannot account for war as a purely biological phenomenon. Its roots lie deep in organic life, but there is no direct development or exclusive development from animal behavior to human. War is peculiarly human. That, in a way, may be accepted as the truth. Warfare as we know it among human groups, as conflict within the species is due in some way to, or is made possible by, the secondary differentiations within species which give to groups, so to speak, a pseudo-specific character. And these differences depend largely upon the conditions that enter into the formation of groups,—upon desires, impulses and needs arising in the social life rather than in instinct as such. These characteristic differences are not variations having selective value, but are traits that merely differentiate the groups as *historical entities*. These secondary variations have not resulted in the elimination of those having inferior qualities, but have shared the fortunes of the groups that possessed them,—the fortunes both of war and of peace. *War, from this point of view, belongs to history rather than to biology.* It belongs to the realm of the particular rather than to the general in human life. War has favored the survival of this or that group in a particular place, but has probably not been instrumental in producing any particular type of character in the world, either physical or mental.

Very early in the history of mankind, in fact as far back as we can trace history, we find these psychic differentiations, as factors in the production of war. There are significant extensions and also restrictions of the consciousness of kind pertaining to the life of man, as distinguished from animals. Animals have not sufficient intelligence to establish such perfect group identities as man does, and they lack the affective motives for carrying on hostilities among groups. They remain more clearly subjected to the simple laws of biological selection, and are guided by instincts which do not impel them to act aggressively as groups toward their own kind. Man proceeds almost from the beginning to antagonize these laws, so that it is very likely that the best, in the biological sense, has always had some disadvantage, in human life, and may still have. The real value that has thus been conserved by this human mode of life consists in preserving a relatively large number of secondary types or individual groups, rather than in insuring the predominance of any one biologically superior type. *Man's work in the world is to make history.* Even though war were a means of making a biologically superior type of man prevail we should not be justified in saying that it is thus vindicated as a method of selection.

Many writers whom we do not need to review in great detail have contributed to the objections to the biological principle as an explanation of war. Trotter (82) examines the doctrine that war is a biological necessity, and says that there is no parallel in biology for progress being accomplished as a result of a racial impoverishment so extreme as is caused by war, that among gregarious animals other than man direct conflict between major groups such as can lead to the suppression of the less powerful is an inconspicuous phenomenon, and that there is very little fighting within species, for species have usually been too busy fighting their external enemies. Mitchell (10) says that war is not an aspect of the natural struggle for existence, among individuals; that there is nothing in Darwinism that explains or justifies wars; that the argument from race is worthless since there are no pure races. M'Cabe (76) maintains that war is not a struggle between inferior and superior national types. Dide (20) also discusses the question of differences of race as causes of war, and the use that has been made of this dogma. Chapman (39) says that no race question is involved in the present war as has been supposed. There is no conflict of economic forces, no nations compelled to seek expansion.

Precisely how warfare originated (assuming that it arose in one way) we shall probably never know, since we cannot now reconstruct the actual history of man.

We think of men as living at first in groups containing a few individuals, and presumably for a long time these small and isolated groups of men prevailed as the type of human society. We can already detect the elements of conflict in these groups, but whether warfare in the sense of deadly conflict originated there we cannot know; or whether it was only in the experience of men as large migrating hordes which had been formed by the amalgamation of smaller groups under the influence of hunger or climatic change, that warfare in any real sense came into the world. We do not know to what extent the small groups of men we find in conditions of savagery now represent primitive conditions. Fortunately, however, some of these problems of origin are of but little practical importance and their interest is chiefly antiquarian or historical.

The assumption that in the behavior of original groups of men war arose as a natural result of the life of the group seems to be an allowable hypothesis. Whether warlike conduct came by some modification of the habits brought up from animal life as instinctive reactions, or whether man invented warfare from some strong motive peculiar to human life, and produced it intelligently, so to speak, under stress of circumstances may have to remain an open question so far as conclusive evidence is concerned. What we lack is a knowledge of the type and form of the instincts of man in his first stages, and the degree and kind of intelligence he had. But the reconstructed pre-human history of man so far as we can make it seems to show, as we have already suggested, that early man could have had no definite herd instincts or pack instincts such as some of the animals have, that his habits were plastic and guided by intelligence rather than by impulse. His social life, his predaceous habits, the habit of killing large game, his warfare must have been a gradual acquisition, and from the beginning have been very different as regards motive and development from animal behavior which judged externally may seem to be like it in character and to have the same ends.

There are already inherent in any group of human individuals that fits into such knowledge of man past and present as we have, all the necessary motives of warfare in some form. There are the reactions of anger made to any threat or injury, fear, the predaceous impulse and habit, originating in hunger, the motives arising in sexual rivalry. These motives are the source of behavior toward both members of the group and outsiders. There is no absolute distinction between these objects. It is of the nature of man to be both aggressive and social. One instinct or motive did not come from the other, since there are emotions and desires at every stage that tend, some of them to unite and some to disrupt, the group. The sense of difference of kind and the fear of the strange on the one hand, and the effect of propinquity and practical necessity in the conduct in regard to the familiar on the other make the reactions different in degree in the two spheres but not different in kind. There is no aggressive instinct or war motive that is directed exclusively toward the outsider. Certain tendencies toward violence and strife, modified and controlled within the group, become unrestrained when directed toward the stranger. Among these motives are those of sexual rivalry, fear, anger, desire, and the play motive as an expression of any instinctive habits of aggression that may have been phyletically established.

Since every individual creature has his needs that can be satisfied only by preying in some way upon other animals of his own species or others, the motives for strife are original in organic life. Every animal lives in a world of which he is suspicious, and rightly so. He is suspicious toward the members of his own kind and group, and toward all strangers he shows watchfulness and fear. There are two motives, therefore, of a highly practical nature that contribute to a general state of unfriendliness in animal life. Both the motives of conflict within the group, the habit of aggression and its complement, fear, and the jealousy and display motive (the display itself probably having originated as a show of ferocity on the part of males) must have been transferred to relations between groups as a natural result of the proximity of groups to one another, although this process is not quite so simple as this would imply, since in part the outside groups are produced by these very same antagonistic motives in the group, for example the driving out of young males because of sexual jealousy. The presence of other groups must have excited all the motives of warfare at a very early stage, and this contrast had the effect of stimulating the social feeling of the group and developing control of impulses on the part of individuals within the group toward one another. So the motives of combat, as shown within the group and toward outsiders, developed, so to speak, by a dialectic process.

Fear and the predatory impulse, the sexual and display motive, play or the hunting activity as a pleasure for its own sake, with a desire perhaps to practice deception and to exercise intelligence, presumably introduced some kind and degree of definite warfare among primitive groups of men at a very early stage of human life, although of course such a conclusion can be only speculative. Increasing intelligence, the power of discriminating and of reacting to secondary likenesses and differences, and especially the recognition of the nature of death, and the advantages of killing rather than merely overcoming an enemy, the discovery of the use of weapons, introduced warfare into the world. Warfare is, then, not simply the negation of some original principle of mutual aid, nor yet an expression of instinctive aggressiveness or cruelty, but it is a product of original endowment, of conditions of life, and of intelligence all together. It is practical, but at no stage can it be said to be *wholly* practical. Changes must have taken place in warfare as in other social reactions as men passed through a number of stages from primitive wandering or a relatively unstable life to a stable life, but the motives of conflict cannot have been added to in any essential way. Through all the course of history all the motives that originally made individuals of a group or the groups as wholes antagonistic have remained, although the mental processes have become generalized, fused and transformed. If Gumplowicz is right we can still detect in any great society to-day all the primitive individual and group animosities, tempered down and held in check by laws and customs, but still existent and by no means overcome and made innocuous.

These motives of warfare might best be traced out in four more or less definite principles of conduct, or four purposes of war that appear throughout primitive life. These are: 1) thievery, including wife capture; 2) the fear motive; 3) cannibalism; 4) the display motive, with the desire to intimidate and to display power (more or less closely associated with the play motive, the love of hunting, gaming and the dramatic motive).

Cannibalism, of course, is a special expression of the predatory motive in general, or it is mainly that. Cannibalism was certainly established early in primitive life, at least early enough to antedate all religion, and although its origin and history are shrouded in mystery, the motive was quite certainly practical. Evidently it was widespread if not universal. Whether it was introduced as a result of a failure of animal food, as some think, or has a still more simple explanation as a part of the original impulse which led men at a certain stage of their development to become hunters, cannot be determined. We know, however, that the alien human being was to some extent included under the same concepts as the animal enemy and prey, and presumably some of the strongest motives that led men to attack animals also included man as an object, since the alien group was regarded as in some degree different in kind from the in-group. It may have been in the great migrations when all the aggressive motives were increased that cannibalism became fixed as a habit.

Cannibalism may well have been the primitive motive of warfare as serious deadly combat, but all predatory habits must have contributed to establishing a more or less habitual state of warfare among all groups of men. The predatory raid, with the reaction of defense, when carried on as a group activity in any form, is in fact war, so far as attack and defense were serious and deadly, and intelligence and weapons were sufficiently developed to make man a dangerous opponent. This predatory motive, of course, extended to all desired objects, and these objects must have included all objects that could most simply be acquired by stealing. They included food, women, and all other possessions. The custom of driving out young males from the group, by the jealousy of the old males, and of preventing males from obtaining females within the group must have been one of the earliest and one of the strongest incentives to predatory warfare. At first all property of the group, for so long as groups were wandering, was to some extent common, and attack and defense must have been common. The objects of predatory raids which produced group combat must have changed with the social life. When habitation became fixed and property therefore more individual, probably the predatory impulse itself became relatively a less important factor in combat.

Two motives grow out of the practical motives of combat, which we may assume to have been the original motives. These are both emotional rather than instinctive. Fear and anger, that is to say, become more or less detached motives for attack. Fear is increased with the increase of intelligence up to a certain point at least—with the increase of the capacity for understanding danger, and of the powers of man to become dangerous. All the experience of combat engenders anger and hatred, and these moods of hatred toward enemies are cumulative, absorb all the detached motives and feelings of antagonism between groups, preserve and give continuity to the memories of conflict, and so produce among groups the fear and hate motive. The feeling of fear arouses the motive of aggression, and the feeling of anger; and these in turn generate more fear, until both the moods of anger and fear and a perpetual state of animosity and warfare are induced among contending groups. Thus out of primitive motives of combat the feud as a more generalized and psychical antagonism is produced, and these states are possible because of the powers of generalization in man which extend to the emotions and make possible the formation of deep moods.

In another direction, also, the practical motives tend to be superseded by more abstract and more subjective motives. Both in the fear and anger reactions and in the motive that originates in the sexual impulse—display of males, and combat with reference to females—consciousness of prowess for its own sake, and the display of it in order to intimidate the enemy, arise. Into this motive of war there enter all the antagonisms that come from self-consciousness, the whole force of the diathesis of developing sexuality, with its jealousy and cruelty, and tendencies to perversion. The force of this motive of prowess must at some period of development have become very great. It extends out into a love of combat for its own sake, reënforces other motives, and issues in the more abstract motives of honor and power that we see playing such a great part in modern warfare.

These primitive motives of war are not merely numerous. They fuse, reënforce one another, and almost from the beginning, we must suppose, create complex states of consciousness, and form moods. War very early, we say, must contain all the motives that ever enter into it. The predatory impulse, the love of deception, of conquest, the love of combat for its own sake, the hunting impulse, the motive of power, of fear and anger, the impulse of display and the more primitive sexual motives, the motives of courage and jealousy, even a beginning of the aesthetic motive, are all there. They become the warlike mood or produce war, in the sense in which we now understand it, only when the intelligence gives to the relations between groups definite intentions and directions, and out of the many impulses that lead to combat, a distinctive motive and mood are derived. So we may say with all certainty that the making of war is not a mere perpetuation of some alleged instinct of murder, surreptitiously retained by man in his rise from an animal state, but it is quite as much a product of his whole social nature. It becomes established as life grows more complex, as specific desires increase in number. Man is not, as thus seen in these genetic views of him, a self-tamed animal. He has not arrived at a precarious and unstable social condition out of a primitive individualism which is the essence of his warlike nature. On the other hand, he has not degenerated from some ideal pacific state. Ages ago he was already divinely human, and possessed those capacities both for coöperation and antagonism out of which war is created.

CHAPTER II

UNCONSCIOUS MOTIVES, THE REVERSION THEORIES OF WAR, AND THE INTOXICATION MOTIVE

There are several interesting theories of the causes of war, now in the field, most of them inspired by our recent great conflict, all of which (but no one perhaps completely or quite justly) may be described as based upon the view that war is an outbreak of, or reversion to, instincts and modes of activity which as primitive tendencies remain in the individual or in the social life and which, from time to time, with or without social cause, may break loose, so to speak, and hurl man back into savagery. These theories of war show us, in some cases, human character in the form of double personality, or liken civilization to a thin and insecure incrustation upon the surface of life, beneath which all that is animal-like and barbaric still remains smoldering. Some of these theories we need to review briefly here.

Bertrand Russell, in answer to the question, "Why do men fight?" which is the title of his book dealing with the causes of war, says, in substance, that men fight because they are controlled by instinct (and also by authority), rather than by reason. Men will cease fighting when reason controls instinct, and men think for themselves rather than allow their thinking to be done for them. This view does not explicitly state that war is a reversion, for man may be at no point better or more advanced than a creature of instinct, but it lays the blame for war upon the original nature of man. Man has instincts which presumably he has brought with him from his pre-human stage, and some of these instincts are, on their motor side, the reactions of fighting.

Le Bon (42) speaks of a conscious and an unconscious will in nations, and says that the motives behind great national movements may be beneath all conscious intentions, and may anticipate them. The Englishman in particular lives, in a sense, a divided life, since there is a manifest inconsistency between what he really is and what he thinks. What these instincts are, Le Bon does not specify; presumably they may be either better or worse than the conscious motives.

Trotter (82) and also Murray (90) consider war from a biological standpoint, regarding it as a herd phenomenon. Trotter's view, especially his interpretation of Germany, which we are not to consider here, is original and important. War is a result of the action of a *herd instinct*, a specific instinct which is peculiar in one respect, in that it acts upon other instincts but has no definite motor reactions of its own. War is the result of the action of the herd instinct in man upon the old instinct of aggression. At least aggressive war is. Men in all their social relations show the play of these instincts; in war it is the old aggressive instinct, the old passion of the pack, that dominates them; and it is the ancestral herd-fears that overcome them in their panics. It is the herd instinct that makes men in groups so highly sensitive to the leader, whose relations to the herd or pack are always dependent upon their recognizing him as one of the group; that is, as acting in accordance with the desires of the herd.

It is by the union of the herd, Murray says, or through the herd instinct, that suppressed unconscious impulses are given an opportunity to operate; when the human herd is excited by any external stimulus, the old types of reaction are brought into play. Curiously, in such times, leadership may be assumed by eccentric and even abnormal members of the group—by those who are governed by perverted instincts; by men who are touched with the mania of suspicion, or who even suffer from homicidal mania.

The essential point of these biological views is that, when the human herd is subjected to any influences that tend to arouse the herd instinct—that is, to unite the herd in any common emotion or action, the old instinctive forms of response are likely to be brought to the front. Whatever the stimulus, the tendency is for the herd to fixate its attention upon some external object, which at once is reacted to with deep emotion. Plainly, if this be true, if herd instinct does throw human society from time to time and from various causes into attitudes of defense and offense with the appropriate emotional reactions, and if in such times leaders are likely to appear, having exaggerated instinctive tendencies, there is always close at hand and ready a mechanism by which war can be produced, war being precisely of the type of mass action, under strong emotion, of a group closely united under spectacular leadership, with attention cramped upon some external object hated or feared.

Nicolai (79), who believes strongly that war is wholly useless, compares it to the play we turn to when the actions performed in the play are no longer in themselves practical. War is a great debauch, perhaps now the last the race will experience. War is like wine: in it nations renew their youth. It is not the war itself, but the mood it produces that we crave, and this mood is longed for because in it old and sacred feelings of patriotism are aroused, and these feelings are themselves survivals, something romantic, archaic, no longer needed in the present stage of social life.

Novicow (83) says something very similar to this. War is a survival, like the classical languages, for example. Men begin to find beauty and glory in these things only after the activities they represent are useless. The principle of their survival is nothing more or less than that of habit. It is habit that keeps war alive; wars are a concession to our forebears, a following in the footsteps of a dead past.

We are presenting these views in a somewhat loose and illogical order, but let us look at still a few more of them. Patrick thinks of war as precisely a plunge into the primeval. War is a reaction, a regression, but still it is something more than a mere slipping of the machinery of life. It is *craved;* and it is craved because it offers relief from the tension of modern life. It is not quite clear whether it is because we are tired and want rest for our over-worked functions, or are merely dull and need renewed life, but in any case, when the desire has accumulated enough, back we fall into the primeval. Then all the tensions and inhibitions of civilized society disappear. Society, relieved of its cross-tensions, is resolved and organized into an harmonious and freely acting whole, seeking a definite object. Life is simplified, and becomes again primitive. Old and vigorous movements take the place of the cramped thinking of our civilized life. All that keeps us modern and evolved is relaxed.

Naturally the Freudians have their own explanation of war in terms of subconscious wishes, repressed feelings and instincts. Freud (78) himself says that war is a recrudescence (and a mastery over us) of a more primitive life than our own. The child and the primitive man, as we have long known them in the Freudian theories, live still in us and are indestructible. We have supposed ourselves to have overcome these primitive impulses, but we are far from being so civilized as we thought. The evil impulses, as we call them, which we supposed had at least been transformed are changed only in the sense that they have been influenced by the erotic motive, or have been repressed by an outer restraint, an educational factor, the demands of what we call civilized environment. But let us not deceive ourselves; the old impulses are still alive; the number of people who have been transformed by civilization is less than we supposed. All society is at heart barbaric. Judged by our unconscious wishes, we are a band of murderers, for the primitive wish is to kill all who oppose our self-interests, and war is precisely a reversion to the method of free expression of our desires in action. Society and the authority of government have suppressed these primitive reactions in the individual, but instead of eliminating them altogether from human nature (which, of course, no legislation can do in any case), government and society as a whole have appropriated all these primitive actions to their own use.

Jones (37), the Freudian, distinguishes two quite different groups of causes of war: the conscious causes, all expressed in the feeling of patriotism; and the unconscious causes, which grow out of the desire to release certain original passions—the passions of cruelty, destruction, loot and lust.

The central thought of all these views, it is plain, is that war belongs to the past. It is a return to something that, in a significant sense, is the natural man—is his instinctive and unguarded self. It is also plainly implied in these views, here and there, that modern man, by thus lapsing into war, is renewing his stock of primitive nature. The modern man is in unstable equilibrium, and whatever upsets that equilibrium sends him back through the ages. MacCurdy (37), having Jones and Freud in mind, protests against these views to this extent: he says that the present state of man, rather than the past, is the natural state, and that at least in reverting to the primitive state man becomes unnatural.

The question upon which our discussion of this aspect of war is going to hinge is whether, or in what sense, the activities and the feelings aroused in war are reversions. Wars, beyond a doubt, do involve to a greater extent than peaceful life certain instinctive reactions. Wars are so impulsive and so persistent that we must suppose very deep motives to be engaged in war; and the fact that in all wars, and on both sides of every war, the feelings and the reactions are fundamentally the same, indicates that war is something less differentiated than the peaceful life. But that war can be explained in terms of instinct as such, or that war can be disposed of as a mere recrudescence of old impulses and types of conduct buried beneath civilization, is very much to be doubted. War, in the first place, in its moods and passions, appears to be too complex, too synthetic a process to be quite what this view would imply. It is too intimately related to everything that occurs and exists in present day society. It means too much, concretely and with reference to objects specifically desired for the future. War is related to the past, but to a great extent, it may be, wars represent and contain the present and look toward the future. The distinctions and differences in the interpretation of war thus implied, and the conflicting understanding of facts about society and individual life cannot be very clear at this point, but that there are involved fundamental problems of psychology, and perhaps divergent ways of thinking of history and society, and of such principles of philosophy at least as are implicated in æsthetics, and finally of the practical questions that are of most interest in these fields to-day, may begin to be evident.

There is one aspect of war, or one question about war, that seems to suggest that its problems are more subtle and less simple than the instinct-theories imply. War has been, and still is, the great story of the world, the center of all that is dramatic and heroic in life. Its mood—and that is the essential thing in it, whatever else war may have been, and in spite of all its horrors—is *ecstatic*. War produces, or is produced by, states of mind that affiliate it with all the other ecstasies—of love, religion, intoxication, art. We may well doubt whether any explanation of war can ever be satisfactory that does not take this quality of it fully into account. One may say, of course, that war is ecstatic just because it does satisfy instincts, that the satisfaction of all instincts is pleasant, or that pleasure *is* the satisfaction of instincts. But there is more in the problem than that. Love, the source of the other great romance of the world, is not exhausted by calling it a gratification of the sexual instinct, or a primitive tendency of all organic life. It is at the other end of the process of development of it, so to speak, its place as a present motive in life, that it is most significant, and it is by no means explained by calling it a product of sexuality.

So with war. Made out of instincts, it may be, but it is not explained as the sum of instinctive reactions. *That, at least, is our thesis.* It is the fact that war is a great ecstasy of the social life, that it holds a high place in art, that history—our selective way of reacting upon human experience—is in a large measure the story of war, that its representations in dramatic forms are almost endless in variety; it is such facts that give us our clew to the nature of the problems of war, and also to the practical questions of its future.

Hirschfeld (98), in a short study of war, has enumerated and briefly described some of the forms in which the ecstasy of war appears, or some of the ecstasies that appear in war. He speaks of the ecstasy of heroism, and the ecstatic sense that accompanies the taking part in great events, the consciousness of making history. On a little lower plane there is the excitement of adventure and of travel that gives allurement to the idea of war in the mind of the soldier, and which also glorifies the soldier; the sensation hunger; the *cupidus rerum novarum*; the ecstasies of nature and freedom, suggested by the very term "in the field." Add to these the ecstasies of battle and of victory, the *Kampfsrausch* and the *Siegestrunkenheit*, and the mood of war in which acts unlawful for the individual become not only lawful but highly honorable when done collectively. There is also in the mood of war the social intoxication, the feeling on the part of the individual of being a part of a body and the sense of being lost in a greater whole. The lusts of conquest, and of looting, and of combat, all contribute to this spirit of war. And finally, summing up all the other ecstasies, the strong inner movement of the soul expressing itself in strong external movements, and in the sense of living and dying in the midst of vivid and real life.

Hirschfeld's analysis of the ecstasy of war discloses deep and powerful motives in the individual mind and the social life. We can find this ecstasy everywhere in the history of war, sometimes as a national exaltation, sometimes as a more restricted phenomenon. Villard (54), speaking of the first days of the war, says that in Germany then one could see "the psychology of the crowd at its noblest height." The exaltation of a people, whatever its content, or its purpose, is an awe-inspiring spectacle. There can be no greater display of the sources of human power. In this particular time of exaltation we can see in action religious ecstasy, the cult of valor, and the stirring of more fundamental and more primitive feelings. This exaltation has its imaginative side. There is a dream of empire in it. There is an exhibition of the forms of royalty, its display, its color and its dramatic moments. There is the spirit of militarism and of great adventure, the excitement of chance, of throwing all into the hands of fate, the æsthetic and the play motives which are never separated from the practical passions in times of great exaltation.

This mood of war differs, of course, at different times under different circumstances. The French people certainly went into the great war with no such exaltation. We should have to look elsewhere in French history for the ecstatic war spirit, when the French are moved by the motives of glory and prestige, or by the vanity and eroticism which Reuthe thinks are the essential qualities of the spirit of France. But taking history as a whole there is no lack of ecstasy in the spirit of war. We find in this ecstasy exalted social feeling, joy of overcoming the pain of death, the exultation of sacrifice, love of display, feeling of tragedy, the ecstasy of exerting the utmost of power, love of danger, the gambling motive, the love of battle, love of all the dramatic elements of military life. These separate ecstasies, taken all together, make up the exalted mood of war. They represent war in its most significant moments.

In this mood of war instincts are exhibited, but they seem to be in some way transformed, so that the whole has a meaning different from the parts. The mood of war is not a mere effect, a reaction to events. It is a longing—plastic and indefinite it may be—but looking toward the future. It is a craving, not for the release of definite instincts, but is rather a force or a desire which, however misguided the expression of this mood or this energy may be, is the essence of what individuals and society to-day *are*. We may find in this mood, upon superficial examination, mere emotions, but in a final and deeper analysis, we may suppose, its content and its meaning will be found to be specific—purposes which constitute what is deepest and most continuous in the individual and in society, but which at the same time give to this mood its generality of direction and of form.

It is the war-mood, then, that must be explained, if we wish to understand the motives and causes of war. And this war mood, so it appears, is related to all the other great ecstasies—of art, religion, intoxication, love. It is, of course, then, a psychological problem, and one having many radiations and deep roots. The view that we are going to take is that in the mood of war we have to do essentially with what, relying upon previous studies of the principles of art and of the motives that are at work in society that produce the phenomena of intemperance we may call the *intoxication motive*. That this intoxication motive is a plastic force, a mood containing desires and impulses that may be satisfied in a variety of ways, since as a sum of desires it is no longer specific and instinctive, is the main implication of this view. It is this generic quality and compositeness of the purpose of the individual and of the spirit of society that obscures the meaning of history and often makes individual lives so enigmatical, and which also makes these purposes of individuals and nations so persistent, sometimes so terribly forceful and insatiable.

As contrasted with instincts, the motive of intoxication we say, is plastic, and its object—and this is one of its most significant characteristics—is to produce exalted states of consciousness mainly for their own sake. At least this experience of exaltation is the main or central thing sought. It is a tendency to seek exalted states, but at the same time, we should say, specific instincts gain some kind of satisfaction, although not at all necessarily by the performance of the external movements appropriate to them. They may obtain a certain vicarious satisfaction. The mood gives conduct a general direction, it provides a motive and the power, it is the source of interest and of desire, but its objects may be indefinite and variable.

Some general aspects of the moods that we have to consider have already come to light, and these may prove to be valuable clews to a psychological analysis of their content. There is the ecstatic state, and the craving to experience it, the love of excitement, the desire to have a sense of reality, the impulse to seek an abundant life, the love of power and of the feeling of power. These are all related, and at least they have something in common, but it is the last mentioned, the motive of power, that seems to be the most definite and to have the clearest biological meaning and implications. Indeed this motive of power (and we must here again depend upon previous studies of the æsthetic motives and other aspects of ecstasy), appears to be fundamental in art, in religion, and in history. It is a concept that gives us a vantage ground for the interpretation of some of the most significant parts of life. The idea of power and the craving for power as a general motive, but also containing and exploiting specific purposes and desires, runs through all the history of art and religion and also through history itself. Religion is based upon the desire to exert and to feel power, and it is the manifest and indeed the expressly acknowledged purpose of all primitive art, and is concealed and implied in all later art. Art is practical, an effort to realize a sense of power, to become a god (just as in his motive of play the child desires more than anything else to realize himself as a man), to influence people, or objects, or gods, to exert magic somewhere in the world. In the feeling of power which the ecstatic state produces, the belief in the power of art is established, and at the same time deep and hidden impulses are exploited. On the feeling side, and indeed in every way, this ought to explain how art, religion, and all states of intoxication have a common element, if they are not primitively the same.

A psychology of the war moods must undertake to trace the history of the motive of power, considering its beginnings as the desire and sense of satisfaction connected with the performance of definite instinctive acts, and with their physiological results, with the exertion of power and the production of effects upon objects. It is in the performance of instinctive acts, in which superiority is inborn, that animal and man obtain their original sense of power or superiority. As capacities are differentiated and multiplied, the experiences of achievement generate a mood and a more general impulse, a desire to exert power for its own sake. The sensory or organic elements tend to predominate in this generalized motive, simply because the specific actions in which the sense of power is obtained cannot so readily, or cannot at all, be generalized. Such an organization of actions and states in consciousness demands nothing new in principle, implies nothing different from that found on the intellectual side when concepts are formed from concrete experiences. The associative processes and the selective principles everywhere present in mental action are all that are necessary to be assumed here. We may take advantage, however, of the special investigations of affective logic, and the like, as giving evidence in support of such a conception of the formation of moods as is here being worked out. We are likely to make the mistake of thinking the specific instincts and the impulses and pleasure states that we find in human experiences, such as ecstasy, as the whole of these experiences, and to overlook the constant process of generalization that goes on in all the mental activity of the individual. For example, we may think of various plays which involve instinctive actions as being wholly explained by, or to be made up of, these instinctive acts alone, whereas in most plays that take the form of excitement, abandon or ecstasy, there are being employed processes which are general in the sense of reënforcing all the specific acts alike, and are yet specific in the sense that they are themselves, or have been, practical: that is, they are in reality processes that belong to the fundamental strata of consciousness—to the nutritional and reproductive tendencies. Out of these tendencies the more complex processes of which we speak are made, but they are no mere repetition of old forms. That, at least, is the way these ecstatic moods appear from our point of view.

It is precisely because ecstatic moods are presumably thus general and composite, and involve fundamental instincts (but in such a way that they are transformed, and no longer present in body, so to speak, but are represented by their organic processes rather than appearing as specific concatenated chains of motor events), with their purposes changed and their whole meaning determined by the present states to which they belong, that we should be inclined to say that to explain any great and powerful movement in the lives of individuals or nations as merely reversions is very inadequate and indeed wrong. They are emotional forces that are at work, composite feelings and moods rather than instincts. They are aspects of the continuity of the life of the present, rather than of the fragmentary past that lives in the individual. These forces are plastic, complex and organized, rather than haphazard and suppressed. They are directive, creative, but incidentally they make amends for and satisfy and exploit the past.

If these principles be valid, their application to the psychology of war seems plain. The central purpose or motive of war to-day is a craving for the realization of the sense of power. This is the subjective side of it, the unconscious, instinctive, mystical motive so often observed. The question of the actual power exerted or displayed is not the most essential point of this war mood. It is the manipulation and the satisfaction of inner factors that make the most significant aspect of these moods. History, we should hold, is in great part an unfoldment of this motive. Nations crave, as collective or group consciousness, the feeling of power. Just as we say the child in his plays wants to be a man, and the individual in his art feels himself a god, so nations in their wars and in their thoughts of wars, feel themselves more real, realize themselves as world powers, and as supreme and divine. To be first and all is indeed the purpose that runs in these moods, and this we believe is true, in its way, of the most insignificant and hopelessly decrepit of peoples. This must be taken account of in the interpretation of history, and in that larger pedagogy, the pedagogy of nations to which we just now look forward.

These moods which, slumbering, become the ecstasies of war are vague, even secretive. They contain aggressive thoughts that are disavowed, vanities that are concealed, fears that present a quiet front. But we must not think that the war mood always intends war. Nations have their subjective lives and inner history, and their vicarious satisfactions. A nation in arms already feels itself victor by reason of its sense of power. Otherwise few wars would be entered upon. Dreams and talk of war may incite to war, but they may also satisfy the desire and need of war. There is a certain narcissism in nations, and this is due precisely to the fact that patriotism as a feeling and impulse necessarily lacks in the group consciousness the mechanisms for externalization, except indeed in war. War is an escape, for a people, from a kind of subjectivism, from the evils of a self-love to perhaps the greater evils of self-assertion.

Nations in war, and even in the thought of war realize their own potentiality, take account of stock of their powers, and create an ideal, romantic and dream world. They make castles-in-air, and these castles-in-air always take the form of empires. War, precisely like art, is at first more and then less practical, and sought for practical purposes. More and more there is a craving for glory, for prestige, for subjective satisfaction and symbols of power. Nations take lands that they cannot use for any good purpose, inflict indemnities that may ruin themselves rather than their enemies, exploit economic relations that are dangerous to the nations' very existence. It is power that they seek, and it is power they thus create, but it is often different in form and in value from what the conscious purpose holds. They are really seeking general and subjective states in part for their own sake. Psychologically it is all one and the same whether we realize this power by actually killing an enemy, or believe we overpower him by the performance of some mystic and ecstatic act, or in some more modern way become confident in our own power and prestige. National life, in order to maintain its integrity, must move upon a plane of intense feeling. It must have objectives, but these objectives are not necessarily of value in themselves. This is the delusion and enigma of history. Peoples enact dramas in their own subjective lives, and these things they do have reference to the desires for inner experiences. We may say that nations, like individuals, crave for luxuries of the emotional life, but to think of these experiences as merely static pleasure-states, after the fashion of a certain conception of the emotions, would be wholly to misunderstand this view which we have been trying to present. These subjective states are full of meaning and of purpose. They are not reactions, but rather, in so far as these collective lives are normal and progressive, these moods and ecstasies are more of the nature of crucibles in which old reactions and feelings are fused, given new direction, new forms and in a certain way a new nature. History is made in these moods of war. They are subjective forces, but they are also objectively creative.

What is it that nations really desire? What is it, we might ask, that an individual desires? On the side of experience it is an *abundant life*, a life full of the feeling of power. This craving for an abundant life is a craving for the satisfaction of many desires, instinctive and acquired, but it is also a craving, in some sense, for more desire. It is not merely to satisfy desires, but to realize more life by creating more desires that experience is sought. That is the philosophy of the life of the superior individual; it is also the principle of the larger individual—the nation. The creation and the satisfaction of desire are the motives of art. They are also the motives of life.

In history, it is the intangible value, the unconscious purpose, the desire to realize empires that are only in part material, the desire for glory and prestige and opportunity that seem to be the guiding motives. There is a general and plastic purpose beneath all the special tendencies and desires directing interest toward specific objects, and also sometimes making the objectives sought indefinite and the purposes in seeking them seem mystical. It is the desire to be a power in the world, or rather to have power over the world, and to experience all the inner exaltation these desires inspire that appears to be the creative force in history. These things, moreover, are not the desires and impulses of the geniuses among nations alone; they seem to be inherent in all national life.

Study of the *intoxication motive* in the individual and as a social phenomenon shows that it is not an expression of the need of relaxation from strain, or a reversion, or something that occurs by a mere release of primitive instincts. It occurs in the great periods of history, and in the strong years of the life of the individual, rather than in times of weakness. It is always a spirit of the times rather than of some past reverted to. It may occur in times of disorder or of repression, but it is an experience in which energy and power are expressed. We see it most dominant when life is most abundant, when there is also a craving to make life more abundant still, when there is already power and more power is longed for. It is true, however, that two opposite conditions may produce the strongest manifestations of this intoxication motive. Something analogous to these conditions we see in the lives of individuals, in the phenomena of intemperance, which belong in general to the virile years. Social ecstasy is produced in times when there is already a free expression of energy, but also under conditions that cause pain, disorder and repression. Under the latter conditions we think of it not as desire for relief from strain but desire to be released from obstacles that impede the expression of the growth force. If all this be true, we see war in a somewhat different light from that in which it is ordinarily regarded. It is not, in its typical forms, a reversion to barbarism, and it is not a political mishap. It is rather a readjustment of tendencies or forces and an expression and product of the living and progressive forces of society—not necessarily a good or even a normal expression of them, but an awakening and a realization of such desires as are to-day at work in everything we do—forces which for the moment are raised to a white heat, so to speak, in which purposes are for the moment fused and it may be confused—but still an expression of what, for better or for worse we *are*, not of what in some remote past time we *were*. We cannot explain war or excuse ourselves for waging wars by saying that we lapse for a time into barbarism, but on the other hand the heroism we suddenly find in ourselves as nations or as individuals, is not so different from that of ordinary life as we may have supposed. We have perhaps no right to say that all war is thus to be characterized. War is a very complex and a widely variable phenomenon, but this is the explanation of that aspect of the motive of history which in general produces war. War may have its abnormalities, if we may speak of a worse in that which is already bad enough. War may satisfy the desperate mind; it may, on occasion, be a narcotic to cover up worse pain, or an evidence of decadence; or even be what those who think of it as a reversion believe. But all these aspects of war, if our view be sound, are the eccentricities rather than the essence of war.

The conditions preceding our recent great war will doubtless in the course of future historical and sociological research, be minutely scrutinized, in the effort to find the causes of the war—factors deeper than and different from the political and economic causes and the personal intrigues that are now most emphasized. If we believe that the war was made in Germany rather than elsewhere, we might look there, especially for these psychological factors of war—for our intoxication motives and unconscious impulses and our causes of reversion, but we should probably not find anything different in kind there from what we should discover in other great countries. Those who have seen in modern industrialism dangers of coming disaster, or who now look back upon it as a genuine cause of the war were probably not mistaken. Industrialism has been producing rapidly, and in an intense form, what we may call the mood of the city, and this mood of the city contains all the conditions and all the emotions that tend to bring to the surface the deep-lying motives of the social life that we are trying to point out. There are both the joy of the abundant life, the craving for new experiences, and the sense of reality, and also the disorganization of interests and motives, the stress and fatigue and monotony which prepare the mind for culmination in dramatic events. There is, in a word, a deep stirring of all the forces that make for progress and expansion, and also conditions that disorganize the individual and the social life. Lamprecht (59) of all German writers seems to have appreciated this. He has written before the war, describing a condition in Germany which he says began in the seventies of the preceding century—a change of German life in which there is a great increase of the activities of the cities, with haste and anxiety, unscrupulous individual energy, general nervous excitement, a condition of neuro-muscular weakness (and he might have added as another sign, over-stimulation of the mind by a great flood of morbid literature).

In Lamprecht's opinion, this period of excitement, this strong tendency to the enjoyment of excitation in general, is a form of socio-psychic dissociation. It is a period of relative disorganization, when the individual is subjected to a great variety of new experiences, when outside influences prevail over the inner impulses of the individual, in which the individual is unsettled and there is a tendency toward pessimism and melancholia. Lamprecht thinks of this state as something transitory, and already as he writes (in 1905) nearing an end. This state of continuous excitement, with its shallow pathos of the individual and its constant and superficial happiness, its worship of the novel and the extraordinary, the suggestibility and the receptivity of the masses, automatic action of the will and the emotions—all this Lamprecht thinks will pass. It is a stage in the process of a new formation. The very elements of dissociation are positively charged, so to speak, and contain creative power. A new system of morals, a new philosophy, new religion begin to emerge. There is a strong effort to reach a new dominant.

This is Lamprecht's psychological interpretation of recent German history. This view and the various aspects of the condition which Lamprecht describes, the relation of the materialism, the pessimism and the melancholy of such a time to the optimistic trends and the deep forward movement need a closer study than we can here give it, but may we not see in it the truth that such conditions as these are prone to cause wars as a phase of the process of the inner adjustment of national life? Wars occur as forms of expression of those impulses which appear in the individual life in times of rapid growth and relative dissociation as outbreaks of intemperance and passion—a culmination, according to our view and terminology, of the intoxication motive. Industrialism itself is perhaps but one manifestation of deep impulses in the life of nations; it is at once an intensification and a formalizing of life. Hence perhaps its paradoxical appearance as an increase of both joy and distress. There is nothing in it that is wholly satisfying.

Germany, says Lamprecht, was seeking, in this transition period, a new dominant, a new religion and a new philosophy. But Germany, let us help Lamprecht to say, since he does not himself draw this conclusion, has failed to emerge upon the level of an exalted ecstasy, failed to produce the philosophical, the moral and religious fruit of its new impulses, *failed, in a word, to find its dominant on a high level,* precisely as often the promising individual fails and has expressed his truly great nature in low forms of activity. So Germany, and the world, dominated by industrialism and all the desires and forces that the rapid development of industrialism has brought into action, has come to a culmination of its efforts in an outbreak unparalleled in history. On the side of Germany we see a nation governed by a mood of war in which the chief modes of thought and action represented are the pseudo-mystical and religious longings for new empire, romantic love of the past, militarism, and all the motives of the new industrialism and the new science.

The best motives of the old feudalism and the new industrialism tried to unite, as we might say, into a new and very great civilization—*and they failed*. What has happened is that the material powers and the cynical moods of industrialism have combined with the mystical elements and the superficial æstheticism of the old feudalistic régime to create a philosophy of life, a temporary stage it may be, in which force and fanaticism and the uncompromising ideals of national honor and brute strength prevail over those of a wider efficiency and a broader devotion which might have inspired a greater and a better Germany. Convention and political motives have done the rest.

Bergson says that in the war spirit of Germany one sees matter arrayed against spirit. One can see some truth in this, but spirit and matter are not two armies pitted against one another. In Germany, as we may believe elsewhere, the spiritual in the sense of creative forces in the subconscious life of nations does try to organize the practical life, with its routine and convention, into an onward moving progress, in which, necessarily, exalted moods (if energies are to get themselves expressed at all) must prevail, and must be full of possibilities, both of great good and of great evil. Life in its collective form will be abundant, because that is its most fundamental craving. It may be terribly and destructively abundant, or benignly, but progress, as history seems to show us—if reason and psychology do not—can never be orderly and complacent. Order and convention must break down to introduce new spirit and new desires which are continually being created in the inner life. These forces may be old instincts which are continually upsetting civilized life, but the desires they produce and the mechanism of their operation seem to be different from what our customary psychology and interpretation of history imply. Just as these moods make the child play and be wholly unpractical when one might suppose he could be useful, and the individual, as man, live a certain life of adventure rather than in security and routine, so this spirit or mood that dominates nations makes them imperialistic, and causes them to crave those things which lead toward war, if they do not crave war itself, when we might think they ought to be most concerned about the economic welfare of the world as a whole.

Whether this spirit of nations be an evil to be overcome, and to suppress, or an untamed force to direct to right objects, or a good that by some logic of events which we do not understand works out the right course of history, we do not know. But here, of course, we come to problems, which, if they are problems at all in any real sense, are philosophical and ultimate.

CHAPTER III

INSTINCTS IN WAR: FEAR, HATE, THE AGGRESSIVE IMPULSE, MOTIVES OF COMBAT AND DESTRUCTION, THE SOCIAL INSTINCT

We have found that the essential, and we might say, primary psychological datum of war is a war-mood, that the central motive of this war-mood is a general impulse which we called the intoxication motive, and that this intoxication motive, considered generically, and in regard to its specific meaning is a craving for power and for the experience of exerting and feeling power. The war-mood is not a mere collection of instincts; it is a new product, in which instincts and emotions have a place. There are several reasons, practical and theoretical, for regarding it as a highly important problem to discover what the actual content of this war-mood is. This mood, being one of the greatest of all powers of good and evil, and one most in need to-day of education and re-direction, it may be, it will probably be controlled, if ever, upon the basis of a knowledge of what it means as a whole, and of what its elements are which appear in the form of fused, transformed, truncated, generalized and aborted instincts and feelings.

Primitive Tendencies

First of all, the highly complex emotions, moods and impulses we find in the social consciousness as expressed in the moods of war, do contain and revert to instincts and feelings that are part of the primitive equipment of organic life, and are usually identified as nutritional and reproductive tendencies. The part played in war by the migratory impulse, the predatory impulse and the like indicates the connection of the war-moods with the nutritional tendencies; and the display elements found already in primitive warfare and, as we have already inferred, in all forms of ecstasy contain factors that are at bottom sexual. We no longer eat our enemies, and we do not bring home their heads to our women or practice wife stealing, but it is easy to observe the remnants of these old feelings and instincts in war. Trophy hunting continues, and we may suppose that even the moods of primitive cannibalism have not entirely been lost. The ready habituation of soldiers to some of the scenes of the recent war seems to suggest a lingering trace of this motive, while the looting impulse which plays such a part in war, and some aspects of the destructive impulses and the like that are displayed, are, with a high degree of probability, closely related to instincts that were once specifically practical and belong to the fundamental nutritional motives. Nor is it a mere euphemism, perhaps, when we speak of the greed of nations, nor solely analogical when we compare the ambitions of peoples with certain adolescent phenomena in the life of the individual. Plainly the social consciousness, as a collective mood, does not command the specific reactions connected with sexuality and nutrition, but we may observe the presence of these instinctive reactions in two phases of war. We see them in the tendencies of various individuals, who under the excitements of the war moods are controlled more or less specifically by instinctive reactions. We see also fragments of instinctive reactions and primitive feeling woven into the total states of social consciousness. The hunger motive may, and probably does, supply some of the elements of the fear and the aggressive moods of war; just as the sex motive provides some of the elements of anger and hatred, and some of the qualities of combat itself.

The Aggressive Instinct

A natural, but somewhat naïve explanation of war is that it is a survival of the aggressive instinct that man has brought up with him from animal life, in which he originated, and that very early in his career was directed toward his fellow men. This aggressive instinct as expressed in the modern spirit of war does not need, on this view, to be thought of as something reverted to. It is still active throughout the social life. Both the purposes and the methods of it remain. We have referred to one aspect of this before, and to the objection that can be made that the ancestry of man does not show us such an aggressive instinct. The nearest relatives of man are mainly social rather than aggressive in their habits. Even the habits of hunting other animals and eating animal food appear to have been acquired during man's career as man, and he never has had the aggressive temper that some creatures have had. Man has acquired a very effectual and very complex adjustment to his environment by piecing together, so to speak, fragments of his original conduct, and developing mechanisms that have been produced in the race as a means of satisfying fundamental needs. Modes of reaction produced originally for one purpose have apparently been utilized by other motives. Of course the more specific animal instincts are not wholly lacking, but it is also true that man through his social life has produced habits that resemble or are substitutes for primitive instincts. The love of combat, especially as it is shown in play indicates the presence of instinctive roots, but it does not show the existence of a definite instinct of aggression. This play is in part an off-shoot of the reproductive motive. These fighting plays of children are in part sexual plays, and we see them clearly in their true light in some of the higher mammals most closely related to man.

One aspect of the aggressive habit of man has been too much neglected. It is highly probable that aggression in man has been far more closely related to the emotion of fear than to any assumed predatory instinct. It is a question whether the predatory habit of man, ending in cannibalism and the hunting of animals for food, did not originate in the time of the long battle man must have had with animals in which the animals themselves for the most part played the part of aggressors. It was not for nothing, at any rate, that our animal ancestors took to the trees, and it is certain that the fear element in human nature is very strong and very deeply ingrained. We see throughout animal life fear expressed by aggressive movements, by the show of anger, as well as by flight. This is seen especially clearly in the birds. With all their equipment for the defensive strategy of flight they express fear instinctively by attacking, and this is apparently not a result merely of the habit of defending the young. The great carnivora also attack from fear, and seem normally never to attack such animals as they do not hunt for prey unless they are frightened. The charge of the rhinoceros and other great ungulates is probably always a fear reaction. They appear to have no other aggressive impulses, certainly none connected with the nutritional motives since they are herbivorous in habit.

The fear motive is probably much deeper in human nature, both in the lower and the higher social reactions than is commonly supposed, the concealment of fear being precisely a part of the strategy of defense. Fear has created more history than it is usually given credit for. The aggressive motive alone, in all probability, would never have made history such a story of battles as it has been. Nations usually attribute more aggressive intentions and motives to their neighbors than their neighbors possess, and war is certainly often precipitated by an accumulation of mutual distrust and suspicion. Nations are always watching one another for the least signs of aggression on the part of their supposed enemies, an attitude which of course is inspired only by apprehension.

Moods of fear and pessimism we say are deeply implanted in the consciousness of man, and we must interpret both his optimism, and all its expressions in philosophy and in religion, and also his aggressive behavior as in large part the result of a conscious or an unconscious effort to overcome his fear. The social consciousness is full of marks of age-long dread and suspicion. Fear of fate, fear of losing identity as a nation, fear of being overrun by an enemy, fear of internal disruption, are strong motives in national life. Fear runs like a dark thread through all the life of nations, and gives to it a quality of mysticism, and a touch of sadness which is so characteristic of much of the deepest patriotism of the world.

Fear is one of the most powerful motives of all aggressive warfare in the world. We find it in every nation, even those which are naturally most aggressive, and in them perhaps most of all. In the history and in the war moods of Germany the fear motive is unmistakable. America is not without it. Nations conceal their fears, presenting a bold front to the foreigner; but beneath the display one can always detect suspicion, dread and intense watchfulness. America has in the past feared Germany, and America fears the Far East; we look furtively toward Asia, the primeval home of all evils and pestilence, for something that may arise and engulf us. Small countries fear; large countries with their sense of distances, have their own characteristic forms of apprehension. Fear is the motive of preventive wars. It makes all nations desire to kill their enemies in the egg. It creates the death wish toward all who thwart our interests or who may in the future do so.

This fear motive runs through all history. Parsons says that men fight not because they are warlike, but because they are fearful. Rohrbach thinks that if Germany and England could each be sure the other would not be aggressive there would be no war between them. It is this aspect of the foreign as the unknown that especially plays upon the motive of fear. This fear is like the child's dread of the dark; it is not what is seen, but what is not seen that causes apprehension. It is the stranger whose psychic nature we cannot penetrate, who causes fear. In small countries having only land borders, this attitude of suspicion and fear must become an integral part of the whole psychic structure of the national consciousness. Fear becomes morbid; nations have illusions and delusions based upon fear. There are reasons for believing that all aggression contains a pessimistic motive, or background, and that this pessimistic background is based upon the emotion of fear. Countries that are most positively aggressive have such a pessimistic strain. Pessimism is a shadow that lies across the path of progress of modern Germany. This fear motive, the quality of the animal that charges when at bay, is to be seen throughout all German history. Germany's fear of Russia must certainly be blamed for a great part of the pessimistic strain in the temperament of Germany, and therefore as an important factor among the causes of the great war. Every war appears to the people who conduct it as defensive, precisely because every war is to some extent based upon fear, and fear in national consciousness is a persistent sense of living by a defensive strategy. It is existence that nations always think and talk of fighting for; it is existence about which they have apprehensions. Beneath all group life there is this sense of fear, since fear itself was a large factor in creating that life. When people live together, repress individual desires and participate in a common life we may know that one of the strongest bonds of this social life is fear. The need of defense is a more fundamental motive in national life than is aggression. A "shudder runs through a nation about to go to battle." The lusts of war are aroused later by the overcoming of fear.

Germany's inclination to preventive wars, her incessant plea of being about to be attacked, can by no means be interpreted as pure deception, or as an effort to make political capital. Germany's army *was* primarily for defense, because a defensive strategy is the only strategy that Germany with her position and her temperament can adopt. Germany's great army was Germany's compensation, in consciousness, for the insignificance of her territory. It was for defense. It was also a compensation for a feeling of inferiority, in Adler's sense. Fanaticism, envy, depreciation of others, aggression, morbid and excessive ambition were all fruits from the same stem. The gloom which many have found in German life, and the pessimism in German philosophy, we may explain in part by the experiences of Germany as the scene of so many devastating wars. Upon the background of fear, in our interpretation of aggressive motives, is erected German autocracy, German ambition and the conception of the absolute State, which may be interpreted as almost a specific fear reaction. It comes in time to have other meanings, and like many instinctive reactions, it may be put to uses for which it was not originally produced, but there is fear concealed in the heart of it. How action can be both defensive and strongly aggressive, then, is no mystery if we see that aggression may be a fear reaction, that even the most ardent imperialism is based in part upon fear, upon the consciousness at some time of being weak and inferior.

Fear and suspicion cause aggressive wars even when the fear may be, in all reason, groundless. There is no more dangerous individual in the community than the one having delusions of persecution, for his mania is naturally homicidal. So with nations. Fear is a treacherous and deceptive passion. We may see this fear, if we choose to look for it, even in the ecstatic mood of war and the spiritual exaltation of Germany during the first few weeks or months of the war. This exaltation was in part a reaction of fear—or a reaction from fear. Germany was afraid, feared for her existence, and the exaltation was in part a sense of taking a terrible plunge into the depths of fate. Germany was afraid of Russia and afraid of England, and that fear had to be overcome, because the presence of the fear itself was a matter of life or death. But the exaltation did not merely succeed the fear. It contained it. And why should Germany, even with all her preparedness and her resources not be afraid? An inherited fear is not so easily exorcised. Germany arrayed against all Russia and all the British Empire, Germany no larger than our Texas experienced a state of exaltation, overcoming fear. But it required something more than courage to overcome the fear; and that other element was mysticism. To the sense of throwing all into the hands of fate which, by all physical signs must be adverse, was added, as a compensating element, Germany's mystical belief in her security as a chosen nation. Fear, by its intensity and depth may, like physical pain, become ecstatic and thus be overcome.

Hatred

Hatred must be considered both as a cause of war, and as an element in the war moods. Many authors have called hatred one of the deepest roots of war. This hatred between nations even Freud says is mysterious. But Pfister, referring to Adler's theory, says that war must be understood precisely as we understand enmity among individuals. A sense of inferiority is insulted, and thus aggressive feelings are aroused. The nation, like the individual, is spurred on to make good its claim to greatness. It is a feeling of jealousy based upon a sense of inferiority that causes hatred. O'Ryan and Anderson (5), military writers, say there are two causes of war: those based upon an assumed necessity, and those based upon hatred. Nusbaum (86) also finds two causes of war, the expansion impulse and the egoism of species, which leads to long enmities.

History shows that we must accept hatred as an underlying cause of war. The reaction of deep anger which may be aroused by a variety of situations that arise among nations, especially when it is, so to speak, an outbreak of a long continued hatred, is a proximate cause of wars. Hatred, the reaction of anger prolonged into a mood, differs as national or group emotion from the anger of the individual in part by being subject strongly to group suggestion, and in part because in the group consciousness there is only rarely a means of expression, on the part of the individuals of the group, of the feelings of hatred. Enemies are far away and inaccessible. Therefore hatred may become deep and chronic.

Hatred between nations is usually based upon a long series of reprisals and a history of invasions. These invasions are primarily physical invasions, but later invasions in the sphere of invisible values, offenses to honor and the like are added.

These ideal values come to be regarded as more vital than material values. Hatred between groups becomes chronic and often seems to be groundless because the values concerned have thus become intangible. The chronic moods of hatred and dislike become explosive forces, ready to be excited to action whenever any difference arises. Veblen (97) says wars never occur except when questions of honor are involved, which is of course equivalent to saying that the reaction of anger is always required as an immediate cause of war. Veblen maintains also that emulation is always involved in the patriotic spirit, that patriotism always contains the idea of the defeat of an opponent, and is based upon collective malevolence. The range of these occasions of crisis is so great, and the feelings of hatred so persistent and volatile, that the mechanism for the production of war is always present. These causes range all the way from violation of property to offense to the most abstract ideas of national etiquette. Violation of international law, of moral principles, we see now, may have very far-reaching effects as infringing the sphere of honor of nations not directly concerned, since the prestige of all nations as participants in creating law and becoming upholders of it is affected.

If hatred and its crises are causes of war, they do not fit into the moods in which warfare is generally conducted. Hatred belongs to the periods of peace and of strained relations, when the cause of war is present, but the means of retaliation are not at hand or not in action. The prevalence and persistence of hatred in war is a sign of imperfect morale. Hatred cannot remain in the war mood of a nation acting with full confidence in its powers. Hatred always implies inferiority or impotent superiority. Dide (20) says that the spirit of hatred does not fit into the soldier's life. It goes with the desire for revenge and is strongest among those who stay at home and can do nothing. Hatred is a phase of apprehension. Hatred is a product of the fear that cannot be taken up into the optimistic moods, and thus be transformed. It remains as a foreign body and an inhibition. It arises when obstacles appear to be too great, when there are reverses, and the enemy shows signs of being able to maintain a long and stubborn resistance, or flaunts again the original cause of the disagreement. Scheler (77) says that revenge, which is a form of hate, is not a justifiable war motive. We should say also that it is not a normal war mood, that it has no sustaining force, but causes a rapid expenditure of energy which may be effectual in brief actions, but is even there wasteful and interferes with judgment and efficiency. Morale based upon hatred is insecure.

Hatred must have been a very early factor in the relations of groups to one another, and presumably we should need to go back to animal life and study antipathies there in order fully to understand the nature of racial and national antagonisms, some of which may be based upon physiological traits and primitive æsthetic qualities. The very fact of the existence of groups, segregated and well bound together for the purposes of offense and defense implies already a strong contrast of feeling between that of individuals of the group toward one another and that directed toward the outsider. This contrast developed not merely as a reaction, but as a necessity, for groups in the beginning must have had to contend against their own feeble social cohesion, and existed only by reason of strong emotions of fear and anger felt toward the stranger. Hatred toward all outside the group must at one stage have been highly useful as a means of cementing the bonds of the group and maintaining the necessary attitude of defense, at a time when all outsiders were likely to be dangerous. Feelings of friendliness toward strangers were dangerous to the life of the group, and so hatred possessed survival value.

The main root of group antipathy is in all probability fear. Hatred is an aspect of the aggressive defensive toward the stranger. Hatred is a part of the aggressive reaction. As an expression of ferocity toward all who are not known to be friendly, it belongs to the first line of defense. Hatred is likely to be strong in the female because the attitude of the female is universally defensive.

In the beginning, as MacCurdy (37) says, the contrasts between groups were sharp, and these definitely separated groups must have felt toward one another not only antagonism but a sense of being different in kind. Intensity of feelings of opposition tends to magnify small differences into specific differences. This sense of specific difference is never lost, not even in the consciousness of enlightened nations in regard to one another, and we may see it to-day displayed as a mystic belief, on the part of many peoples, in their own superiority. Nations are always outsiders to one another, and the sense of strangeness perennially sustains defensive attitudes and moods of hatred. The friendship of nations can never be very secure, because the old idea of difference of kind is never quite abandoned. Some degree of enmity seems always to be felt toward the foreigner; that is, toward all who are not interested in the protective functions of the group. MacCurdy thinks the intensity of suspicion and hatred of peoples toward one another belongs to the pathological field, and that one expression of this is the peculiarity of the mental processes by which nations always justify their own cause in war. This, however, is perhaps an exaggeration, since we can trace these states of mind in all the history of the race.

How deep-seated the enmities and the sense of strangeness among nations may be is seen in the fact that national groups living in close proximity to one another tend to become less friendly rather than to become affiliated. These feelings gradually produce conceptual entities, which stand for the reality of the foreign. These concepts are deposits, so to speak, from a great number of affective reactions, and they always contain imaginative content based upon enmity and suspicion. This underlying enmity between neighboring peoples is not something rare in the world. All foreigners, even in the minds of the most intelligent of peoples, are reconstructions, caricatures. These feelings and attitudes are strong and deep and they prevent genuine friendship among nations. We tend to think of all foreigners as in some degree malicious, as designing, and lacking in the good qualities and right habits which we ourselves possess.

Many authors have commented upon the entire inability of nations to understand one another. There is a deep reason for this, which we have already suggested. They do not wish to understand one another. It is a part of the archaic system of defense to maintain an attitude of distrust and misunderstanding and even fear. The fear of the enemy is a protection—against invasion from without and disruption within. Nations do not dare to relinquish their fear of one another, and we see something of this voluntary cherishing of fear and enmity in the present hesitation about entering into leagues on the part of many nations. Nations really wish to hate one another, it would seem. Other evidence of this we have observed in the cult of hate that has been promulgated to keep up morale in the recent war. We see enmity maintained when the differences among the peoples holding it are superficial and must indeed be exaggerated and caricatured in order to make them support feelings of dislike. Small differences in the customs of closely related peoples are sufficient sometimes to maintain intense antagonism. As Collier (68) says, it is precisely the bad manners of a people that cause conflict. These bad manners are of course manners that are *different from our own*.

Germany's outburst of hatred and its frequent exhibition during the war and its promulgation as a cult and a religion appear to have excited the interest of many writers on the war. As a chapter in the psychology of war it has suggested new problems and points of view, and it has also appealed to many as an interesting problem of national psychology. If our explanation of hatred as especially related to fear and to the sense of inferiority is correct Germany of all nations must have been affected with a disorder of morale, or some perversion of national consciousness.

The hatred of Germany for England is not the only example of international enmity in the world, but its expression in the war has made it peculiarly interesting. The grievance against England is first of all that England is great and prosperous, and lives in comfort upon the unearned fruits of empire, while the German has toiled hard through the centuries and has caught nothing. England is hated because in many ways she has stood squarely in the path of Germany's progress and because in the history of European diplomacy, doors leading to wider empire have been again and again slammed in Germany's face, usually by the hand of England. Germany hates England, according to German writers, because England, a kindred race, tried to betray western civilization into the hands of barbarism. Germany hates England because, to the German mind, England is hypocritical. The Englishman criticizes in others precisely what he does himself; Puritanical talk covers a sinful heart. Germany hates England because in her sea-policy England has been high handed and arrogant. The Germans often call England a robber nation, with the morals of a burglar who, having enriched himself by his trade, and having retired from business, now preaches honesty.

It is not merely the hatred of England on the part of Germany that is of interest for a psychology of war but the fact that Germany has taken her hate for England with a peculiar seriousness, believed it unique, has been to the pains of justifying it morally, has covered it with religious exaltation, made it a cult and even expressed it in a formula, and made it an educational program. There are many German writings justifying the hatred of England and encouraging hate as a weapon of righteousness. Smith (47) (64) has given us the titles of forty-four German publications in his own possession, having for subject Germany's hatred of England, and says that there are sixty-five more known to him. Some of these expressions of hatred are extreme. There is, or was, a pastor in Hamburg who declared from his pulpit that his people were doing God a service in hating England and in taking every step possible to wipe so pestiferous a nation from the face of the earth. Frau Reuter says that it is impossible now more than ever to love our enemies, that England who professed love for Germany and then betrayed her love must be hated. Stern, in his studies of hate in children found that hate may be strong without any clear content, in the minds of German children. That some of this hatred of England is a direct effect of the teachings of Treitschke can hardly be doubted, when we recall the great influence his teachings have had, and the peculiar bitterness of that dramatic personage for England, for England's pretentiousness, her middle class satisfaction, her insular conceit.

The further details of the cult of hatred in Germany need not detain us, since the purpose is only to suggest here the connection of hatred with the national pessimism, the fear and the inferiority motive of Germany. We see a similar attitude in Austria, where there is a violent race hatred toward the Serbians, which Le Bon has regarded as the motive from which Austria went to war. Ferrero comments upon the fact that hatred is conspicuously absent in America, and says that the greater hatred in Europe is due not only to the obvious result of nations being crowded together, but also to the caste system which limits the freedom of the individual and tends to engender deep passions. Dide (20) says that in Germany preoccupation with the idea of injustice is a cause of war, and Chapman (39) also remarks that Germany had gone mad thinking of her wrongs. That jealousy and fear are in general the substratum of national hatred is deeply impressed upon one in studying the psychology of Germany. All the hate motive of the late war might well be found in Germany's prayer *"Gott strafe England."* Germany appealed to God to punish England, of course, because Germany herself could not. Both the appeal and the hatred are reactions of fear and a sense of impotence. Germany hated England because England was secure behind her navy, upon her island, beyond the reach of the war machine which is Germany's symbol of power and the compensation for her sense of inferiority and weakness.

The Instinct of Combat

We may distinguish in the motives of war between the aggressive tendency, which we have already discussed as a reaction of fear or of anger, and a more specific instinct of combat as a possession of the individual, less subject to suggestion, less closely related to the phenomena of the herd. The aggressive reaction we associate, or some writers do associate it, with the *predatory instinct,* practical in its motive, having in part an economic basis. The love of combat which appears especially as a play motive in the child and the youth is expressed as a desire for conquest and in the pleasure of overcoming an enemy.

Some see in war a recrudescence of the instinct of combat, and indeed think of war as mainly such a return to primitive instinct. The life of peace represses this motive too much, they think. Life is too organized and coöperative and the individual craves release from it. The general objections to such an interpretation of war we have already stated. We think rather of certain specific movements as avenues of approach to highly complex states of ecstasy, and of these states of ecstasy as representing or containing the real craving for war, so far as there is one. The war mood exploits these movements and gives room for instincts to display themselves, and these instincts, in their expression, are pleasure-toned because they are archaic and have once been well organized and habitual forms of activity having practical objects. But to say that men have a profound but concealed desire to kill one another, that the fighting impulse remains intact in some original animal form, is a travesty upon human nature. It is precisely because in war killing is depersonalized, so to speak, that it is a moral duty and is performed under conditions in which there is a summation of many strong motives leading to the act that, as we see it, men find joy in battle. The instinct of attack, or the hunting instinct that is involved in this activity, can become pleasure-toned only because of the presence of other motives, and because the object is dehumanized for the time. Otherwise we should expect all soldiers, once having their aggressive instincts aroused in battle, to become dangerous to the community.

That there is, however, a residue of pure love of physical combat and a survival of the instinctive movements of combat is shown in play, although here too the motives are mixed. The desire to fight, to kill, to hunt are still present but for the most part are sublimated in adult life into desire for competition in general, love of danger, and the hunting and gambling impulse. But we can here and there in human conduct see certain roots of pure instincts having definite coördinated reactions. These undoubtedly do play a part, but probably a very small part in the present moods of war. So far as they remain purely instinctive their place as a general motive of war seems negligible. It is a question, in fact, whether even in the state of savagery any pure instinct for killing ever played a considerable part. There were already practical motives, motives of fear and anger, and presumably also complex states of pleasure connected with beliefs, customs and ceremonies as well as with battle, so that even then men cannot be said to have acted upon anything like purely instinctive impulses.

Numerous accounts have come from the scenes of the great war about men who appear for a time to be dominated by irresistible instincts. Gibbs (80) says there are some men in every army who like slaughter for its own sake. They find an intoxication in it. They love the hunting spirit of it all. We have the story of a French soldier of peaceable disposition who appeared to experience an ecstasy of delight as he lay concealed in a shell hole and was able to pick off many of the enemy. This was not the exhilaration and abandon experienced by men while making attack, when violent muscular exertion produces an intoxication of mind, but a dominance of the mind by something which seems very much like the hunting spirit, under circumstances in which, we may suppose, the enemy had undergone some process of dehumanization in the mind of the hunter. We may suppose also that there are individuals in every army who have pathological impulses or perversions, which show themselves in instinctive reactions of a specific nature and in excess of the normal.

Both the Germans and the French are accused by French and German writers respectively with being the real lovers of battle. German writers say that the Germans are peculiarly peace-loving and by nature lacking in the battle spirit, but that the French love battle for its own sake, and that this is shown clearly by their history. Others see love of conflict, aggressiveness and cruelty in the German disposition. Boutroux (13) wishes to place among the causes of the great war the native brutality of the German disposition, a trait existing from long ago, and now become a disciplined cruelty—a *zuchtmaessige Grausamkeit*, regarded as right and meritorious. Many think they find this love of fighting, bloodthirst and love of destruction in the German soul. Many attribute pure aggressiveness of a pronounced type or an exaggerated predatory instinct to the Germans. Chapman (39) says that the war is a flaming forth of passions that have covertly been burning in the soul of Germany for several decades. He adds that with the Germans war is instinctive; there is no *casus belli* at all. War 'is for war's sake, and is a need of nature with the German. Smith (64) declares that the German is innately brutal, and as one proof of this he shows the statistics of brutal crimes in Germany. He writes of the truculent aggressiveness of the Teutonic race, of the hatred and love of destruction displayed by the robber knights of the Middle Ages, and regards quarrelsome aggressiveness as innate in German character. Dide (20) thinks that such aggressive warfare as is practiced by the Germans always goes with a pessimistic disposition. Thayer (58) connects bloodthirstiness with the paganism of Germany, and says that bloodthirstiness crops out again and again in German history. Nicolai (79) also refers to the craving for blood in the German character, and says that it has been shown throughout the history of the Germans. The old sacrifices which grew out of cannibalism and are due to the persistence of the craving for blood show an instinctive desire for slaughter, or at least a confirmed habit of killing that dies hard. But in all these characterizations of national temperament there is no clear distinction among various motives of conduct. Anger and fear reactions, love of combat itself, the motives of display are all intermingled.

There can of course be no precise way of estimating the place of a pure instinct of combat among the causes of war, or in the war moods. We have seen reason for believing that although these instincts remain as fragments in the individual and especially are utilized in higher processes of the social life, they are less influential in determining motives and conduct than is sometimes believed. We cannot at least explain war as a sudden release of these instincts. That primitive passions for violence, as MacCurdy (37) maintains, reënforce the herd antagonism, and in the midst of the apprehension at the threat of war, give rise to a desire for war, may be true, but such primitive passions are not all of the forces that are at work in causing modern wars. To say that in the individual of modern society a savage still lives is an exaggeration, and does not properly express what social consciousness is or has done. The social life is not a balance in which primitive instincts are held in leash by other instincts or feelings, but a new product in which there is a synthesis of impulses in which the original form of the impulses may be greatly transformed. We live in composite situations to which there correspond composite moods. Often motives which clearly reveal to analysis their instinctive character have no tendency to express themselves in the definite instinctive movements corresponding to this instinct-feeling, having permanently become dissociated from the primitive reactions, either by a process of generalization and fusion of states and processes in the individual, or by the inheritance of structural changes. There are, it is true, all degrees of amalgamation of old and new elements or of transformation of old elements, but to think of instincts as remaining intact and unchanged in modern life seems wholly wrong.

After all man is no longer an animal, and even the distance between man as a member of the present complex organized society and man as primitive or savage is considerable. The difference is not entirely in the associations themselves but in all that the associations have done, or that they represent, in modifying instincts, which no longer exist in their original form and distinctness. Man is a creature of feeling, but not of instinct we say, and this distinction is important in many ways. All analogies between animal and human life have an element of danger in them. To explain human conduct in terms of herd instincts—instincts of aggression and the like—is misleading, since the instincts that are assumed do not exist as such, and perhaps never did. The psychology of the crowd, and the psychology of war, cannot be contained in the psychology of the herd, however attractive the simplicity of these concepts may be. That primitive instincts may remain as remnants, that the crowd shows some of the characteristics of the herd and the pack cannot be denied, and that in the spirit of war these fragments and traits play a certain part may well be believed. But the synthetic and highly complex mood we call the war spirit, and the causes of war, however archaic some of their elements may be, are very different from any mere sum of instincts. There is no specific craving for combat that we can call a cause of war, or that, in our view, plays any considerable part in the causes of war—combat as apart from practical motives and the complex moods into which, in its modern form, it enters. Some writers appear to be deceived because they assume that war is itself primitive, and do not see that in spite of its conventions and its old forms, it is not far behind civilization, not because civilization has made no progress, or is so insecure, but because war, chaos though it be, in some respects contains all our modern feelings. Kerr says that war is due to a superfluity of animal force that must vent itself, but such explanations of war seem certainly to be very far from the truth. That theory is far from being adequate as an explanation of play. It is much less so as an explanation of war. The other theory of play that is most prevalent and which is offered as a theory of war—that play and war are reversions to primitive instincts, is also insufficient. War is neither an overflow of energy nor a reversion to primitive states. Rather it is caused by and involves all the present and active motives of man and all his essential human qualities.

Social Instincts

Whatever the specific causes of war may be, war is of course possible only because there exists a mechanism or instinct or feeling, because of which great groups of people act as a unit in the common interests of all. We usually speak of this collective action as the result of *social instincts* or a general *social instinct*. It is the place of this "instinct" in the causes and moods of war that we must consider. War is a social phenomenon: it is a movement directed toward an object, but the force that drives the movement is of course social.

Several writers, among them MacCurdy (37), Murray (90), and Trotter (82), have dealt with this social aspect of war, and have interpreted war as a herd reaction. All these theories are simple. Trotter maintains that in man there are four instincts and no more: self-preservative, reproductive nutritional, and herd instincts. The peculiarity of the herd instinct is that it does not itself have definite motor expression, but serves to intensify and direct the other instincts. This herd instinct is a tendency, so to speak, which can confer instinctive sanction upon any other part of the field of action or belief. The herd instinct, for example, gives instinctive quality to the social organization and social proclivities of three different types of society, which appear as national characters. These are the wolf, the sheep, and the bee types. The aggressive type of social organization is represented by the Roman and now by the German civilization. This is a declining type, but it was because moral equality could not be tolerated in Germany that the rulers were obliged to cause Germany to revert to the primitive aggressive form of gregariousness. China would be a good example of Trotter's herd of the sheep type, for here the defensive instinct seems to be the dominating social reaction. War becomes, in such a herd, a great stimulus when, and only when, it is a threat to the whole nation, and when, therefore, the individual fears for the whole herd rather than for himself.

The third type is the bee type, well represented by England, although still imperfectly. This is the type toward which the world as a whole tends, but as yet there is no complete form of it. At present the capacity for individual reactions to the same stimulus has far outstripped the capacity for intercommunication. Intercommunication in the biological sense has been allowed to run at haphazard. When once a great gregarious unit of this type shall have been thoroughly organized, and be subject to conscious direction as a whole, there will appear in the world a new kind of social mechanism and a new biological form. The interest in war will give way to a larger and more dramatic field of interest and of conquest than the mere taking and re-taking of land. But there is as yet no such society. Even in times of a great war, there is an internal differentiation that cannot be overcome, an individualism that creates antagonism, and a type of leadership which is conservative and static rather than progressive.

If we may safely apply Trotter's generalization to the present antagonism among groups (within nations, and also national groups) we might say that the rapid differentiation of the human species has had an effect of creating within the species *man* a large number of types of sub-specific value, and in this respect man differs greatly from any other species. Differences recognized by groups of the same species of animals are generally not sufficient to create antagonism among the groups, but in the case of man these differences have had precisely the effect of marking off groups with antagonistic interests. The animal society dominated by a few instincts directed for the most part toward external objects preserves a state of peace within the species. Man by reason of his intelligence and his capacities for specialization and the great number of his desires tends to prey upon his own kind. This segregation is in part artificial, becomes conventional and is subject to the effects of leadership that tends to fixate artificial distinctions, but it is also in part an effect of the exigencies of the wider life of man, of his superiority of which variability of conduct is an essential aspect. This differentiation is one of the conditions of a firmer organization in the society of man than any animal society can attain, but at the present time the two processes of differentiation and organization are to some extent antagonistic to one another.

Trotter maintains that the tendency of nature is to increase and maintain the homogeneity of the species, but we should say rather that the whole process of differentiation and organization is upon a level in which the biological processes that make for or against homogeneity have but little effect. The task before man is social. It is not so much a consciousness of his destiny as a species that man requires, but of his work as an organized group. It is due to a rapid differentiation and increase in man's desires that he has become a species in which there is internal warfare. It must be by the control of these desires in a conscious process of organization that he will become, if ever, a well-ordered and homogeneous group. Trotter thinks of such a change as a biological phenomenon, as being one of those momentous steps which a very few times have been taken in the development of organic life in the world.

We cannot discuss fully here these biological views, as they relate to the future organization of the world. That the explanation of wars within the human species this view affords is correct so far as it goes one would admit. Men fight among themselves as animals do not, because of their differences. We should prefer to think of these differences, however, neither as a phase of biological differentiation as structural change nor as functional adaptation by differentiation of reactions to the same stimuli, but as the effect of the new consciousness of desires that came with the rise of man from the animal stage, and the conditions under which these desires could and must be realized. It is the complexity of interests that has given to man his antagonisms and his differences, and these secondary differences have been utilized as a means of still further developing the desires and satisfying them, or justifying their satisfaction. It is man's intelligence and his capacity for being governed in his conduct by many desires that teaches him to make war upon his own kind, and the very same qualities make his associations firm and lasting. *But just in this way the human group ceases to be a herd and to be dominated by herd instincts.* To interpret war, therefore, as an effect of social instinct or herd instinct upon the instincts of aggression or of self-protection, or as the effect of aroused instincts of aggression and self-protection exciting the herd instinct, is unsatisfactory because it is too simple, and erroneously undertakes to explain human life in terms of instinct and also carries biological analogies too far. These views, if we understand them, seem to have the characteristic faults of all purely biological sociology.

That, however, the "herd instinct," or the social feeling or the cohesive force in groups, whatever it may be, is exceedingly strong and persistent is shown by the recent war. We see a world highly differentiated, and with wide associations which seemed to have become permanent becoming at once a world in which the lines of cleavage are based upon propinquity and political organization. All ties, except national ties, were broken up. The nation, conscious of itself, becomes a unit or personality, and the sense of personality of a nation becomes greatly intensified in time of war. The individual becomes unimportant, both in his own estimation and in the eye of the law. It is the life of the nation as a whole that is felt to be threatened and under this threat the group as a whole becomes an object of devotion and solicitude. Nicolai (79) comments upon this *Massengefuehl* and says that, when not counterbalanced by higher elements of social consciousness, it may be a low and dangerous element in the consciousness of groups. Sumner (70) also speaks of the extraordinary power of gregariousness, and says that when the movement is upon a vast scale, the numbers engaged being very large, there is always an exhilaration connected with the movement, and that if the causes involved are believed to be deep and holy, the force of this gregarious mood may become demoniacal.

There are two especially remarkable changes that take place in the social life in war or in the act of going to war, and which represent the social instinct or feeling at its highest point. These phenomena are types of social reaction, but the question may be raised whether they do not represent something more than reactions in the ordinary sense. We see in times of war, first, a greatly increased sensitiveness to leadership, a craving for devotion to a leader, indeed, which is sometimes pathetic in its effort to transform really commonplace men into religious objects. The leader as a concept and an ideal is a product of the social mood itself, which does for him precisely what romantic love does for its object, exerts a creative effect upon him. The leader is magnified to heroic size and held up before the enemy as a threat. It is plain to be seen that this devotion to leader and imaginative treatment of him is in part a defensive reaction. The individual hides behind this colossal figure, and thus feels himself safe. But this protective impulse that creates the invincible leader is not the only motive; at least it is probably not the only one. The leader represents the ideals and the ambitions of the people, and his prestige and the forms that surround him, especially everything that is aesthetic or suggests the heroic, symbolize the craving for power in a people. The strength and the peculiar abandon and perversity, one may say, of the affections of a nation toward the leader in time of war make the rise of such a leader dreaded by the political powers in every country. Newspapers, in every war, find some heroic figure whom they exploit as a coming dictator, and changes of leadership in the field apparently sometimes have reference to these popular currents. But a nation in love with its leader is strong in defense, and readily becomes aggressive, and this relation of mass to leader is of course one of the main foundations of military morale.

The second universal social phenomenon of war is the greatly intensified feeling of solidarity as shown in comradeship and united feelings on the part of the people. This too is in part, and only in part, a protective reaction. The individual becomes safe by becoming a part of a whole which then alone seems to have real existence and true value. The individual loses himself in the whole, but the whole group also becomes absorbed and taken into the sphere of protection and interest of the individual. The individual becomes highly sensitive to everything that happens to the group, and peculiarly affected by the social mood of comradeship. This spirit of comradeship becomes one of the most conspicuous qualities of the social life in time of war. Comradeship in arms is of course the highest point of this social solidarity. The mass action, the close physical relationship, subjection to the same narrow routine and the common experiences of danger, induce social states that represent the most complete expression of pure social feeling, and excite moods which, upon occasion may reach the highest degree of ecstasy or intoxication and lead to acts of the most exalted heroism.

These changes in the social life in time of war are striking and fundamental. To explain them would mean to explain social feeling itself. We may say that these phenomena of the social life are precisely the *herd reactions* the biological writers speak of, but to do so would mean, from our point of view, to ignore some very significant aspects of human social life. It would ignore first of all the ecstatic quality of the higher social life, which is indeed the essential quality of the social spirit of war. Instead of saying that this intensity of feeling is merely a reflex of an instinctive reaction, we should say that it is the expression of, and in part the satisfaction of, desires that are fulfilled in the social experience of war. The intense social life is craved, not as an instinctive reaction, but as a complex state expressing explicit desires. The craving for this social solidarity and ecstasy of social feeling is a factor in the causes of war. What we experience socially in times of peace is a society in which social feeling is narrow and provincial, in which we are conscious of many antagonistic motives. This social life fails to satisfy the desires which are seeking expression in the social life. That war is in part a creation of the social impulse seeking expression may be assumed from the nature of the social feelings that are excited in war. That such social feeling is a creation in the sense that it is desired, we see if in no other way in the fact that social ecstasy is the most universal form of satisfaction of all those impulses which fuse in the intoxication impulse, where we recognize it as the craving for an abundant or real life. Life is most real in its intensely dramatic social forms. Social ecstasy is in part a conscious adaptation. It is something that is desired and induced, and artificially cultivated in various ways, especially by a variety of aesthetic social experiences, and in the cults of intoxication. Alcohol has been used specifically throughout the world and from the beginning at least of the historical period for the purpose of creating social feeling. Patriotism is in part, we may say, a cultivated, social emotion, and in the art of manners we see the social life given forms which will increase its susceptibility to suggestion, its persuasive force and its organized expression. Such facts show us social emotion which is something more than the feeling side of an instinctive reaction.

This is hardly the place to try to elucidate the fundamental principles of the psychology of the social feelings or instincts, but it may be helpful to suggest in outline certain divergences in the theory of the social life that seem to be in point. We see on one side many writers who tend to regard social phenomena as mainly the result of instinct, as the expression either of a single instinct or of a combination of several specific instinctive tendencies. Contrasted with these views are the theories according to which social life is something that is mainly created by reason, based, so to speak, upon the observation that in union there is strength. Neither of these views seems to be satisfactory. That social feeling is based upon instinct is clear, but that it is also something created, synthetic, and subjected to selective processes seems also evident. Precisely what the instinctive basis of the social life is, perhaps one cannot with any certainty determine, nor can we say how many specific instincts enter into it. But that social feeling in its higher levels is a very complex mood, in which, although there are several instinctive reactions or feelings, there is to be discovered no social instinct as such, is the conclusion which we reach.

Social behavior is a development of all the fundamental tendencies of the organism. It has its roots both in the reproductive and the nutritional motives. These fundamental tendencies have issued phylogenetically in specific reactions that enter into the social life at all its levels, and in the life of the individual these reactions, expressing needs and desires, issue in highly complex moods, in which fundamental feelings are present but do not constitute the whole of the social moods. The individual does various specific things with reference to his fellows which are of the nature of instinctive reactions, but both in the phyletic development and the development in the individual, elements that enter into the modern social life as instincts have tended to lose their specific character, have become general or merely organic, have been transformed and have to some extent lost their original significance.

The motives of hunger, the reactions of the reproductive mechanisms, reactions to visual impressions and to sounds, warmth reactions, the huddling of fear, the influences of suggestion, susceptibility to all the stimuli of the social object enter into social feelings, and remain to some extent as instinctive reactions in the higher social processes. But we do not seem to find any general social instinct, or any specific herd instinct or any definite and broadly acting protective and aggressive instincts. As compared with some other views of the social feelings ours assumes in one way more and in another less of instinct in the social life. There is more instinct in the sense that more specific instinctive reactions are recognized in it, but less in assuming that these reactions are derivatives of primitive reactions of the organism, and also because they become transformed and fused and lose their original forms. They have come from common sources in organic life, we might say, and they meet again in the general moods which they help to create.

Conclusions

It is an important point to observe that most if not all of the specific instinctive reactions and feelings engendered in war, or occurring as an incitement to war, are capable of inducing ecstatic states. There are several of these movements and states, each of which can become, so to speak, a foundation for the development of ecstasy. Combat may and must do this, and probably war could never be carried on at all unless danger and death had qualities which arouse ecstatic moods. There is a joy in fighting, in killing, and in the tumult of battle that becomes one of the most important of military assets, and is one of the main elements of morale in the field. This capacity of human nature to make over that which is intrinsically painful into the pleasurable is one of the paradoxes of human life to be explained and taken into account in the study of the psychology of war. Fear itself may induce an ecstasy, both in the individual, as we know from many reported cases from the late war, and as a social mood in which the fear contributes a quality of intensity and ferocity to patriotism. The gambling mood, which is in part a play with fear, is another ecstatic reaction seen in war, and it is often the means of clearing the way, so to speak, for free and uninhibited action.

Of course all the purely æsthetic elements in the social life have this effect of arousing exalted moods, and indeed that is precisely their function. All social impulses tend in this same direction, and there is induced in all intense social states an intoxication mood. In these social states, the reproductive motive is often clearly discernible, but partly by common consent and convention, and partly because of the composite and fused form of impulses in the social mood, robbed of its specific reactions and converted into a new product, regarded both as conduct and as feeling.

All religious states aroused in war tend to become ecstatic. Their work is to overcome the sense of tragedy of war, and it is only by becoming intense and voluminous, so to speak, that they can accomplish their work at all. Either they must end in a mysticism which includes or takes the form of exalted moods, or they must, as can be accomplished in some temperaments, become dynamic states by inspiring a fatalistic attitude, which is at bottom a sense of throwing oneself unreservedly into the hands of fate.

We may best think of these complex war moods as the forces out of which wars are made, and the spirit in which they are conducted, but not as by their own initiative creating wars. These intoxication moods or ecstasies are forces which contain desires that are general, we say; they are mental processes that act as a means of greatly increasing the volume of all social actions. When we analyze them we find specific desires in them, and evidences of instinct and primitive feeling, but they are not in themselves tendencies toward specific reactions and in fact the motor tendencies they contain more or less inhibit one another.

In general, these war moods of which we speak are *precipitated* by definite and incisive reactions of fear and anger. These emotions of fear or anger seem to be the necessary positive stimuli to induce the moods of war. Fear and anger, no one can maintain, are the sole causes of war, and they are far from being the sole factors of the war moods, but they are the usual precipitants of war.

Fear and anger as social emotions cannot sustain organized and effectual social activity upon a large scale; we see them always, in war, taken up, transformed, absorbed in moods which are at once more practical, and more exalted and which, as complex processes, can be sustained over long periods of time. But these primitive reactions of anger and fear enter into the ecstatic moods, become associated with or induce æsthetic and religious states of consciousness, gain moral justification or religious exploitation, become aspects of directive and dynamic moods and so give force and efficiency to morale and strategy.

War appears as a breakdown of certain modes of volition. Certain types of conflict are abandoned, and aggressive activities become more simple and powerful, but war is no reversion to primitive instinct, or to any number of instincts. The resulting states of mind are too rational as means, and too exalted and ideal to be thus primitive. New content is introduced into social consciousness and new purposes come to light in these ecstasies, even though the consciously sought objectives may be archaic and conventional and the mental states traceable to more elementary states, and the conduct be similar in purpose and type to the simpler forms of conduct we find in the animal world What we are trying to impress here is the well known truth that the whole of a thing is not necessarily contained in its parts. It is the meaning of the war-mood as a whole, as a summation of many factors of the mental life, and as a direction of social consciousness as a whole that is its most important characteristic.

CHAPTER IV

AESTHETIC ELEMENTS IN THE MOODS AND IMPULSES OF WAR

That experiences and motives which belong to the field of the aesthetic play an important part in war can hardly be doubted. The whole history of war shows this, and even in the beginning war seems to be an activity carried on in part for its own sake, and not entirely for its practical results, and thus has qualities which later are explicitly aesthetic. We cannot of course separate sharply the aesthetic motive from everything else in studying so highly complex an object as war, but that war does partake of the nature of what we call the *beautiful*, and that the craving for the beautiful is a factor in the causes of war seem to be certain. The relation of art to war is of course no new theme. War has often been praised because of its aesthetic nature, and its dramatic features. It is called a beautiful adventure. It is reproduced in pictorial art, represented in music, and thus glorified and adorned, showing at least that it can readily be made to appear beautiful if it does not in itself possess beauty. Those who think of war as related to play also connect it with art. Nicolai (79), who condemns war, says that it is when war as an instinctive action is no longer useful, but is performed for its own sake that it becomes beautiful.

We cannot undertake to enumerate all the aesthetic qualities of war, or to show all the relations of the aesthetic aspects to other motives of war in detail, since to do so would mean to work out some of the fundamental principles of aesthetics. We may begin, however, by saying that war as a whole, as a movement in which there is complete organization of social forces shows already the marks of aesthetic experience and of art. As such a unification of interest in a strong and uninhibited movement, as a coördinated expression of deep desires, a multiplicity of action with a unity of purpose, so to speak, war is aesthetic in form although to mention such very general qualities does not go very far toward characterizing an object.

In its meaning as *tragedy* war contains and exerts a strong aesthetic appeal. With all its horrors, war fascinates the mind. As fate, death, history it inspires awe, and creates a sense of the inevitableness of events and of the play of transcendental and inexorable forces in human life. When, under any influence, these feelings appear as an accepting and willing of evil, we have the tragic movement as we find it in art. The death *motif* in war is the center of a variety of states which are ecstatic and have aesthetic quality. The religion of valor, the passion that is aroused by abandoning oneself to fate, the absolute devotion of service are aesthetic in form as experience, whatever else they may be. The relation of these motives to love and to the reproductive impulses has often been noticed. Devotion and death appear as beautiful; their representation in art is in part a recognition of this fact; in part it is an effort to transform them into the forms of the aesthetic. Art celebrates, but also creates, this luxury of feeling, and war also in its own dramatic movement transforms ugly and plain facts of life by including them in ecstatic states, and surrounding them with glory.

The ideal of glorified death plays a large part in the spirit of war. In war the fear of death is not only in great part stilled, but there is a longing to tempt fate and also to experience death itself, and this desire may become ecstatic. Here we see in effect one of the most important functions of the aesthetic, which is to carry on a *drama of the will* in which something that is in itself painful becomes pleasant and desired. The desire for war is to some extent a desire for death, a longing for a form of euthanasia in which the individual dies but in a sense lives—lives as glorified in death, and also in the continuance of the life of the group and of the country into which he has been absorbed. It is of course its relation to death that more than anything else has made it necessary that war should appeal to art, and take an aesthetic form, and without the aid of the aesthetic, war could not maintain itself in the world. As a sheer fulfillment of duty war could not survive. By the strength of its aesthetic appeal war must control and overcome the instinct of self-preservation.

War appeals to the human mind as the great adventure of life. To the healthy normal man this appeal, under certain circumstances, may be compelling in its power. Man feels the call of adventure in his blood. War may seem at times the natural expression of what is most real and most essentially masculine in human nature. War is the essence of all the dramatic and heroic story of the world. The past lives most vividly in this theme of war, and the sense of remoteness in time lends an aesthetic coloring to all the story of war, and is in part its fascination. The dead heroes of to-day are glorified by linking their names with the great heroes of the past.

To the glory of the individual, which is an aesthetic appeal, is added the still stronger appeal of the ideal of national glory. The image created in the mind which sustains the devotion of the individual is also an aesthetic form. It is the idea of a nation transformed by story, symbol and eloquence that is established. The dimness and mysticism of the long ago, all dramatic scenes of the national life, the forms of royalty are used in transforming reality into an ideal. The consciousness of a nation is indeed an artist which creates an ideal nation, glorifying and transforming the past, and painting a vivid picture of the empire that is to be. No little part in the German idea of the fatherland has been taken by the revived image of the old German Empire, and the story of Charlemagne, the Ottonides, the Hohenstaufen and the Hohenzollern which has been woven into the life of the present and has become an aesthetic setting for the idea of future greatness.

In the religion of valor, also, we may find aesthetic elements. Valor represents in this cult the spirit of the superior man. It is an aristocratic idea. Military life is full of this theme. The ideals of *noblesse oblige,* honor, the spirit of sportsmanship, enter into it, and all these concepts are in part aesthetic in nature. It is neither as moral nor as practical ideas that they have so deeply influenced society, but because of their appeal to the sense of the beautiful. All this aspect of war and military life, both in its motives and in its forms, is closely related to the pure beauty of art. The play spirit also, which in some of its developments at least is aesthetic, enters into the motives of war. War, we say, is the great adventure. It is the realization of power. It is an expression of the love of the sense of freedom. It is the great game, in which everything is staked. The love of danger and the love of gambling with life that it contains have roots that are also roots of various forms of art.

Another element, aesthetic in motive and form, obviously related to the reproductive functions of the individual, is the display motive. This motive of display is concerned especially with the idea of courage. It is of course a deep desire of the male to display courage before the female. This display motive must be the main motive of the *uniform* and all the other ornamental aspects of military life. Rank, titles and decorations belong to the same movement. They are indications of the advancement of the man in those essential qualities of the soldier, the chief of which is courage. The aesthetic forms in which courage is represented help to sustain it, and are an important element in morale, and they also serve a purpose in creating or adding to the allurement of the service and the fascination of war. It is the craving for the display of courage, the desire of the man "to show the stuff that is in him," that gives to war some of its most persistent aesthetic forms, and these aesthetic forms help both to make the display of courage effective and to create courage.

Among these aesthetic elements of war must be considered of course the rhythms, the forms, all the concerted action, the marching (which may be regarded as one of the forms of the dance), the parade, the maneuvering and drill that enter into military life. Already in primitive warfare these aesthetic forms begin to appear and indicate clearly both their practical significance as means of affecting the will, and their relations to the religious and to the reproductive motives. The warrior tries to create in his person the appearance of power, and also by the aesthetic forms he introduces into his warfare, the feeling of power. He believes indeed that through these aesthetic forms he actually creates or exerts power. This is the motive of the war dance, which as an aesthetic form produces this ecstasy of the feeling of power. This power is often conceived to be magical; the women dancing at home are supposed to exert an influence upon the men in the field or upon the enemy, and the savage believes that in his own displays he actually overcomes the spirit of his enemy. Art is here plainly serving a purpose. Display is a means of creating an impression in the minds of the enemy. It also has the purpose of creating an effect in the mind of the soldier himself. The art in military life is, indeed, to give the impression of power to all who must be affected by the exhibition of force.

All social life contains elements that appeal to the aesthetic sense, and these aesthetic elements are by no means solely ornamental. The universal development of etiquette and manners has reference to very practical aspects of the social life. Their function is to influence the will. The highly developed etiquette of military life is not merely to facilitate the military functions, and it is no explanation of the formalism of the military life to say that this is a sign of its archaic nature. Formalism in this life is one of the means taken to cover up all the details of militarism that are repugnant: the hardship, the lack of freedom and the like. Etiquette acts persuasively upon the will, it helps to make military life desired, and to make men submissive under control of absolute leaders. All formalism in social life, considered in one aspect of it, is a symbol of the resignation of the will of the individual. As thus a symbol it may either convey or mediate social feeling, and when social feeling is absent the art of manners may become a substitute for this social feeling, and in both these ways it is a means of giving to society cohesion, order and form.

Such considerations as these help to explain the longing for war or its equivalent which persists in the human heart. It helps us to realize the truth of Cramb's (66) assertion that the whole history of the world shows that man has lacked not only the power but the will to end war and establish perpetual peace. There are still motives in the mind of man that make him approve of war. War is perpetuated because of its heroic form, as a form of experience in which the meaning of life is felt to be exploited, in which life is transformed and glorified, in which the tragedy of life, which in any case is inevitable, becomes a tragedy which, because it bears the form of art, is acceptable and even longed for. This is the allurement of war, its persistent illusion, perhaps. The aesthetic forms of war take war out of the field of reason, and on occasion make it transcend or pervert reason. So we may understand why it is true that sometimes those who but little understand why they are to die on the field of battle may display the greatest courage and the greatest enthusiasm for war, and we must not say that these causes are fatuous because they exist in the realm of aesthetic values.

If we take war too realistically, with reference to its practical motives, its mere killing and looting, which we may suspect are related to the nutritional motive that we always find running through human conduct, and leave out of account those aspects of war which seem to belong mainly to the reproductive motive, to the enthusiasm and intoxication and art of the world, we shall to that extent misunderstand it. These motives cannot, of course, be separated definitely from one another in analyzing conduct, but we cannot be very wrong in differentiating phases of war which belong predominantly to the reproductive motive. It is because, at least, all deep tendencies of life are involved in war that it is so hard to eliminate it from experience. If war were an instinctive reaction it might be controlled by reason. If it were an atavism or a rudimentary organ some social surgery or other might relieve us of it. But war is a product of man's idealism, misdirected and impracticable idealism though it may be, but still something very expressive of what man is. It is this idealism of nations, leading them to the larger life, that makes them cling to war, whether for good or for evil. It will avail little to prove to the world that war is an evil, so long as war is desired, or so long as something which war so readily yields is desired. Statistics of eugenics and proofs that war ruins business will not yet cure us of our habit of war, and not at all so long as there is a vacancy in life which only the dramatic experiences of war can fill. When war is abandoned, it will be given up probably not because economists and sociologists vote against k, and we see that peace is good, but by the consent of a world which, once for all, is willing to renounce something that is dear to it and held to be good, if for no other reason, because it symbolizes what life and reality are. The world appears to have two minds about war, or at least it does not hold consistently to any one attitude toward it. Beneath all judgments about the evils of war, there is the allurement of these aesthetic motives which must be reckoned with in any psychology of war, or in any practical plan for eliminating war from the future experience of the race.

CHAPTER V

PATRIOTISM, NATIONALISM AND NATIONAL HONOR

Many authors find in patriotism or in national honor the chief or the sole cause of war. Jones (37), the Freudian, for example, says that patriotism is the sum of those causes of war which are conscious as distinguished from the repressed motives. Nicolai (79) says that patriotism and chauvinism would have no meaning and no interest without reference to war, and that for the arts of peace one needs no patriotism at all. Hoesch-Ernst (32), another German writer, says that patriotism has made history a story of wars. It has developed the highest virtues (and the worst vices), but it creates artificial boundaries among peoples, and gives to every fighter the belief that he is contending against brute force. Veblen (97) says that patriotism is the only obstacle to peace among the nations. MacCurdy (37) speaks of the paradox of human nature seen in the fact that the loyalty we call patriotism, which may make a man a benefactor to the whole race, may become a menace to mankind when it is narrowly focussed. Novicow says that what shall be foreign is a purely conventional matter. Another writer remarks that patriotism is the guise under which the instincts of tiger and wolf run riot.

Several writers, Powers (75), and especially Veblen, place questions of national honor among the main causes of war. Veblen would hold that wars never occur unless the questions involved are first converted into questions of national honor—and are then, but only then, supported as moral issues. Other writers are to be found who make the same claims for honor, saying that wars are always over questions of national honor—honor always meaning here, let us observe, not moral principle but prestige, dignity, analogous to what we call personal pride in the individual.

Broadly speaking, we may say that such views of war base it upon the fact that nations are individuals, having personality and self-consciousness, and are moved by emotions such as dominate the individual, although such analogies between individual and group are never free from objection. But that the consciousness of the group as an individual may be exceedingly intense, full of aggressiveness, intolerance and pride, of great sensitiveness to all outside the group, is, of course, obvious from the history of nations. Groups thus endowed with a sense of solidarity and sensitiveness become highly vitalized and persistent personalities which stalk through the pages of history with tremendous power and tenacity of purpose. Nations thus live intensely, and in their intense feelings and personal attributes there are expressed purposes and ideals, conscious and unconscious, analogous to those which make the individual also an historical entity.

There seem to be two aspects of group personality that need to be investigated in detail in any study of war, and which must be distinguished from one another, as they may be by referring to the primitive or central emotional quality which each has. These are patriotism and the sense of honor, the former, for our purposes, to be regarded as the sum of the affections a people has for that which is its own; the second a sum of those feelings and attitudes, the emotional root of which is *pride*. These feelings are the affective basis of the idea of *nationalism*.

Patriotism, or love of country or feeling of loyalty toward country, is a highly complex emotion or mood, and its object, an ideal construction, is formed by a process of abstraction in which certain qualities of home, environment, social objects selected by those feelings are made over into a composite whole. Patriotism is immediately connected with the fact that men, by some biological or other necessity are formed into groups, in which the consciousness of the individual in regard to the group and its members and its habitat is different from the consciousness in regard to everything outside. Patriotism is devotion to all that pertains to the group as a separate unit, and its form and intensity are dependent upon what the group as a unit does. The size and organization of the group to which the patriotic feeling may go out may, it is obvious, differ widely.

There appear to be five more or less distinct and different factors in patriotism; or, we might say, five or more objects of attachment, the love of which all together constitutes patriotism. These objects are: home, as physical country; the group as collection of individuals; mores, the sum of the customs of a people; country as personality or historical object, and its various symbols; leaders or organized government or state, its conventions and representations.

The deepest of all strata in the very complex feeling of patriotism, one which is concerned in every relation among nations, is the devotion to, or habituation to—or we might say identity with—the great complex of ideals, feelings, and the like which make up the customs, folkways, mores or ethos of a group. The individual as a conscious person is to such an extent created by these conscious factors that we find that the reality sense is in part produced by them. We have already referred to the belief on the part of many peoples that they alone are real. Foreigners with different mores probably always seem less real than our own people: they may even be looked upon as automata, as not being moved by the feelings and purposes that we ourselves have. The language of the foreigner, the uneducated man is inclined to think of as having no meaning. Every group has its own ways, and whatever else war may be, it is in every case an argument for the superiority of the ways of the group. Each group in war feels that its own most intimate possessions, its morality and its genius are attacked. It guards these instinctively, and a part of the purpose of aggression is the desire to make these things prevail in the world, because they are felt to be the only right, true and sensible ways. This preference for our own ways, and participation in them, is the basic fact of nationality.

The feeling of patriotism is thus primarily an æsthetic appreciation (or at least an immediate and intuitive one) of the totality of the life of the group. Just as standards of normality and artistic form in regard to the human person and its adornment vary from group to group, and are produced in the consciousness of the group, so there is a reaction of pleasure to, and attachment for, the whole of the life that surrounds the individual. This appreciation is wider than moral feeling, which indeed is in part based upon it, and is a sense of the fitness of any act to belong to the whole of the conduct that promotes the welfare of the group.

Patriotism is best known, or at least it is most celebrated, as an attachment to the native land as *place*. This is the poet's patriotism. It is, however, something more than a mere love of the homeland as landscape, and we cannot, indeed, separate out any pure love of physical country. The love of country seems to be an expansion of the attachment to home, as the place in which the family relations are experienced. The sense of place is the core of the love of home, but it is supplemented and reënforced by the personal affections. The attachment to place has also its biological roots, the sense of familiarity of place being, of course, as the basis of orientation, a deep element in consciousness. Fear of the unknown increases the attachment to the known. The land as the source of livelihood is loved, and there are also older elements in the love of the land as is shown by myths and folklore. There is in it the idea of ownership but also the idea of belonging to the land. So there is both the filial and the parental attitude in patriotism. As fatherland or motherland country is superior to and antecedent to us; as possession it is something to hold and to transmit, to improve and to leave the impress of our work upon. As historic land there is the idea of sacred soil, of land which persists through all time. Ancestor worship enters; the soil as the resting place of forefathers acquires not only a religious meaning, but there is attached to it such feeling of an æsthetic nature as is attached to everything that is full of tradition. The protective attitude is prominent in this patriotic love of land. There is in it the fear of invasion, a sense of the sacredness and inviolability of the body of a country when it has once been established as an historical entity. A study of the psychology of invasion and of homesickness would no doubt throw further light upon the still unknown aspects of the intricate moods of home love.

A third element in patriotism is social feeling. This is primitive, but whether it is a herd consciousness or a radiation of the social feelings connected with blood relationship and community of immediate practical interests it is not especially important to decide in this connection, except that the assumption of a specific herd instinct as distinguished from social feeling or instinct appears to be unnecessary. Loyalty of the individual to the group, which is accompanied by or is based upon intensified or ecstatic feeling is one of the strongest elements of patriotism. Social feeling as an attachment to the widest group, the nation, is in general a latent feeling or an undeveloped one. We see it becoming active and intense only under circumstances in which the whole group is threatened or for some other reason is compelled to act as a unit. The recent psychology of the soldier shows us that absolute devotion to or absorption in the whole may be produced automatically by the proper stimuli, and may be controlled as the mechanism of morale, and that elementary sensations enter into it. The wider social consciousness as devotion to the whole group, the nation, is based upon such reactions, and can probably not be fully, developed without them.

This transformation of the individual is something desired and sought by the individual. It comes as a fulfillment of impulses that are latent in the social life, and these impulses are tendencies to seek exalted states of social feeling, rather than to perform specific social functions. War is seized upon by the social consciousness, so to speak, as an opportunity to extend itself and become more intense, and indeed in war we see the social consciousness performing a work of genius, overcoming apparently insurmountable obstacles and aversions. Under such circumstances, social feeling becomes strongly fortified against many suggestions that tend to break it down. An intense ferocity is directed toward any disloyal member of the group, a fictitious character may be attributed to the enemy, and there is an imaginative interpretation of all his acts in a manner favorable to uniting the sentiment of the group. This does not appear to be merely a defensive reaction or a result of fear, but an awareness of the precarious condition of the social feeling itself, when it is widely extended. In its moments of most extreme and fanatical intensity it is likely to be most unstable. It has been said that the surest way to break down social feeling is to make it include too much. The conditions of war always create that danger. Patriotism is greatly intensified, but it is in danger of collapse. The mild patriotism and yet secure cohesion of peace is replaced by a social consciousness increased in breadth and depth, but which is liable also to sudden contraction. All nations when at war appear to be quite as much afraid of themselves as they are of the enemy. It is in part this susceptibility of social feeling to rapid and extreme variation that makes patriotism so mysterious a force. It may be extended in a moment to unite supposed incompatibles, or again apparently strongly cemented groups may fall into disunion. This seems to be due to the fact that social feeling is plastic and is subject to control and is a force and not merely an instinctive reaction.

The fourth element of patriotism is devotion to leader, to government, or to the idea of state. Devotion to leader must have been one of the earliest forms of loyalty. The prestige of the leader is acquired as the result of any action of the group under stimuli that produce either fear or anger. Just as the necessity for strong action creates the leader out of average humanity, so continuation of this necessity, that is the whole historical movement of the life of the group such as a nation continues to add elements of prestige to leadership. The exaltation and typically to some extent the deification of the leader is a natural consequence or aspect of the dramatic life of the group. The leader becomes symbolic of the group, and of its purposes and meaning, so that in devoting itself to a leader the people do more than sustain an emotional relation to a superior person. They transfer their own individual nature, so to speak, to the leader so that he becomes the essence or the spirit of the people.

The dynasty is the connecting link between the leader as the object of devotion of a people and the abstract idea of the state as an entity. The prestige and all the supernaturalism contained in the ideas of divine rights and divine descent that have become attached to the idea of kings are transferred to the government, or extended to the government or state. The illusion of superiority and remoteness is kept up by various forms and ceremonials. Becoming an abstract form, the organization or the office remaining while its personnel changes, the state acquires the character of a religious object. It takes on the character of the eternal, while still it retains all the persuasive and suggestive qualities that belong to individuals. The idea of state thus commands a very high degree of loyalty, and is in a sense itself a product of the feeling of loyalty. Once established the state becomes a medium through which patriotism may be subjected to control and also be manipulated for political ends. It can be extended, transferred, contracted according to what at any time may be subsumed under the government that has thus come to be the central and coordinating factor in the object of patriotism.

Another element of patriotism appears in the form of a deep reaction of the mind of the individual, usually under the influence of social stimuli that take the form of artistic or dramatic situations, to the idea of country as a historical personage. This stimulus may be symbolic—the flag or any other emblem signifying the life or the spirit of a country; or it may be concrete, historic, a story, and this story, which is the content of the idea of country, is in general a narrative assuming a certain artistic form in which facts are treated at least selectively, and usually imaginatively. This work of portrayal of the life of a nation by its story is consciously or unconsciously an appeal to the will; it is given artistic rather than scientific form for this reason. Its purpose is to present a national spirit, or ideal, or principle, and also to persuade the mind to become loyal to this spirit of country.

All countries, as the object of the feeling of patriotism, tend to be personified, and it is thus as a person that country commands the deepest loyalty of the individual. Hence the personified representation of country whenever the will of the individual is appealed to most strongly. Redier (30), a French writer, illustrates this very clearly when he pleads that the interest of the motherland must be placed first. It is not for liberty, or for the civilization of the world that the French are fighting, he says, but for France, "that most saintly, animated and tragic of figures." It is by this process of personification of country that the patriotism of the individual becomes most complete. He thus becomes loyal to a living reality representing an idea, a spirit. To defend the honor and the integrity of this person, one is willing to sacrifice everything that is individually possessed, in causes that can affect one materially in no important way. The desire for personal identity and immortality may be transferred to country as thus idealized, and the individual is satisfied to lose himself that country may live. The common man realizes in a simple and concrete way, in regard to country, the Hegelian conception of state as the reality of mind in the world. About this idea of country held by the truly patriotic mind, as we find it expressed in history and in literature, there grows up a religious sentiment, which protects from criticism the qualities of the ideal personage. A certain pathos of country attaches itself to all who as great individuals represent country, and to all its portrayals and symbols. All these symbols acquire a high degree of suggestive force because of the depth of sentiment and the richness of the content of the ideas that have produced them.

Patriotism, then, is a very complex idea and feeling which we realize as love of country—or, as we might better say, it is an animation by the idea of a very complex object which is country. It is a profound attachment, rooted in the most original and essential relations, and appears to be natural and necessary to every normal mind. The individual consciousness is complete only by including the attachments, in narrower and broader relations, to precisely the elements that enter into patriotism—to place, to the fundamental ways and appreciations of the social surroundings, to persons, to authority, to traditions. The composite effects of these attachments may be greater or smaller, as determined by a totality of conditions, but the foundations of patriotism, whatever its object, are deep in consciousness.

The presence and persistence of patriotism in the world as a deep and intense feeling raises questions that are of both theoretical and practical importance. Here we are interested mainly in the relation of patriotism to war. There is a widespread view that may be expressed somewhat as follows. Patriotism and internationalism or cosmopolitanism are two *opposites*. Patriotism delimits groups, whether rightly or wrongly, and therefore produces antagonism in the world, and either causes wars directly or maintains a continual threat of wars. On the other hand there is cosmopolitanism, a very little too much of which might destroy civilization by removing the inspiration that country gives. Patriotism, standing for the integrity of historic entities, makes the world a world of nations having separate and conflicting wills. Thus we have a choice of evils—between a world of ardent, quarrelsome, but efficient groups and a world in which the chief motive of progress, the vital principle of national growth, is left out.

What is the truth about this? What is the relation of patriotism to war? Confusion and difference of views are likely to arise from a failure to distinguish in the idea of nationalism as a whole, between two very different emotions and purposes. Psychologically, patriotism is a sum of affections. As such, it has a distinct character, constitutes a mood, the possession of which may characterize an individual, and dominance by which may be the main fact in life. As a devotion to certain objects, this motive of patriotism enters into the sphere of motives of war, but it does so mainly, in our view, as a powerful and highly suggestible energy which becomes aggressive only under the stimulus of threat to its objects. Patriotism is indeed tolerant by nature, and one may well doubt whether a genuine love of country is possible without a profound realization of the value of other countries as objects of devotion, and of the validity of the patriotism of every group. True patriotism must always be to some extent devotion to patriotism itself as a progressive force in the world, and it is, therefore, by the very fact of becoming intense and pure, a motive of internationalism.

Such patriotism seems to be free from most of the delusions of greatness that affect national consciousness. Its mood is optimistic and its spirit tolerant and just. We should say that, instead of causing wars, by any initiative of its own, it is itself caused by wars. It grows in a medium of defensive attitudes. It may, of course, play into the hands of all the aggressive motives of war; there are always circumstances creating the illusion of danger, and it is possible, even, that there would be little war if there were no patriotism as love of country to support it. But on the other hand patriotism itself does not seem to be a cause of war. We should say, indeed, that patriotism, to the extent that it becomes intelligent and is a devotion to an ideal of country, and so is not dominated and influenced by other motives is a factor of peace in the world, and is moral in its principles and its nature. This is not the place in which to speak of internationalism as an ideal, but we may at least observe how, conceivably, patriotism may be cultivated, be greatly deepened and intensified, while at the same time and indeed because of this deepening of patriotism all international causes are also served. Such patriotism may leave us with the danger of wars, since it leaves us with a world of individuals having wills and self-interests. But this world, with such a danger of wars, would be better after all than a certain kind of cosmopolitanism in a world such as, for example, might be arranged by an unintelligent socialism.

National Honor

There is another aspect of nationalism, which is psychologically distinct from patriotism as love of country, because primitively it is based upon a different motive. Emotionally it is expressed finally as national pride, as we use the word mainly with a derogatory implication. Just as patriotic feeling is intensified and crystallized by fear, and is in a sense an overcoming of fear, by devotion, so this motive of pride rests upon a basis of jealousy and of hatred, and is essentially a movement in which display is used to obtain prestige, to overcome opposition and to defend consciousness against a sense of inferiority. As a display motive it contains the feeling of anger, and the impulses of combat, and its relation to the reproductive motive is obvious. It is as an aspect of a deeply pessimistic strain in national life, as a process in which an original and naïve sense of reality and superiority, challenged and attacked and brought into the field of opposition and criticism and thus negated by a feeling of inferiority, that this motive becomes of special interest to the psychology of nations and of war.

The roots of this pride and honor process we can find in the impulses which lead groups to demonstrate power and prowess to one another, and in the original feeling of reality which is accompanied by the belief on the part of the group that its own ways are normal and right. We might mention as significant the widespread belief on the part of very primitive peoples that they alone are real people, or are the superior people of the world. The Lapps, Sumner (70) says, regard themselves as "men" as distinguished from all other peoples, a form of self-consciousness which lingers in all such antitheses as Jew and Gentile, Greek and barbarian, and the like. This basic idea of difference in reality is not confined to a few peoples, but there is a tendency for every group to divide the world into two parties: selves and outsiders, and this feeling of difference readily develops into the moods in which there is a mystic sense on the part of a people of being the chosen people, and into those specific theories of superiority that run through the history of most if not of all nations. It belongs to the psychology of Greeks, Romans, Arabs, Chinese, Japanese, and also to Americans as well as Germans; and we learn that Russian books and newspapers sometimes discuss the *civilizing mission of Russia*.

That the motives of display and pride have been peculiarly active in Germany in the last few decades has been maintained by many writers. German writers are inclined to believe that the motive for the "attack upon Germany" was jealousy on the part of her enemies, that Germany was supreme in everything and other countries could tolerate this no longer. Germany has talked about her virtues, her rank, her coming place in the world. Bergson says that Germany's energy comes from pride. Some see the source of this alleged conceit of Germany and her excessive self-consciousness in Germany's hard experiences—the recent slavery, Germany's position as the battle ground of Europe, her late arrival among the great nations. Germany still lacks, they say, the quiet assurance that an old culture gives. Some call Germany morbid and quarrelsome. Again we hear the pride of Germany called an adolescent phenomenon, and they say that Germany is fighting not for principle but to see who is superior. Bosanquet (91) thinks that the lack of political liberty in Germany has had the effect of producing self-consciousness, and a morbid interest in small distinctions of title and rank, and that it is thwarted national ambition that has expressed itself in such writers as Treitschke and Bernhardi. Bourdon (67) thinks Germany is jealous of the culture and the glory and the political and literary prestige of France. Collier (68) says that Germany is forever looking into a mirror rather than out the open window and even sees herself a little out of focus. The seriousness of the Germans, others think, is an indication that Germany takes *herself* too seriously.

But national vanity, we see, is certainly not confined to Germany. The Germans at least think France is highly self-conscious, always thinking of her dignity, glory, prestige and of revenge. Wundt (85) feels much the same about the English. He says they always want to be first in everything, and to dominate the earth. We know that the Confederacy of the United States, at the outbreak of the Civil War, appealed to the world on the ground that it had reached the most noble civilization the world had ever seen. The Japanese (73), we have heard, believe that they are of divine descent, and that they are supreme in manliness, loyalty and virtue. Every nation presumably has somewhere in the back of its mind a belief in its own supremacy in something, and has a sense of being or having something that makes it unique in the world.

We can now see in part how the idea of national honor arises out of the pride of nations. Certain fundamental feelings issue in the form of claims of superiority or supremacy, which may be either vague and unclear or very definite and self-conscious. This claim to superiority is precisely what we mean by national vanity. With this consciousness there goes a knowledge that these claims are in general not recognized by other nations, or that the prestige which the recognition of this superiority presupposes is at least insecure. Since, of course, these claims to supremacy cannot all be valid, there must be a great amount of inferiority parading in the world as superiority, many fictitious and presumably half-hearted assumptions that must not only be defended against outsiders, but must also be *internally fortified*. The pride and the conceit must be justified by the creation of a fictitious past, and of an impossible future. The motive of these falsifications on the part of race consciousness is clear. A nation is defending its claim to superiority by first establishing the claim in its own mind. These claims being really unfounded must be placed beyond criticism. They must be given a religious form. But also external forms and relations of an artificial nature must be established. Nations always hide behind barriers of formality. They make displays to one another. In this way the feeling and the appearance of superiority are kept up. Everything external to the group and not participating in its illusion of supremacy must be *kept* external to it. The belief which the nation itself assumes in regard to its virtue must be demanded from all outsiders with whom the nation has relations of any kind. At least the forms of the recognition of the claim must be insisted upon. This is the principle of national honor. It is a defense of certain ideal or fictitious values in which nations insist that others should recognize these claims and values. National honor is an artifice for defending a claim to superiority and concealing an actual inferiority, and it relates to values which, in general, do not exist. Its work is concerned with the maintenance of prestige.

These ideal values and the integrity of the appearance of supremacy, are sustained by the assumption of the forms of empire or the imperialistic attitude. Empire is indeed what is dramatized in the forms which nations assume, and this dramatization of imperial form is the background of all the ideas of honor. The maintenance of the integrity of the imperial form, as an ideal realization of the supremacy a nation assumes, becomes more important than even the securing of material possessions, for the imperial form is the very reality and existence of the nation. It is at bottom merely the assertion that its own mores are supreme and entitled to be universal. To admit that this is not so would be to become to some extent unreal, and to lose something essential to a sense of personality. Therefore, there can be thus far no intimate relations among nations. They must present to one another symbolic representations of themselves. It is their flag, the symbol of their place in the world and of their military prowess and courage; their ambassadors, the representatives of their dignity and the symbol of their pretended friendliness; their display of royal forms, which is the sign of their prestige and their imperial nature, about which they are most sensitive. Offenses to these symbols of what a nation assumes itself to be and demands that others should think it, tend to be *mortal* offenses, because they invade the sphere of what nations hold to be their reality. So the relations of nations to one another must, as we say, always be formal. Nations can allow no intimacy. Why they cannot one can readily see, for it is not difficult to detect the fear, the jealousy, and the inferiority motive behind all this assumption and display. Treitschke shows us what national honor may mean when it is carried out into a philosophy of state. Here is the idea of national self-consciousness at its greatest height. The state must not tolerate equals, or at least it must reduce the number of equals as much as possible. The state must be absolutely independent. The state, furthermore, cannot have too keen a sense of its dignity and position. A state must declare war if its flag is insulted, however slight the circumstances may be.

National honor, its codes and standards and its justification and vindication by combat, present so many resemblances to the practice of dueling and the idea of personal honor once so generally held by the upper class, and still existent where the military spirit prevails, that we ought to study the dueling code with reference to the psychology of war. There are psychological features that appear to be identical. The idea of personal honor is associated with a feeling of superiority that must be defended. Any offense or affront to the individual was a mortal offense. The superiority in question was first of all superiority of ancestry; it was this that constituted the value of the individual and set the standards that he must maintain. This superiority was to be judged not so much by conduct as by an assertion of it represented by certain external forms. The individual by his manners declared himself a gentleman, and laid claim to forms and considerations that must not be omitted in relations with him. The virtues he defended so rigorously did not exist as a rule in calculable or practical form, since they did nothing objective. They might be ornamental or purely fictitious. They existed in the form of claims, and the values assigned to them were arbitrary. The man declared himself possessed of superiority, and was ready uniformly to prove this claim by acts purporting to indicate willingness to die.

This code and belief belonged to a day when relations among individuals were simple and, so to speak, external. They were relations that were readily codified and made invariable, since they had no essential practical content or function. Manners were significant as substitutes for friendly relations, since the system was lacking in moral and social sentiments. Manners were a means of fitting together individuals who really belonged to no functioning whole, except when, for example, they might be united in military exploits. Everything was unitary and independent of everything else in this society.

Now this code and this philosophy of life have declined precisely to the extent that the conception of ideal human life has changed, from that of something ornamental and personal to that of something useful and moral. Life has become organized, and relations have become more practical, so that the values of conduct may now be estimated, and one no longer may maintain a claim to virtue based upon forms expressing intangible or subjective or unreal virtues. The virtues of a man in a democratic society are, indeed, more or less obvious and open. Pride of family, an ornamental mode of life, and a scorn of death are no longer necessary and sufficient guarantees of worth. Evidence of value is both possible and required; before value is admitted it must be shown. Self-defense in a legal and moral society are in the main superfluous, and the values of individuals are so changed that to justify them by the duel would seem out of place. Its service being to defend artificial or arbitrary claims to distinction, it ceases or it falls into disuse when the individual's reality and value come to depend upon his functional place in society. It would be highly illogical to put to test social values by a process that appears to have nothing but anti-social elements in it.

That nations exhibit the same type of relation toward one another that we find in dueling and its code seems to be clear, although we must always avoid pressing any analogy between individual and nation too far. A claim to superiority that is deep and irrational, and which appears on the surface as sensitiveness in regard to honor and vanity, keeps nations always in defensive attitudes, quite apart from the actual fear of aggression. This superficiality or at least externality of relations is the source of actual conflict. The forms employed to maintain these relations are obviously ornamental, are elaborations of the forms of courtesy among individuals, are little dramas of friendship, so to speak, little plays representing friendliness, while the diplomatic motives are simply to obtain everything possible, each nation for itself, without war, and to maintain prestige. These relations are substitutes for social feelings that do not exist. Generally speaking, nations are never friends. They never really share in anything. They are all highly conscious of their own prestige and dignity, and they always communicate with one another in a formal way. In it all, we see the signs of emotions and habits that extend far back to the beginnings of social life and indeed into animal life. The display which takes the form of social relations among nations, represented well by uniformed diplomats, is so plainly archaic and its real meaning so obvious that we can hardly fail to understand what it is all about. That the attitude is really defensive, and the purpose to keep up appearances before strangers, so to speak, can hardly be doubted.

The fact that these questions of national honor are in some respects detached from the main realities of *political relations*, and are, indeed, fictitious and exist in the region of the imagination, that they pertain to the conventional and ornamental sides of national life, might be supposed to indicate that they could easily be done away with, and all these fertile causes of war be eliminated. That must not be assumed. Vanity has deep roots. The ornamental in life symbolizes the real. It is the point of entrance to the deepest motives. Conventional and archaic forms do not die out, just because we discover that they are irrational and harmful, and the causes they serve seem to us to be unreal. This kind of unreality in the consciousness of nations is in fact the ideal for which nations live. Nations play at being great, and fight to defend their prestige—but this play, as we know, is oftentimes terribly real.

CHAPTER VI

"CAUSES" AS PRINCIPLES AND ISSUES IN WAR

The causes for which wars are fought, or which are asserted to be the causes, make one of the important psychological problems of war. Sometimes these causes are elusive, sometimes they may give occasion for cynicism and a pessimistic view of national morals; again we see self-deception, again ideals seeking for light, peoples trying to find something to live for or to die for. We see in the recent great war as in other wars, a great variety of causes for which men are said to be fighting. Some would say that the war was entirely a war of principles; some take a purely political point of view and say that principles are not involved at all, and others that nothing was displayed at all of motives except primitive passions which are equally devoid of moral issues or any principles.

It would be interesting from the psychological point of view to make, if possible, a complete collection and classification of the causes that have been brought forward as the fundamental things fought for in the late war. Many widely different and divergent views are held. The forms in which the issues of the war have been stated are almost innumerable. New definitions and new statements of old conventional ideas appear continuously. Every writer seems to see the war from a different point of view from all others. Eventually, we may suppose, all this will be clear, since these "causes" of the war will be one of the great themes of future philosophical history. At present we can only formulate such a view as may be suggestive with reference to general interpretations of the place of principles and causes in war.

Let us examine a few of the opinions about the issues fought for in the recent war. MacFall (56) says that the whole strategy of the civilized world is bent upon creating permanent peace. Many speak of the war as a war to overcome war; we are told that one of the most conscious motives of the soldiers in the field has been to make the great war the last war the world should ever see. Something of the same idea is involved in the view each nation has that it was attacked, and that the purpose of the war was to defeat and punish aggressors. Apparently every nation and every army engaged in the war has had the feeling that it was fighting in the interests of world peace.

The German explanations of the war and of its issues have been very numerous and widely varied. The German has had his own interpretation of the "white man's burden," Tower (57) calls attention to the German hybrid word "Sahibthum," expressing the mission of a people. Each nation has its essence, which becomes a deep impulse. The German's impulse is translatable in the words "Be organized." The German has been eager to organize the world. He-believed in all seriousness that he was fighting the fight of order against chaos. It was the fight of the spirit against that which is dead and inefficient. The German believed that the systematic exploitation of the world was his peculiar mission. Ostwald is the great apostle of this view. He said that the war was a battle of the higher life against the lower instincts. Germany represents European civilization. The German emperor said that Germany should do for Europe what Prussia had done for Germany—organize it. In the German philosophy of life this principle of order had become a serious principle. An inefficient and disorderly world had need of Germany. Everywhere there was waste and stupidity, and a want of reason in the world. System was to be the cure. The fundamental fault in all this disorder the German mind recognized as an excessive individualism. Individual instinct and the social order were in eternal conflict, as Dietzel expressed the issue, and Germany stood for the social order, for reason, since reason is precisely the denial of the instincts and the desires of the individual in the interest of a foreseen result.

Shortly after the beginning of the war, we remember, a manifesto appeared signed by three thousand German university professors and other teachers, saying that they, the signers, firmly believed that the salvation of the whole of European civilization depended upon the victory of German militarism. Hintze (49) said that Germany was fighting for the freedom of everybody, meaning presumably according to the German principle that freedom consists in voluntarily submitting to order. This freedom is also in Hintze's view a principle of freedom and equal rights for all nations, in so far as these nations have reached the necessary stage of civilization. The mission of the coming central management of mankind (*Menschheitzentralverwaltung*) implied in the most ideal theory of Germany's mission is the true German burden. Haeckel says that the work of the German people to assure and develop civilization gives Germany the right to occupy the Balkans, Asia Minor, Syria, and Mesopotamia, and to exclude from those countries the races that occupy them. Schellendorf says that Germany must not forget her civilizing task, which is to become the nucleus of a future empire of the west. Koenig says that the spiritual life of Europe is at stake, Germany's fight is the fight of civilization against barbarism—against Russian barbarism he means. This ought to be the cause of all Western Europe, but England and France have betrayed the western civilization into the hands of the East. This belief gave to Germany's cause a deep impulsion (12).

Another way in which Germany's cause was frequently stated was that Germany was a pure, virile and young race which was fighting the older civilizations of the world. Vigor was assured of victory in any case, but young life had a duty to perform—that of clearing the way for new growth. This has found numerous forms of expression among German writers, some of them highly dramatic and exaggerated; as, for example, that the human race is divided into two species or kinds, the male and the female, assuming that the German is the male among the national spirits.

With these views of the nature of the German ideal or cause there have gone, of course, interpretations of the conscious motives and principles of other nations. In general other nations had no principle. German writers have tended to believe that both England and America were hypocritical and that their pretended democratic cause was at heart only party and political aspiration. These nations, they said, claimed to desire the world to enjoy the rights of democracy, but each country assumed that it itself must be the controller of that democratic principle. Another frequently expressed view of the purposes of England and America is that they have purely sordid interests, that they are capable of fighting only for advantage and material gain.

Many of these German views of the war imply a principle that runs through many fields of German thought—that values are something to be determined objectively. It is a scientific principle. Its conclusions rest upon proof, rather than upon subjective principles of valuation. There is another argument which is in part based upon an interpretation of scientific principles, but is in part also a fatalistic doctrine—confidence in the issues of battle as a means of testing the right and the validity of culture. The right will prevail, on this theory, because the right is the stronger or because in some sense strength *is* the right, and because the method of selection of the best by struggle is a basic principle, and may be applied to everything that is living or is a product of life.

If the German interpretation of the German cause has been dominated by an ideal of objective proof, we hear on the other side much about subjective rights and subjective evaluations—the right, for example, of every people to determine its own life, to have its own culture, to decide upon its own nationality. The Allies have believed that they were fighting to establish this principle throughout the world, and that this principle is diametrically opposed to the German principle. The thought of centralization, of a hierarchy of nations and the like, is wholly foreign to this democratic principle. Bergson (17) finds in the idea of industry the cause of the war and the principle of opposition in it. The Allies, he says, have been fighting against materialism with the forces of the spirit. Germany's forces are material. A mechanism is fighting against a self-renewing spirit. The ideal of force is met by the force of the ideal.

Boutroux (13) says that France, in the war, has had before her eyes the idea of humanity; France was fighting for the recognition of the rights of personality—rights of each nation to its own existence. France is a champion of freedom; she wants all the legitimate aspirations of peoples to be realized. Germanism, with its ideal of force, is contrasted with the ideal of Greek and Christian culture and philosophy. A cult of justice and modesty is contrasted with the cult of power; in the former, sentiment and feeling have a place as criteria of values; in the latter the appeal is to science and to reason.

Hobhouse (34) says that the war is a conflict of the spirit of the West against the spirit of the East (precisely the same as the German view, we see, but with a very different identification of the champions). Germany has never felt the spirit of the West. The war is for something far deeper than national freedom; it is a war to justify the primary rules of right. Burnet (18) thinks that the great conflict was a conflict between Kultur as nationalistic, and humanism as something international—that Germany, in recent years, had abandoned an ideal of culture for that of specialization in the service of the State. England's answer to the call was not to the specific need and appeal of Belgium, but because England felt that there was something in Germany incompatible with Western civilization.

Le Bon (42) says that we must always remember that the Teuton is the irreconcilable enemy of the civilization of the French and of all it stands for, and that he must always be kept at a distance. Durkheim's view is that Germany's ambition and energy and will antagonize the freedom of the rest of the world, and the rest of the world felt this and the war was the consequence. Dillon (55) says that the future for which Germany has been striving is a future incompatible with those ideals which our race cherishes and reveres, and that we must make a definite choice between our philosophy and religion and our code on one side and those of the German on the other. Drawbridge (19) says that the war has been a conflict between the ideals of gentleness and tact, on one side, and of brutality and ruthlessness on the other. It is the Christian spirit against the Nietzschean.

Again we have been told that the war was simply a war of autocracy against democracy, of mediævalism against modern life, of progress against stagnation, of militarism and war against peace, of the Napoleonic against the Christian spirit. Occasionally we hear more personal and subjective notes. Redier (30) says that France was fighting solely to retain mastery of her own genius, in order to draw from it noble joys and just profits.

The American point of view has been expressed in several forms by the President of the United States. For example, he has said that we are one of the champions of the rights of mankind. The world must be made safe for democracy. And again, that America is fighting for no selfish purpose, but for the liberation of peoples everywhere from the aggression of autocratic powers. This view that the war was remedial, that it was in the interest of progress, to prevent that which is belated in civilization from gaining the upper hand, and that it is on the part of America a war of participation and aid in a cause which though supremely good might otherwise be lost, is the prevailing idea. That this spirit of the championship of causes and of justice to other nations is a stronger motive in the Anglo-Saxon peoples than in others appears to be an opinion that history on the whole can confirm.

It is relatively easy to obtain the opinion of philosophers about the "causes" represented in the war; it would be of interest also to know what the millions of men in the field think. Data are not altogether wanting, but there appear to be no general studies. That many men, in more than one army, have no clear knowledge of any cause for which they have fought, except as these causes are nationalistic is certain. That there is ignorance even among the men of our own army in regard to the causes and purposes of the war has been made evident. Knowledge and enlightenment can hardly have been greater elsewhere. German soldiers are credited with believing that they are defending Germany from attack. The French soldier was fighting for France. The invasion of his country left him no doubt and no choice. The English soldier has often said that he was doing it for the women and the children, and one writer says that the deepest motive of two thirds of the British army was to make this war the last. The American soldier, from the nature of the circumstances under which he himself entered the war has been more conscious of a motive of helpfulness and of comradeship with other peoples who are in distress and danger. Probably the idea of America's honor, and the more abstract idea still of the cause of freedom, even though this idea has been, so to speak, our watchword, have not been the most influential motives in the mind of the individual. Germany was attacking people who were in distress, and the American soldier went over to make the scales turn in the direction of victory for the oppressed.

There is, of course, a literature of the war produced by the soldier in the field, in which there are expressed high ideals, abstract conceptions and firm principles. The French soldier has written about liberty, the German soldier has had considerable to say about a Kultur war. An American volunteer in the British army has written, "I find myself among the millions of others in the great allied armies fighting for all I believe right and civilized and humane against a power which is evil and which threatens the existence of all the right we prize and the freedom we enjoy" (24). But in general the consciousness of the soldier, from all the evidence we have, was concerned, as presumably was that of most of us, mainly with the most obvious qualities of opposing forces, their concrete actions, and the personal motives of rulers.

Leaving aside so far as one can one's own partisanship and mores (which is not a very easy task), what causes can we say, with a considerable degree of certainty, have actually been issues in the present war? To some extent what one thinks these causes are will remain matters of personal opinion and preference. Are there also principles which, when once observed, will be accepted as the fundamental "causes" of the war? There seem to be three at least which characterize wide differences in the ideals and the civilization of the opposing forces.

There is, first of all, an issue between the ideals of a relatively autocratic form of government and a relatively more democratic form of government. This was a cause of the intellectuals, but it was also a popular cause. Men in general like the form of government under which they live. From the standpoint of those who hold that a democratic form of government is right, the war seemed to be a conflict between a modern and progressive régime and an old and vicious one. So far as this autocratic principle aimed to suppress the rights of individuals, or to menace the liberties of small nations, so far as it was aggressively militaristic and had imperial ambitions, which could be achieved only by force, it stood clearly opposed to democracy. Democracy and autocracy were plainly at war with one another, and yet if we look closely we shall see that neither one can offer any actual demonstration of its validity as the most superior or the final form of government. In part they may appeal to the observable course of history for their justification, but the final source of judgment seems to rest in the mass of opinion in the world. Questions of form and taste are not wholly absent. But the believer in democracy and the believer in autocracy will both assert that deep differences in principle are involved. They will not admit that democracy and autocracy are superficial forms, and are questions of taste, and they will not agree with Munsterberg, who says that the two forms tend inevitably toward a compromise, by a process of alternation in which first one and-then the other is the dominant form in the world.

The war, in another aspect of it, has been a conflict between the idea of nationalism and that of internationalism. It is a conflict between an ideal of state, represented in the German philosophy of state by the principle of complete autonomy of the individual nation, and one which assumes that states, while retaining their rights of sovereignty are to be governed by laws which regulate their conduct as functioning members of a society of nations. The difference is that, relatively, between a state of anarchy among nations and a state of order. To some extent there has been a conflict between the idea of rights and the idea of duties of nations. This internationalism is not merely a sociological principle, something academic and scientific, as a theory of state or society; it is an ethical principle, which contains some recognition of justice as a subjective principle. It has some roots in theory, but it is also based upon the immediate recognition of the rights of peoples to their own individual lives. Its ideal is a world containing many nations, coördinated by natural processes and not a world in which a single nation or a few may hold the supreme place, except as this supremacy might come by a process of natural development.

The third conflict of the war was one which we may call a psychological conflict. It was a conflict between two ideas of life, one based upon a belief in the supremacy of reason, the other implying that the final test of values in life remains in the sphere of the feelings, or is a matter of appreciation. Germany, in her recent history, has stood conspicuously for the belief that human society may and indeed must be controlled and regulated by definite principles—principles that must be determined according to the methods of science. These principles take the place, in this philosophy of life, of certain typical human reactions that are believed to be demonstrably irrational. In its visible and most practical form the application of this principle is through organization.

This characterization of German life reveals something very much like a paradox in the principles of the war. We see a conflict in one direction between a certain mediævalism in government and social forms and a more modern and progressive type; we see also a conflict of a modernism of an extreme form, represented by a scientific civilization, united with this mediævalism, and in opposition to a conception of life which is in some respects more naïve and more primitive. The explanation of this paradox is that Germany offers an illustration of a phenomenon of development that has been seen before in history, of an excess of development and specialization in a direction that appears to be off the main line of progress, or at least is an anachronism. Germany has shown us the effects of rationalism, some would say a morbid and hypertrophied reason. This rationalism is certainly in part a product of systematic education and propaganda, a conscious exploitation of science, and it is in part temperamental. Such a result is always possible in a small state with a highly centralized form of government. It is a notorious fact that Germany's type of civilization can be spread neither by persuasion nor by force. If we may apply a biological analogy we may say that German Kultur in its modern form cannot survive. That this German civilization has been felt by the world at large to be abnormal and of the nature of a monstrosity we can hardly doubt, and that therefore to some extent there has been a sense, on the part of the enemies of Germany, of fighting to root out a dangerous and rank growth. Germany, seeing in her own civilization only the appearance of modernism, has been inclined to regard all other civilizations as decadent.

Germany, governed by the ideals of rationalism, has assumed that history can be made, wars conducted, life regulated in accordance with a program. On the other side we see a very general acceptance of a philosophy of life in which many evils of disorder and waste and the necessity of an experimental attitude toward life are accepted as necessary consequences of the life of freedom. We see implied in this philosophy of life a belief in a morality and a religion that are based upon feeling rather than upon objective evidences, and a way of judging conduct more or less naively and simply or according to methods of appreciation that are essentially æsthetic, using the term in a wide sense. This mode of life is accepted in the belief that order in due season will come out of relative disorder, by a natural process or by a gradually increasing organization and voluntary adjustment. If we accept the validity of this attitude in life we shall be inclined to regard rationalism as it is manifested to-day in German life as an evil. We may believe that in the end the cure for this rationalism will not be less reason but rather more, but we shall see also that it is possible for reason to outstrip and pervert life, and indeed involve life in an absurdity, simply because as a method of dealing with the whole of life it cannot be sufficiently comprehensive.

Are these and all such issues that we find in war, causes of war? Do nations fight for principles? Opinions certainly differ on this point. Some think of wars, we say, as essentially conflicts of principles; some interpret wars wholly in terms of political issues. We should say that the truth lies between these assertions or is the sum of their half-truths. Wars are not in their origin wars of principle. The political, the personal, the concrete aspects of the relations of nations are always in the foreground in causing wars. Wars become wars of principle after they have been begun for other reasons. Sanctions and motives appear after the fact. Fundamental differences of mores which include the raw material, so to speak, of principles and causes are factors in wars in so far as they create misunderstanding and antipathy, but in so far as these differences of nature and of principle do not enter into the sphere of politics and of national honor, they do not as such cause wars Those deep moods which accumulate in the minds of peoples and enter into the causes of war are not convictions about principles. They are more generic and natural. History does not seem to show us wars caused by pure principles. We sometimes say that the Civil War in our own country was fought over a principle, but that is something less than the truth. The fundamental question at issue was plainly that of the rights of certain states at a particular time to be independent and free.

Principles emerge in war, we say, and then they become secondary causes. And it is precisely this emergence of principles from fields of battle that perhaps constitutes the greatest contribution of wars to the civilization of the world. We need to reflect upon this deeply, since the whole philosophy of history is concerned in it. The virtues that nations discover in themselves in war they elaborate in peace. Nations at war become conscious of their spiritual possessions. Since their existence, they believe, is at stake, it is a part of their self-defense to justify their value in the world. They discover in themselves that which is most characteristic of them, and this becomes their principle. The principle of a nation is that which the national consciousness fixates itself upon as the title of the nation to continued existence. Nations do not go to war over their causes, or about their distinctive virtues and missions in the world. Rather it is their likenesses that precipitate wars,—their resemblances and identities in being the same in ambition, and having the same conceptions of national honor and the same motives for war and desiring the same objects. Nations in general do not go to war over principles because they are not motivated by principles in their historical course. The principles of nations are aspects of their inner development. The "causes" of nations at war, according to our view, are these inner qualities of which they have become conscious. Nations discover them in the stress of war, and it is quite natural also that in such times they should not always judge them fairly, and that they should often make for themselves a fictitious character.

CHAPTER VII

PHILOSOPHICAL INFLUENCES

Philosophy, in the minds of many writers, must be given a high place among the causes of war, and a considerable fraction of the literature of the late war is devoted to the problem of discovering, in the field of abstract thought, the influences that led to the great conflict. Nietzsche, especially, seems to have been held responsible for the European conflagration. As the philosopher of the New Germany, as the chief expositor of the doctrine of force, the inventor of the super-man and of the idea of the beyond-good, Nietzsche seems to stand convicted of furnishing precisely the concepts that have become the German's gospel of war; and since the German is prone to be guided by abstractions, the evidence, even though circumstantial, seems to many to be convincing.

Schopenhauer, also, as the great pessimist; Hegel, with his doctrine of the supremacy of the State as the representative of the Idea on earth; Kant, as the discoverer of the subjective moral principle; English utilitarianism as the doctrine of the main chance; empiricism, as the philosophy of inconsistency and dual principles of thought and conduct; even the whole spirit of the English philosophy, which Wundt says is nothing but an attempt to reconcile thought with the ideas of peace and comfort—all these have been charged with being instigators of the war.

Bergson (17) takes a different view. He says that the desire comes first, the doctrine afterwards. Germany, determined upon war, invokes Nietzsche or Hegel. Germany in a moral temper would appeal to Kant, or in still a different mood to the Romanticists. Le Bon (42) says that nations are pushed forward by forces which they cannot understand, and that rational thoughts and desires play but a little part in war. That appears to be true. We cannot say that philosophies do not enter at all into the causes of war, but among these causes they must be insignificant as compared with other causes that neither arise from abstract thought nor are greatly modified by reason in any way. Consider the influence of Napoleon (himself so little a product of any philosophical influence), as compared with Hegel; or of Bismarck as compared with Nietzsche, and this will be apparent. There are in the course of the centuries books and men that, as rational forces, do exert profound effect upon the practical life, but they must be rarer than is sometimes supposed. It is all too easy to assume a relation of cause and effect when there is only a similarity between thought and subsequent conduct. Rousseau may or may not have inspired the French Revolution. Probably he did not. The recent great war, we might say, has occurred in spite of philosophy, and if Nietzsche's influence gravitated toward war, it can hardly be thought to have had any deciding force in turning the scales already so overloaded by fate. Philosophy failed to prevent war. Nietzsche's philosophy did not cause it. His philosophy affords a convenient phraseology in which to express a philosophy of war, granting sufficient misinterpretation of his philosophy. Probably what influence he has had has been due rather to his literary impressiveness than to his thought as a contribution to philosophy.

Darwin, as the great force behind a new and varied development of science, has had the fate to be, in some sense, a factor in the moods and the new habits of life that led toward the final issue in the great war. It is not so much that his principle, misapplied, or applied uncritically may become a justification of war or even its basic principle that has made him so great an influence, but precisely because his thought, by becoming one of the great coordinating principles of all the natural sciences has given power to a movement which has had various practical consequences, not all of them good, or at least not all yielding fruit for our own age. Darwin's great influence as a force turning scholarly interest toward naturalism and away from classicism, as a factor in modern materialism and even pessimism, as a background, if no more, for the Haeckels and Ostwalds of science is no inconsiderable factor in the scientific and objective spirit of the day.

Facts must be faced. It is not such influences as that of Schopenhauer, who expresses a logical or at least an abstract and we might add literary form of pessimism, that in the generations just past have transformed most of the conceptions of religion, with all the effects upon the practical life that have followed, but the force of our modern science combining with tendencies which it fosters but perhaps does not create, giving momentum to industrialism and specialization,—it is this change in the ideas of men that we must suspect of being implicated in the present catastrophe of the world, if any influence from the rational life is to be counted at all. Hegel and Kant hover in the background. The author of the plan for universal peace provides us with a subjective principle of morality which can be distorted into a philosophy of moral independence and even of independence from morality, and Hegel must have helped to establish the German theory of the State, although with Treitschke and with the practical state-makers like Frederick the Great and his followers, we can hardly believe Hegel indispensable. The causes of war are too general, too old and too fundamental to be greatly added to or detracted from as yet by philosophy. Philosophy is the hope of the world, it may be, and by no means a forlorn hope, but it is not yet one of the great powers. When philosophy is a mere endorsement by reason of some motive that has arisen in the practical life, or is a literary expression of views about life, it may give the appearance of being a profound force in the world. But this is not real philosophy, in any case. Philosophy has not as yet shown itself highly creative even in the calm fields of education and the moral life.

No! Philosophy is a factor in the motives of war rather by reason of what it has not done, than because of its positive teachings. To-day we ought no longer to be under illusions on that point. Neither Christianity nor philosophy can make or prevent wars as yet. They have not been able to cope with the practical forces of the world which make for nationalism, partisanship and personal interests. It would require a greater amount both of religion and of philosophy than we now can bring to bear upon the world to offset the influence of Napoleon alone in the practical life of nations. It is the Napoleonic spirit that still governs Europe. Philosophy has been thus far a science of being an explanation of the world after the fact, and not even to any great extent a science of its progress, except in so far as, we may say, beginning with Hegel and with Spencer, there has been some development of the methods and the most formal conceptions of such a science. It is asking too much of philosophy, in its present stage, to expect it to preach the gospel, or to teach school, or to direct politics, and for the same reason it is unjust to charge philosophy with having created the greatest catastrophe of history. If philosophy cannot wield any great power now in those parts of life that are by their nature presumably most amenable to reason, its effect upon those events that express the supreme force of human passions and the totality of life will not be very important. The influences of philosophy are academic, and presumably any doctrine of life that preaches achievement, virility and unmorality will include in some degree war among the interests that it will affect, within the limits of its academic nature. But youth is inherently warlike, because above everything else it seeks to realize life in its fullness, and war at least does symbolize this reality and abundance of life. A philosophy which preached peace would hardly become a great influence with youth. A philosophy advocating the cause of war would form a natural background for the essential motives of youth. If the scales were evenly balanced, it might turn them. It is hard at least to see the relations of philosophy to the practical life in any other light to-day. Philosophies are tenuous and adaptable things. We see them used to support opposite causes, and they change color under the influence of strong desires. Bosanquet (91) shows us how Hegel's noble conception of the State, if we but substitute for its central thought of welfare of the State, that of selfish interest, may be made to change before our eyes into the meanest of maxims. This process is, however, not unique in the history of the relations of thought and life.

A detailed study of the relations of intellectual factors to war would need to consider the effects of a great number of more or less philosophical ideas which throw their weight on the side of war. So far as these ideas are simple and clear, and especially if they can be conveyed in the form of the phrase, their influence cannot wholly be ignored. Some we have already referred to. The doctrine that might makes right, the conception of state as supreme, the belief in the divine right of kings, the belief in the ordained rights of aristocracy, belief in militarism as a social institution, the doctrine that life may be controlled by reason, all intellectual pessimism, skepticism, any form of concept-worship, whether Hegelian or other, acceptance of the methods of science and the results of science as applicable to all the problems of life—all such principles which inhabit the region, so to speak, between philosophy and the practical life manifestly have some relation to the spirit of war. In a very general way they may be counted as philosophical factors in war. For the most part, however, those ideas that have been accused of abetting war are exaggerations and perversions of philosophical ideas. Nietzsche, Darwin and Hegel have all been exploited and made to stand sponsor for specific philosophies of war. In the new philosophy of life which Patten thinks has greatly influenced German conduct, and which may be expressed in the words *Dienst*, *Ordnung*, and

Kraft, we can see both the effects of impulses that have grown out of the new life itself, and the influences of formal philosophy. That such ideas have had relatively a greater influence in Germany than elsewhere must be admitted, but that either this devotion to ideas or the ideas themselves have been derived from philosophical interests and from philosophies that have played any important part in the history of thought we may well doubt. We should suspect that the same practical interest that works unceasingly to distort and popularize philosophy would help to create such pseudo-philosophy.

Von Bülow (65) says that the German people have a passion for logic, and that this passion amounts to fanaticism:—that when an intellectual form or system has been found for anything, they insist with obstinate perseverance on fitting realities into the system. Durkheim (16) says that the Germans' organized system of ideas is a cause of war. It is also true, we should say, that the tendency to organize ideas and even the fundamental ideas by which the Germans have been guided are deeply rooted in temperament, in history and in the social order of the past. Boutroux (13) says that the Germans themselves regard the war as the culmination of their philosophy. We should say on the contrary that the whole war philosophy of Europe is almost wholly a product of strife and comes from impulses that arise irresistibly in the practical life. Into these movements philosophy fits or may be made to fit, and the presence of ideas in a society in which the academic life has great prestige, ideas which coincide with beliefs readily gives an illusion of an order governed by the higher reason. The fact that Germany's recent wars had all been highly successful, the fact that Germany had learned to depend upon her good sword in time of need are the chief sources of Germany's doctrines of war: the Hegelian background in the light of what we have learned in recent times about the psychology of nations, must seem to be rather of the nature of the ornamental. The ideal of the Prussian State to be a power directed by intelligence suggests Hegel, but it seems highly improbable, to say the least, that Hegelian philosophy has had much to do with shaping this ideal. Behind all this is the necessity of shaping German life in the form which it has taken—necessity if we accept, at least, Germany's national temperament itself as a necessity. That other belief, widely held by German intellectuals and officers that war is the testing of the validity of national cultures would also probably never have appeared on the scene had not Germany been secure in the belief that she herself had both the right and the might on her side. It is possible, of course, that the war has distorted our vision so that the relations of the practical life and the life of reason have all been thrown out of focus, but when we see what forces have been at work, and what they have done, it is difficult to escape the conviction that we have been inclined to believe too much in the power of mere ideas. This may be the great lesson of the war. We may learn from it how to make ideas become the power that hitherto they have failed to be.

CHAPTER VIII

RELIGIOUS AND MORAL INFLUENCES

That war and religion have always been closely associated with one another is one of the outstanding facts of history. This is true both of primitive warfare and of warfare to-day. Yet we cannot say that religion as such has been a cause of war. Religious wars are almost invariably also political wars, and as soon as religion and politics are separated, religion no longer appears to be a war motive. When religion becomes associated with worldly ideas which it supports and makes dynamic it may become a strong factor in the spirit of war, but as a means of segregating men, and giving them unity of action religion can no longer be regarded as a power, if it ever was. Any motive that will not so segregate men and break up all other bonds cannot be said to be a very fertile cause of war. Religion as a cause of war belongs to a day in which the spirit of nationalism was weak, and when religious empire had a visible and political position in the world. Nationalism, growing stronger, became the supreme force dominating the motives and interests of men and governing the formation of groups, or at least the actions of groups as interrelated units. In the recent war we have seen how the sense of national unity has been able to hold in check all other motives. Neither religion nor any class or clan or guild interests could trace the faintest line of cleavage so long as the motive of war remained.

The mood of war always contains a religious element. Not only is this shown in primitive wars, where the relations of religion, war and art are indicated in such phenomena as the war dance, which is of the nature of a magic weapon, but we see it also in the complex moods of the present war spirit of the world. The idea and mood of valor have a religious significance. Cramb says that we can trace in Germany before the war, showing through the transient mists of industrialism and socialism, the vision of the religion of valor which runs through all German history. The craving for a valorous life, for reality, the desire to lose one's own individuality—these moods of war are religious or mystic whatever else they may be or contain. The inseparable relation of war and death necessarily inspires a religious consciousness. Without exalted moods which in some way contain religious faith—faith on the part of the individual in the eternal values which he represents and in his own security in the hands of fate, and in the immortality of the country which he serves, war could not exist.

The mood of war always contains a religious sanction, and every important religion sanctions war. This explicit relation between religion and war is seen very early. Wherever there is ghost worship, and the warriors justify war and fortify themselves for it by believing that their ancestors still participate in the combats of their children, and that in waging war they are doing a duty in keeping up the traditional feuds of their race there is found the root of the relation between war and religion. Every war is a holy war; it is but a change in degree from these primitive wars in which the ideas of ghosts must have had almost the clearness of reality to our modern wars with their deeper but more indefinite religious sanctions. Since war always creates the need of moral justification, the war mood at all times tends to seek religious sanctions. Christianity, the doctrine of peace and good will, very readily lends its support to war, since wars are almost invariably regarded as defensive by all who participate in them. War in the service of the weak and endangered can always invoke the spirit of Christianity. The logical ground for this has been laid for us by many writers; Drawbridge (19), one of the most recent, finds no support in Christianity for the doctrines of pacifism. All nations, when they fight, fight for God, for liberty and the right, with the implied belief that their own country has a mission in the world, supported by divine authority.

All governments have in them a strain of theocracy. We see this in many degrees and forms, from the original totemistic belief in descent from animals that are also gods to the vaguest remnants of the habit of interpreting national interests as guarded by divine powers that we often see in the language of practical statesmen. The doctrine of the divine rights of kings of course had its origin in that of divine descent. The most striking revelation of the place such theories may have, even in modern times and in enlightened nations, is to be seen in the revival and deliberate use of the doctrine of divine descent as a fundamental principle of the government and theory of State in the New Japan. All nations hold something of this philosophy; God and State are always related and all wars, whatever else they may be, are waged in the service of religion and with the sanction of it. This spirit is not wanting even in the most modern democracy. The historians of Germany have shown us to what an extent the theory of the divinity of state and its divine mission may be intermingled with practical politics and have helped to bring to light the psychology of this movement in history.

Several writers, but especially Le Bon (42), have written about the relation of mysticism to war. Le Bon said indeed that the main causes of war, including the most recent one, are mystical causes. By mysticism he means unconscious factors which are religious in quality and which contain a race ideal which is both powerful and irrational. German mysticism appears to have attracted much attention during the years of the war. Germany has presented the picture, we are told, of a people becoming dangerous by couching national ambition and honor in terms of religion. This mysticism of the German contains a powerful belief in race superiority, and in the supremacy of the culture of their own nation, beliefs which have the clear marks of mysticism about them. The traces of the theory of divine origin still cling to them. Boutroux (13) says the Prussian State is a synthesis of the divine and the human. Another writer observes that the Germans believe in the altogether unique and quasi-divine excellence of the German race, and of Germanism, and that the Germans have a new religion which they believe in spreading by the sword. Some see in Germany a serious demand for the revival of the religion of

Odin and Thor, the religion of conflict of primeval forces, and of the triumph of might. Literary expressions of this religion are certainly to be found, and it may fairly be maintained that Germany has never become Christianized to the extent that most modern nations have.

That mysticism has been a large factor in the war spirit of the Germans in the late war can hardly be doubted, or at least that a religious element of some kind has played a great part in it. The war began as Germany's holy war. A cult of State and of self-worship are involved in it. If not, innumerable expressions of Germany's cause among German writers are simply literary exaggerations. The Germans have believed that they are God's chosen people, that they represent God, and since the German civilization grew up in antagonism to the Graeco-Roman civilization, God must have adopted the one and discarded the other. One German writer says that we must eliminate from our belief the last drop of faith in the idea of a progressive movement of humanity as a whole. Reality is represented in one nation at a time, and the chosen nation is the leader of all the rest.

While such mysticism as this (if it be mysticism) is most conspicuous in aristocratic and imperialistic nations, we find it elsewhere. It is a powerful force in imperialistic Japan and in Russia. We find it everywhere in history in some form. In France it is still the "saintly figure" of France that inspires the soldier and induces a religious mood. There is no longer a vision of an empire of the future, perhaps, and this mysticism of France has not in recent history shown itself in the form of aggression, but French mysticism clings to the ideal and the hope of a glorious future for a deathless France soon to be renewed. All peoples that have declined or suffered an adverse fate, even the pathetic remnants of the American Indians, expect the return of their lost power. Such mysticism is, we may think, the only condition under which national life in many cases can continue. The religious or the mystical mood of nations is created by the need of making belief dynamic, of overcoming doubts and fears. Hence the exaggerated and irrational claims peoples make in regard to the value of their culture and about their mission on earth. By their mysticism nations justify their aggressive wars and fortify themselves in their defensive wars. Thus nations acquire a feeling of security. They believe in their star of destiny. They feel that their life which is of supreme value to the world cannot perish. It is this spirit that nations take with them into battle. It is a mystic force, and this mystic force is, in great part, we may believe, one of the by-products of the tragedy of history. Faith and hope have one of their roots at least in fear and pessimism.

Moral Motives and War

That the attitude of nations toward one another is not, generally speaking, an ethical attitude and that moral principles do not motivate the conduct of peoples we have already suggested. Sumner (70) says that the whole history of mankind is a series of acts open to doubt, dispute and criticism as to their right and justice. Differences end in force, and the defeated side always protests that the results are unjust. And yet wars are always conducted with moral justification and in the belief that moral principles are involved. These moral principles, however, are not the points of difference upon which the beginning of wars depends. Nations never go to war for purely moral reasons. Moral feeling may coincide with the interests of state, and a defensive war may of course be conducted in the spirit of deep moral right and duty, but plainly it is never the sense of right and duty alone that is the motive of defense. Perhaps after all this question of the moral element in the causes of war is a futile one, and leads to casuistry. There are always political and other practical questions involved, whenever strain occurs between nations, so that wholly moral issues can never arise.

If wars are not moral in the making they are always justified morally, whatever the motives may have been that caused them. Without this moral sanction it is doubtful whether wars could be conducted at all, although this moral sanction may be based upon very superficial grounds. The higher patriotic feeling runs, says Veblen (97), the thinner may be the moral sanction that satisfies the public conscience. On the other hand moral sentiment may often be strong and deep in the minds of the masses of people in a nation, and the public feeling of obligation to enter a war may be strong, but in general such moral feeling does not lead to war. Righteous indignation lacks initiative. Honor as moral obligation requires the aid of honor as national pride and dignity. The relations among allies may at first thought seem to be moral relations, but when we observe closely we see that usually nations go to war together because their common interests are endangered. When their common interests are not involved they usually break treaties and so do not stay together. Actions directed offensively against one member of a coalition are usually directed against the others, so that in most cases the allies of a nation have no choice, but must defend themselves.

The relative importance of moral principles in the motives of war may be observed by comparing the motives assigned by the nations that participated in the late war with the motives which a study of the history and political situations of these countries reveals. There are wide disparities between these historical causes and the assigned causes. These need not, however, lead us to take a cynical view of history as many sociologists and students of politics do. We have as yet no organized world in which moral principle can operate. The world, we might say, is still infantile or immature. The world is still unmoral. We cannot say that nationalism as the principle of the conduct of nations is a wholly selfish principle as contrasted with a moral or altruistic motive, since such an analogy with individual morality fails to take into account the complex nature of nationalism, and overlooks the social qualities of patriotism.

England's purpose in entering the war has been freely discussed in England. The popular impression is that England declared war upon Germany in order to defend Belgium and to keep her treaty obligations. If we consider conduct in a certain abstraction from the practical setting in which it is performed such a conclusion can be drawn. There was a moral stirring in England, and several writers have commented upon the fact that England subverted her own conscious purposes by her unconscious and instinctive morality. There was a strong feeling against war, even a widespread moral sense that England had become too civilized to wage war. There was a shrinking from the economic hardships that war would entail.

Against these strong tendencies there prevailed, at least in popular sentiment, a profound feeling that in some way Germany's civilization was incompatible with England's, and this feeling was in part of the nature of moral aversion. Dillion (55), at least, sees a profound ethical motive in Italy in the late war. After a pro-German party had won out in favor of war, he says, a *deus ex machina* in the shape of an indignant nation descended upon the scene. But after making allowance for all moral feeling and the unusual and dramatic manner in which moral issues, to a greater degree than ever before in modern history, were brought to the front, we must admit that the political and diplomatic interests and manners of nations have taken their usual course in the war. Nations have been governed by the motives that have always dominated the relations of groups to one another.

Germany presents the most glaring example of the contrast between public opinion and expressed motives and political facts. Such expressions as these: that Germany's ideal is one that does violence to no one; that humanity and all human blessings stand under the protection of German arms; that, where the German spirit obtains supremacy, there freedom reigns; that in regard to England's downfall, there can be but one opinion—it is the very highest mission of German culture; that Germany's war is a holy war—such expressions as these, which are psychologically explicable without questioning their sincerity, seem out of harmony, to say the least, with what we know of Germany's political aspirations. Germany's desire for England's downfall does not appear to us to be based upon a moral motive; Germany's war seems far from being a holy war, and it is hard to see in it a means of spreading culture abroad in the world. We cannot give any place in the causes of this war to a moral desire to make the world better. However much Germany may have been convinced that Germany was destined to be a civilizing force in the world, the moral obligation thus aroused, we may be sure, did not become the real motive of the war.

The moral justifications of war are very numerous, and that this belief in war has some effect upon the spirit of war and helps to perpetuate it, and is not a mere reflection of the warlike spirit itself, may of course be admitted. Many believe that war accomplishes work in the world; war is a great organizing force. There is also a view that war is good as a moral stimulant, or as a creative moral force. War is often regarded as the means of moral revival of a people that has become sordid and dull. Schmitz (29) says that war gives reality to a country. War strengthens national character, some think. It purges nations. In war people grow hard but pure. Irwin (25) says that such war philosophy as this is to be heard broadly in Europe, chiefly in Germany, but also in France and in England. Mach (95) says that disintegration takes place in times of peace. Schoonmaker says that war has taught men socialization. Again we hear that wars are just and right because they are necessary. Redier (30) says that war is a way of giving back courage to the men of our times. This praise of war which comes from the depths of feelings, we must suppose helps to give continuity and force to these feelings.

Institutional Factors

If the spirit of war is to any extent educable, and is created in national life and is not merely something instinctive, it is presumably modified in one way and another by all those institutions that are educational in their effect. Perhaps one of the most pressing problems of education in the near future will be that of the relation of education to war. We shall need to know what the school has done to cause wars, what changes should be made in the future with reference to this influence of education upon the fundamental motives of national life. The schoolmaster has been indicted among other instigators of war. We must see how much truth there is in this allegation. We must understand also how the whole educational process, as we may see it now after the war, may be made if possible to become a greater factor in life than it has been in the past, if it is at all an important element in the development and the control of the psychic powers of nations.

Schmitz (29) says that the eighteenth century and the French Revolution were dominated by the phrase, the nineteenth by money, and that there was a danger that the twentieth century would be dominated by the schoolmaster and by the concept, but that this danger is past because life has become so full of realities. Russell says, we know, that men fight because they have been governed in their beliefs and in their conduct by authority. If this be true the authority exercised upon the mind of the child by all his teachers may be suspected of having been in one way or another an influence in creating the moral attitudes that prevail in regard to war and peace. We have heard the question raised as to whether in the past the teaching of history as the story of wars, and the presentation of the facts of history from the nationalistic point of view, have not been morally wrong.

German schools, and the method of public education the sinister effects of which we have abundantly felt—that is, the propaganda, show us educational phenomena that are psychologically of great interest and which are also unique from the educational point of view. The influence of schools seems in general so negative, and there is so little connection between what is learned as fact and conduct in the practical life that, even in the case of the German teaching of war philosophy we must suspect that this teaching has been successful only because it has gone with the strong tide of feeling in the popular mind. That the German schools have directly and indirectly fostered the development of ideas that lead in the direction of war there is no doubt. Even more influential than the specific ideas that have been implanted, is the spirit of these schools: it is their militaristic and routine life, the great authority assumed by the teacher, the specialization, that has helped to nourish the warlike spirit of Germany, quite as much as the fact, for example, that Daniel's Geography teaches that Germany is the heart of Europe, surrounded by countries that were once a part of Germany and will be again.

German education, we say, seems to be unique in the extent to which it influences public sentiment and national conduct. In general, education has appeared among the influences that lead to war rather by default of positive teaching than by anything positive it has done. Even in Germany, we should say, the spirit of war has been made to flourish less by the teaching of a narrow nationalism, by inculcating hatred, and implanting wrong conceptions of German history than by failing to provide youth with means of deep satisfaction, by failing to coordinate deep desires of the individual, and to organize individuals in a normal social life. This is true everywhere. Education has not affected life as a whole, and it has not thus far been an influence which, to any appreciable extent, has accelerated the development of peoples in their especially national aspects and relations. It has nowhere fostered any conception of the whole world as an object of social feeling. It has everywhere accepted a certain provincialism as natural and necessary, and has tacitly assumed that national boundaries are the horizon of the practical life of the child. The school has in fact failed to take advantage of its unmatched opportunity to use the imagination of the child to develop his social powers. Sociologists say that if sociologists had been more diligent in spreading abroad information about the social life, the great war would perhaps never have happened. That we may certainly doubt; something more profound must be done by education than to disseminate knowledge, if it would undertake to be a power in the world and to do anything more than add its influence to the tendencies of the day, or perhaps temporarily change the direction of these tendencies.

CHAPTER IX

ECONOMIC FACTORS AND MOTIVES

Thus far we have considered the motives of war mainly from the psychological point of view, discovering its main movement and development in the world to be a product of the psychic forces in the social order. This method, however, did not exclude the objective facts, and did not ignore the practical motives. We found that war is a manifestation of many tendencies, and in fact is related to all the deep movements in the life of society and of the individual. War comes out of the whole of life in a way to preclude the interpretation of it in terms of any single principle, or at least to prevent our finding a single cause of war. We ought to try to see now how such a psychological view of war stands in relation to certain more objective views of it, which in a very general way may be said to be centered in two closely related views. One is that war is almost exclusively an economic phenomenon, and the other that war is the work of individuals. One is the economic interpretation of history, and the other is the great man view of history.

We still see a lingering theory that war is a result of the ancient migratory or expansion impulse—that over-population and the pressure of various economic conditions are the source of the impulses that lead to war. We have seen reasons for believing, however, that war, even in the beginning, has not been a wholly practical matter. Hunger, pressure of population, migratory movements because of economic conditions, will not explain the origin and the persistence of wars. Wars are not simple as these views would imply, at any stage. That at the present time economic advantage, whether or not it be the motive of war, is in general not gained seems to be very clearly indicated. The taking of colonies and other lands may be a detriment rather than a gain to the conquering nation. The industry and the finance, of all concerned in war, are likely to suffer disaster. Peace is the great producer of wealth. War is a terrible destroyer of it. Ross says that as industry progresses, wars become continually more expensive and less profitable, that the drain is not upon man power so much as upon economic power; nations bleed the treasure of one another until some one of them is exhausted and must yield.

The theory that war is caused by the pressure of population, especially as applied to the recent war, now appears to have been very naïve. It was maintained that Germany needed more room for her growing population, that Germany must have more land at home and more colonies. Claes (46), among several writers, shows that this is not true. Germany had no pressing need of more land, except for political purposes, or such land as provided the raw materials for her military industries. Bourdon (67) maintains that it is not true that Germany's population was becoming excessive. Le Bon (42) says that this theory of over-population is a myth. Still others have shown that in a country that is rapidly becoming industrial, as was Germany, where population is becoming massed in the great cities, emigration ceases; and that actually, in Germany's case, labor was imported every year, and that there are great tracts of arable land in Germany still but sparsely populated. Nicolai (79) also attacks the theory that war is sought for economic gain and says that an economic war among the European states is an absurdity.

The need of colonies is often put forward as a real and also a legitimate motive for war. Colonies must be provided, they say, for the overflow of population from the homeland; colonies are the foundation of the trade of nations—trade follows the flag. They think of colonies as the offspring of nations, and nations without colonies seem sterile and destined to extinction. We know that Germany's desire for colonies is one of the causes of the European crisis, and that the colonial question has been a fertile cause of trouble in Europe for many years. And yet we have evidence that in the present economic stage of the world, colonies do not perform to any great extent either of the functions that are claimed for them. Trade does not in general follow the flag; industrial nations do not need colonies either to provide for over-population or for commercial reasons. The acquisition of colonies does not as such benefit the great industrial and financial interests. Why, then, do nations so ardently desire colonies; and why, without colonies, do they feel themselves inferior and at a disadvantage? Why, in a stage of industry, in which it is presumably more to their advantage to conduct aggressive campaigns in countries already densely populated, are nations so willing even to fight to obtain colonies? Powers (75) says that the desire for colonies comes from the idealistic tendencies of nations. This appears to be true. Correspondingly we find that colonies are of more interest to general staffs and admiralties than to captains of industry. Colonies are wanted for military reasons, more than for trade reasons. Colonies are desired as bases of operation in the game of empire building by conquest. There is still another reason. The race for colonies perpetuates an ideal which has grown out of an earlier stage of the life of nations. Colonies were once actually the means of the greatness of nations. The longing for colonial possessions, for the extension of commerce, the great jealousy and apprehension of peoples in regard to their trade routes, and the fear nations have for their commerce, quite out of relation to present needs and conditions, hark back to an old romance of the sea. The waterways of the world, the islands and new continents have a traditional appeal, which comes down to us from the days when the small countries of Europe, one after another—Portugal, Holland, Spain, England—became great in wealth, and grew to be world powers, by their commerce and their colonial possessions. In those days the expansion of nations was not at all due to economic pressure at home. The landowners, the rules, the privileged class in general were interested in colonies, because in that direction stretched the path to fabulous wealth, and because over the seas were the lands of adventure. The seeking of colonies was both the business and the pleasure of the nations. To-day the gaining of colonies may be only a loss to nations economically, but they satisfy the craving for visible empire, and also a longing that is deep and intense because tradition and romance are deeply embedded in it.

Probably no one now believes that war among modern nations is due to a pure predatory instinct or to a migratory instinct which is supposed to have led primitive hordes to seek new habitats and to prey upon other peoples. Hunger does not now drive people in companies from their homes and pour them into other lands, although it is true that any threat which excites the old hunger-fear tends to arouse the war spirit and to stir the migratory impulse; and a deep sensitiveness to climatic conditions and a claustrophobia of peoples have remained long after the need of land urged as the main cause of war, and we hear war justified on the ground that crowded peoples require more land. This *land hunger* is an old motive and it still remains deep in the consciousness of peoples long after its economic significance has ceased. Just as we say the threat of hunger is often imagined, and the fear of hunger and a deep and persistent fear of peoples and the sense of danger of being engulfed and destroyed by other peoples linger in consciousness, so the consciousness of the old struggle for land remains as one of the most powerful of traditions, and any threat, near or remote, to a nation's land arouses all the forces of the war spirit, and the thought of aggression as a means of conquest of land is always alluring.

Land was once the main possession and the main need. To-day it is the chief symbol of the power of a nation. The possession of it is desired when it gives nothing in return, certainly when there are no valid economic reasons for taking it. This land hunger becomes the excuse of nations for their sins of aggression. A differentiated society, so organized that only the few, if any at all, can by any possibility profit by the taking of lands still hungers for this primitive possession. To a great extent land as a national possession has an ideal rather than a practical value. It was one of the original sources of prestige and distinction, having become the main material interest of man as soon as he came to have fixed abode. The whole historic period of the world has been a story of a struggle for land. It is the memory of this land struggle, which is one of the deep motives of war, which often determines the strategy of war, and the policies of nations.

Precisely how the system of great land ownership originated is obscure. Sumner (70) says that the belief that nobles have always held lands, and are noble by reason of this possession, is false. Nobles have in one way and another enriched themselves and bought land; or rather having acquired land they have succeeded in acquiring titles of nobility, and establishing their lines. In all nations which have retained any traces of the feudalistic form, and to some extent everywhere, land continues to be the basis of wealth, and also of power, and the land-owning classes are still mainly the ruling classes. This land-owning class is still dominated by the old traditions of the landed aristocracy. It is the fighting class, and supplies great numbers of officers for the armies. It upholds the idea of national honor in its ancient forms as related to private honor; it provides the great number of diplomatic and decorative officers. Japan, Russia, Germany and to some extent England, at least up to the time of the war, have retained feudalistic institutions, and the land interest still remains as a motive of war. In all these nations, certainly in those which have remained feudalistic in fact, it is the aristocratic and owning class that usually represents the war interest. It both rules and owns. It sends out the peasant and the worker to extend the state. It is the protected class. Laws and constitutions favor it. Taxes fall lightly upon it. Originally this was the class that received all the benefits of war. To-day it suffers less from war than do other classes. Even when it does not gain by war in a material way, it is likely to gain in power (100).

We have seen this system of class rule at work in very recent times, and it is a question whether the old ideal of land possession did not work to the ruin of Germany economically, and indirectly antagonize the industrial interests of the nation. German politics had been trying to serve two masters, who were not entirely in agreement. Germany was still a country of landed proprietors, and these proprietors always have thrown their weight to the side of war. They were by no means dominated by a motive of pure greed, and they did not seek war entirely for their own advantage, but because, we might say, they are ruled through and through by motives that can be satisfied only in a militaristic state of society. Their gain from a successful war is mainly a gain in prestige and distinction. An unsuccessful war, as we have seen, threatens their extinction as a class. All democratic movements tend toward land division, or is indeed in part precisely this process. Aristocracy without land cannot maintain itself.

The economic theory of war comes to its own in the view that industry now controls the world, that industry is the power behind politics, and that industrial needs are the real energies that make wars. We live in an industrial age, they say, and industry rules. Plainly to find the whole truth about this relation of industry to war is no simple matter. There are at least three more or less separate questions involved in it. We need to know whether an industrial state of society, or the industrial stage of economic development, is especially prone to cause wars, as distinguished from more general political and economic interests. We need to know whether wars, in an industrial stage, do really serve either the interests of industry or countries as a whole. Finally, there is the question whether those who control industry and finance do actually create wars.

In the industrial and financial stages of economic development new conditions arise which certainly must be taken into account in any theory of war. There are deep changes in national life. The moods of the city become a new force or a new factor in national life. Socialistic ideas and new aspects of nationalism and patriotism appear. There is a spirit of unrest; both pessimistic and optimistic tendencies in society are increased; the motive of power takes new forms, and there is a deep stirring of fundamental feelings and impulses. The crowd instincts, the old hunger motives, are felt beneath the surface of life. This is the effect of industrialism upon the psychic forces of peoples in their collective aspects. Nations also become as wholes more specialized in the industrial life; they are dependent upon one another as never before. All the ancient motives of commerce are stimulated, and the minds of nations revert to the old fears and the old romance connected with the thought of the seas. The growing interdependence of nations produces a peculiar and paradoxical condition. Competition in regard to markets arises, with all the complications and strains that we have seen in recent years. There are new motives of aggression, but at the same time the need and motives for peace are increased. Industries in general thrive best in an era of assured peace. They live upon the wealth and prosperity they themselves create. Intrigue, not force, is their proper weapon. Le Bon (42) says, that the desire to create markets was not the cause of the great war, because expansion went on very well in the time of peace. Germany had no aggressive designs except commercial designs we are told. Mach (95) tells us Germany's whole future, the success of her carefully laid plans for industrial development and supremacy, depended upon continued peace.

That such views of the relation of industry to war are in the main correct can hardly be doubted. Industrial relations create strains among nations, but when as a result of these strains war occurs it must be regarded as a disaster from the point of view of the industrial interests. Industry we say thrives upon the wealth that it creates. A war which destroys half the wealth of the world must be a calamity for all great industries except at the most a very few having peculiar relations to the activities of war.

But there is another aspect of the relations of industry to war. Industrialism as a great institution and movement of modern life becomes in itself a political power. Howe (100) says that with the end of Bismarck's wars personal wars and nationalistic wars came to an end. The old aristocracy of the land merged with the new aristocracy of wealth and this wealth has become the great political power in the world. But this is only a half truth. Industry has become a factor in the foreign relations of nations, and has become a power in politics, but the motives and powers we call political are exceedingly complex, and the interests of business, industry and finance are by no means the whole of or coincident with political interests. There are of course certain industries and financial interests which may even instigate wars, and some writers give them a high place among the causes of war. Especially the makers of munitions and armaments are credited with a baneful influence in the world. With their international understandings, their influence in legislative bodies, their control of newspapers, they are open to the charge of manipulating public sentiment, and bringing influence to bear upon governments. They are accused of equipping small countries and setting them against one another, of deliberately encouraging the race for military and naval supremacy. No one can doubt that their opportunities for trouble-making are many and enticing, but to think of these influences as anything more than the incidental and secondary causes of war seems to be a curious way of understanding history (100).

The inside history of the great financiering projects would no doubt give us some of the main clews to the present diplomatic relations of nations to one another. If we take into account the various intrigues in connection with the building of the Bagdad route, the financing of the Balkan States in their wars, the bargaining of the Powers in Turkey for financial concessions, the great business interests involved in the Russo-Japanese war, the loans to China and all the rest of the financial history of a few decades we should have in hand materials that no one could deny the importance of for an understanding of current history. Diplomacy has had added to its already complex duties the art of securing financial advantages. In general the art of this diplomacy is to secure these advantages without war, but there can be no doubt that financial relations have multiplied the points of contact and strain among peoples, and that these financial relations have become the main occasional causes of wars. Howe (100) thinks that surplus capital is to blame for a great many of the great disasters of modern times—that it destroyed Egyptian independence, led France into Morocco, Germany into Turkey, and into the farther East, embroiled the Balkan States; and that the great war has been a conflict over conflicting interests of Russia, England and Germany in Turkey. Under the guise of expansion of trade this invisible wealth has been exploiting the most vital interests of foreign countries. Veblen would go so far as to say that wars are government-made, that patriotism is exploited by governments in advance of pre-arranged hostilities to produce the spirit of war (97).

If we hold that these economic causes are now the most important causes of wars, it is easy to accept the conclusion that the most fundamental, and even perhaps the sole cause of war is the evil principle of ownership, as is actually maintained by many economists. If men in cliques, and men as individuals did not own privately great parts of the wealth of the world, these conflicts in which wealth and its distribution are the most vital interests would not take place. Many socialists, we know, hold these views, asserting that wars are due solely to industrial competition among nations, and to the fact that industrialism is based upon the wholly wrong principle of private ownership. Hullquist, a socialist, says that wars are likely to become more frequent and more violent as the capitalist system of production approaches its climax. The working classes, the socialists say, who have nothing permanent, are the natural enemies of war; the capitalists, who have much and want more, are constantly placing peace in jeopardy. The protective system of tariff also receives much abuse from these writers. Novicow (71) places the tariff system high among the causes of war. The belief that it is good to sell and bad to buy, he says, is the great trouble maker in the world. This was also the principle of Cobden the great English free-trader of the middle of the last century. The Manchester school of which he was the leader would do away with wars by making the world economically a unit.

Veblen (97) charges the price system with being a fundamental cause of war, and says that it must now come up for radical examination and perhaps modification. The theory of the rights of property and contract which have been taken as axiomatic premises by economic science may itself fail, or at least be thrown open to question. Either the price system will go, or there will be wars between nations in the future as there have been in the past, because of the need of protection of ownership rights, and because of the nationalism these rights create. To some extent these rights of property *have* been curtailed, Veblen remarks; the old feudalistic rights have in large part been annulled, and the world is at least owned by more people than was once the case. That these changes and readjustments of property rights will be carried still further he thinks there can be no doubt.

Stevens draws similar conclusions about the evil effects of property rights. The great war and all wars, he asserts, are based upon existing social conditions—upon the organization of the family, the school, the state, the church, upon the institution of property, with its corollaries of foreign markets and other industrial relations. Protection of trade, which works in the interest of the owner classes, indirect taxes which fall upon the consumer, the labor system by which, at the present time, the laborer receives but a small share of the profits, but must become when necessary the defender of the interests in which he does not share—all these things we hear being charged vigorously with being the causes of wars, including the recent great conflict. This system is blamed not only for our great international wars, but it is looked upon as the germ of wars to come, internal wars, when international wars shall have ceased, or temporarily have been abated. When, perhaps, the restrictions that assume that the gain of one country is the loss of another have satisfactorily been adjusted, the system that maintains that the capitalist can prosper only at the expense of the laborer will come up for final settlement (97).

All these views, from a psychological point of view, seem to be open to the criticism that they tend to consider the world one-sidedly and by a certain abstraction. They are dealing with a world governed only by economic laws. It is easy to construct these ideal worlds. They are simple and they lend themselves readily to the purposes of a political calculus. Finding economic motives in individual life, in the social life and in politics, and in history it is tempting both to explain the past and plan the future in terms of the entities and principles of economics. But after all it is only when we consider economic motives in their relations to all the motives behind human conduct that we are likely to see the economic motives in history in their true light. Then we shall very much doubt whether property has been in any real sense the cause of wars, or that the abrogation of property rights will be the means of establishing perpetual peace. We shall see that economic motives themselves are but aspects of deeper motives, and involve desire for objectives that are not sought for their material value, and also objectives that are not material at all. The process of development of present human society, so far back as we can see, and as far into the future as we can with any confidence predict, seems to contain as a necessity some form and degree of human slavery. This appears to be inherent in the fact itself of the existence of individual wills, having in any degree individual or personal interests as they must, and the impossibility of devising any social order or government that will give to the individual an ideal freedom, if such a conception be indeed possible at all. We may conjecture at least that in a world in which every trace of an economic motive had been removed, if this were possible, there would still be slavery of some kind, and the inexorable logic of individuality would in the end produce conflict and war.

Nations, like individuals, live, and they pass through certain stages that seem in a general way to be necessary phases of their development. During this process of development certain objects become, one after another, of the most vital concern because they are necessary to the satisfaction of the motives which guide the lives of these nations. But these objects are never so definitely marked off that they become to the exclusion of other motives the causes of wars. The social life is never so simple as this would imply. The past is always involved in the present. One after another certain types of economic objects-become more or less central in the interests of nations, but the minds of nations, like those of individuals, are always influenced by the tradition. Objects are desired with reference to the satisfaction of motives that represent complex and general desires. There are ideal objects as well as material objects; and the material object is often sought because of its possible use as a means of satisfying the desire for ideal values. First food, then land, then commerce, then industry, then wealth itself,—this has been the order in which economic values have become objects for the consciousness of people as groups, and have become involved in and more or less completely represent the relations among peoples we call political. That which is, relatively speaking, an object of necessity at one stage tends to become an ideal or romantic object of the next stage. The relations of economic objects to the desires of nations and to war are complex and not precisely what they may on the surface appear to be. Nations, like individuals, do not know what they need, and they do not even understand clearly what they desire. Their desires are complex: elementary economic motives, political motives, personal motives, the motives of industry and finance, the motive of power and the craving for certain states of consciousness all exist together, and to some extent antagonize one another. The present practical desire is confused by the traditional object. The will of a nation is a composite will, and its history is full of contradictory impulses, and also full of surprises. Nations often think they are fighting for economic reasons when their real motives are plainly to gain military distinction. The reputation is quite as satisfying as any material prosperity gained. There is an illusion and a delusion about it all. All these economic advantages that nations are always seeking have something unreal about them. Nations seek them long after they represent real values. Nations seek colonies when, if business is what they want, it could better be obtained nearer home. Finance looks for advantages overseas, when there are quite as safe investments at home paying quite as large profits. Nations have desires to do great things, not merely to live and prosper.

That is the way these economic problems of war appear, at least when they are examined in relation to other aspects of war and of society. These economic problems are merged into and subordinate to the political or the historical problems, and economic causes of war must be considered with reference to the psychological principles that are at the bottom of all social development.

CHAPTER X

POLITICAL AND HISTORICAL FACTORS

We think of political causes of war mainly as an aspect of the fact that nations desire always certain *geographical objectives*. These desires are represented in part by the policies of governments and leaders, but we must also think of nations as a whole as having desires, and as being moved by profound purposes. At once the question arises whether we shall think of these political objectives, and the wars the desires for them cause, as essentially the objects and the work of individuals. Do individuals in any real sense create history? This, of course, is a profound question and involves fundamental theories of history. Shall we accept the "great man" theory of history, and say that history is mainly the work of a few who are able to shape events with reference to policies of their own, or shall we think that forces that determine history reside rather in the instincts or desires of the common life of the people?

A psychological study of history inclines us to the belief that the forces that make history are mainly forces that do not exist as conscious purposes and are therefore not essentially political forces. One of the conditions of leadership seems to be that the leader shall seek his own personal ends and realize his own purposes for his country only within the field of the traditional and common objectives which are held by the people as a whole as their purpose in history. These are the materials with which the leader must work. Historically his work may seem decisive. Psychologically it is to be regarded as a complex effect of lawfully related social reactions. The motives of leader and people must have large common factors. The leader holds his power and his prestige by embodying in his own will and representing in his own conscious policies the will of the people and their idea of country as an historic entity. The leader is leader only in so far as he is recognized as representing the will of the "herd." As genius, this leader is manifestly creative, but the true genius in statesmanship is even rarer than genius elsewhere. The great leader is an artist. He must take certain vague or clear ambitions of the people, must accept the nation's historic objectives as the foundations of his policies, and working with these objects and desires make his own page of history. His glory and his prestige depend upon his fulfilling deep desires of his people. The forces with which he deals are plastic, but only within narrow limits. Leadership at best is a fragile thing. However autocratic the power, it is after all dependent upon the good will of the people, and the acceptance of the leader as one who is serving the interests of the people.

When we consider the nature and the objects of the ambitions and desires that the statesman or leader must fulfill, we see why the relations of ruler to people are difficult to understand. Nations do not know with clearness either what they desire or why at heart they desire the objectives that seem of most importance. People give economic and political reasons, but the consciousness of nations is subject to deep moods, and is influenced by remote events and traditions. Nations have generic desires as well as specific ones. They always crave empire; they all desire to have rank. They are always ambitious, jealous and watchful of one another. These general and more or less subconscious desires make their desires for specific objects intense, but they also make them peculiarly irrational. The heroic examples of history, hereditary emotions and the effects of specific events in the history of peoples complicate their politics, and often make rational politics impossible. Nations will not act in their own best interests, because they are governed by irrational motives. In this way certain disparities are often produced between the people and their practical statesmen, but history seems to show us that when these disparities exist in the region of fundamental desires and policies it is the leader who must yield. History seems to show us also that wars, coming in general out of the deeper motives of nations, do not belong to such an extent as is often supposed to the realm of politics. Political causes are often incidental causes and determine the time and place of wars but do not create them. Cramb (66) says that wars persist in spite of their unreason, because there is something transcendental that supports them, and this transcendental purpose is the desire for empire. Powers (75) says that nations fight for tangible things and also for intangible things. The tangible things are existence, commerce, independence, territory; nations also desire objects that are not useful, the worth of which consists in their satisfaction of taste. The ambition to own colonies, Powers thinks, is of this nature. Colonies are quite as much ornamental as they are useful. They convey the feeling and impression of power.

That these deep desires of nations as expressed in the ambition to reach certain geographical objectives are exceedingly strong, often if not always irrational, brutally arrogant and tenacious, the whole course of history teaches us. These desires are indeed the forces behind historical movements. They create politics and policies. War preexists in these irrational purposes. These purposes are charged with emotion, with prejudice, and tradition. It is with these motives that all practical politics must contend, and these motives are the forces that the statesman must use and make more rational.

The purposes of nations are usually if not always we say obscure and deep, existing in the form of ideals and tendencies, and likely to take the form of visions of empire wholly unrealizable. And yet there are always certain perfectly clear objectives upon which all the force of these half understood motives impinge. These objectives may or may not be economically rational or morally justifiable. We always know with certainty certain of these objectives for which any nation will if necessary fight. These objectives have often a long history behind them. They are surrounded by tradition, sincerely and even religiously sought. They are ideal objects which nations feel they have a right to possess. Every nation apparently believes itself the logical possessor of something it does not now hold (99). All peoples have their longings for these possessions, which are their vision of a greater self. These objects are often desired for reasons that are clear enough to all; but they are also often but the symbols of deeper desires. As such, nations act toward them with almost instinctive compulsion.

We may suppose that no great historical event is ever enacted that is not determined more by traditional desires than by conscious politics. A thousand years of strife have provided the motives for the great European war. Memories of time-honored objectives have arisen in the consciousness of many peoples, and these memories cannot be recalled without exciting passions that make all rational politics unavailing. Europe has been fighting over again her battles of the past, and at the moment of the present writing is carrying them into the conference of peace. The plans of statesmen and the intrigues of finance have but little success in contending against these forces. Since the leaders themselves are not free from the prejudices and the compulsion of traditions and the unconscious desires and deep impulses which move their people, they can with but dubious success bring international politics into the sphere of reason. They do not represent merely the selfish desires of their people. They are not merely spokesmen of the interests of class or individual. They are embodiments of the whole history of their nations.

All history, and all the present relations of nations to one another may, of course, be considered in terms of the desires for specific objectives caused by the imperial desires of peoples, these desires themselves being regarded as a sum of motives, the effects of past political relations, and containing both rational and irrational elements. The world is a vast field of stress in which the powers at work are national wills rather than political forces as the projects of rulers and the diplomats. These powers, when fully aroused, are quite beyond the control of statesmen acting in their ordinary capacities, and their final issues no historian ought now to try to predict. History has been full of surprises because of the nature of the forces which create history, and these surprises seem to have been sometimes the greatest for those who were most intimately concerned in making history. Events seldom run smoothly according to well laid plans.

It would not fall within the scope of a psychological study of war to describe or analyze the complex system of strains that exist in the world to-day, and to point out the conditions that led to the great war would be for the most part unnecessary, since they must be obvious to all. The main items in such a study of history, however, may well be recalled to mind. One would need to show the effects of England's irresistible development through several centuries; the struggle for the control of the Mediterranean; Germany's efforts to extend her empire toward the East, and the closing of doors against Germany's advance; Russia's pressure upon the Teutonic peoples, the ancient and terrible dread of Russia on the part of the nations of Western Europe, the shadow under which Turkey, Germany, and England had lived because of the presence of the great Slavic state, with its mysticism, its dynastic ambitions and its great growth force, its need of open ports, and vital interest in the amalgamation of the South Slavic peoples, and the determination to own Constantinople and to succeed to the place of the Turkish Empire. We should need to take into account the long history of the struggle for colonies, the colonial trust of Russia, England and France, the ambitions of France for empire in Africa, the operations of French finance in the Balkans and elsewhere, Austria's aggressive hatred of Serbia, and her effort to prevent the revival of Poland, the conflicts of Germany and Austria with Italy in regard to the Ægean and the Adriatic and their shores, the fierce irredentism of Italy, and the ambitions of Italy that have brought her into conflict with the Teutonic powers and with Turkey, all the conflicting purposes and ambitions of Greece, Roumania, Bulgaria, and Serbia, and the added strain in the Balkans because of the vital interests of all the Great Powers there, and many other conflicts and causes of conflicts. These conflicts we see repeated in kind in the relations of Japan, China and Russia and the other powers interested in the geography of Asia, and in the waters of the Pacific, and once more in the growing strains between the East and the West (99).

Taking our world as we find it, and viewing the nature of nations in the light of their history and of their persistent antagonisms, one might readily believe that the causes of war and war itself will continue into a far future. No war, the pessimist might well argue, will destroy national vitality or neutralize the many points of strain. There may be great coalitions and even Leagues of Nations, but these may only make wars more terrible when they come. The friendship of nations will still be insecure and shifting. The great strategic points of the world will remain. Small countries will continue to be ambitious and jealous of one another. Island countries will still be faced by coasts that contain possibilities of danger. The Constantinoples and the Gibraltars will remain; Suez and Panama will be left, and Verdun will still be something more than a historic memory (99).

That these objectives might all be brought into a permanent state of equilibrium, by some ideal world politics, that nations *ought* to abandon their ideas of empire or at least see how crude these ideas are, how out of relation to our modern ideas of value, and how out of place in a practical world—all this we can readily understand, but who will expect nations to become very different from what they are now, and who shall say how many imperial eggs there are in the world yet to be hatched? There are many ways of justifying these ambitions—Germany justifies hers by reason, and the researches of her great historians—the Treitschkes and the Mommsens; Russia bases her claims upon her religion and her ethos; Japan brings her divinity and her traditions, her vitality and her intelligence; England offers her justice and above all her proved genius for government as a justification of empire. But after all, these desires for empire lie deeper than proof and reason can go. Poetic, dramatic and religious elements enter into them. There are geniuses among nations. The creative force in a nation is its life force, its essence and its reality. In some sense the desire to be an empire is the whole meaning of a nation, for without the ambition to be supreme, peoples, some of them, would be nothing. It is the vision of empire, however forlorn and hopeless, that keeps many nations alive, perhaps all. Nations seek to express in visible form the evidence of their inner and potential greatness. The historic and time-honored art of empire-building is the only art they know. Whether this is the tragedy of history, the world's fate and the condemnation of it to perpetual warfare—or is but a term in the logic by which nations rise to other and higher forms; or finally is a crime or a mistake which it is within the power of the will of man to abandon or amend—these are problems of the philosophy of history.

Historical Causes

Historical causes of war are in part the sequences of events that the political causes of war produce (political as the causes inherent in the wills of nations), and we must suppose they are mainly this. History, from this point of view, is the working out of the motives or the desires contained in these national wills. The causes of our late war, for example, are to be sought mainly in the wills of the great powers that are concerned in it. Economic forces, the laws of the growth of nations (both psychological and physical laws), the conditions of the geographical distributions of peoples over the earth—all these are involved in the cause of wars. There are also great personages whose actions must to some extent be considered apart from these general laws; these personages contribute factors to the causation of any given war that are not entirely inherent in the laws of growth or the psychology of nations. Shall we say also that there are fortuitous factors, historical causes that are not contained in any logic of human desires? Can we say, perhaps, that these fortuitous causes are indeed the main causes—in a word that wars are not desired, mainly, but are the product, indeed, either of the mere logic of chance, or of a design that transcends human will altogether? Are wars willed, or are they the results of the complex, the illogical and uncontrollable factors of the world's existence and movement? These may not be practical problems, but they are serious problems, since in the end they implicate the whole of philosophy.

What place shall we give, in the laws of history, to the sudden and chance turn of affairs; to the quick shift of the wheels of fortune; to the incidents, the accidents, the mis-judgments of rulers and the slips of the diplomats? Are wars after all a product of the logic of life, or are they mere fortuitous syntheses of events which in their particular combination make a total that is not involved, either as desire or as tendency, in the sum of the particulars that enter into the whole? How completely, in a word, do the interests and purposes of nations determine wars? May we speak of motives that always tend to produce wars, but never seem to will them?

History seems to show us that wars are less directly willed than we have sometimes supposed, and perhaps that there is a large element of chance in them as regards a given war at any time and in any place. War in general is inherent in, or is a natural effect of, the laws of development of nations. Wars as historical events are not completely describable in terms of these laws. It is the old contrast between the historical and the scientific explanation of things that appears here. Nations have deep and vague desires, we say. They want satisfaction of their honor; they crave a dramatic life, even military prestige and glory, but we do not often find war itself definitely willed. The desires of nations, we repeat, tend to be too fundamental to be specific. Their specific desires are indeed and for that reason likely to be contradictory. They desire both war and peace at the same time, and have interests that may be served by both. They live in indecision like individuals. Motives conflict. They hesitate, and doubt, and fear. They shrink from taking the plunge. It requires the sharp and clear event, the chance event, most often, to precipitate them into wars. It is always to-morrow that they are to wage wars. So wars do not usually occur by the rational plans and devices of any man or any historical sequences of men, we may believe, and it is a question whether wars are very often intended in a real sense by any one. Wars occur as crises in events. The strains that produce them are certainly inherent in the relations of nations at all times, and even in the motives of personal politics, but in general these relations as consciously governed relations are in the direction of seeking the greatest advantage with the least show of force. The conditions must all be present, both the match and the powder, before war can take place. There must be a condition of strain, having certain psychological features none of which can be missing, the condition being something complex and not readily analyzable, at any given time. In addition to these strains events must take place which, in all their appearances, are fortuitous.

One might argue from this that the cure of war consists in eternal watchfulness to see that the match does not touch the powder, that we must watch these events that precipitate wars and safeguard peoples from being affected by them. This, of course, is more or less the method of diplomacy; to some minds the league of nations is a device for doing this on a larger and more systematic scale. But when we study history and see what these war-causing incidents are, how numerous and how variable, we can see that diplomacy and statesmanship undertake an impossible task when they try to steer the world along its narrow historical course, with only historical landmarks for guides.

The war that is so vividly in mind now furnishes us with an illustration of the complexity of the causes of war, and allows us to see clearly contrasting views of the causal factors in great wars in general. We see here a closely fitting series of events, each in itself having but little reference to the great crisis, all fitting together, and for want of any one of which, if one takes the purely historical view, we might suppose the war would never have happened, or might have been postponed indefinitely. If Venezelos, to go back no further than that, had remained in Crete and had been content to be an island politician, would not the course of events in the Balkans have been very different? Out of his course came events which no one could have foreseen, but which, without similar actions on the part of individuals producing other links in the chain, would not have taken place. If some diplomat or some foreign office had made a decision slightly different from what was actually decided; if the three emperors had had a little more reliable information about one another; if the statisticians of the German service had computed a little better England's resources, and had put the moral factor into the sum—would the war have happened at all?

In this direction, of course, lies the chaos of history and its madness—and also its philosophy. We may be driven on the one hand to think of all history as a matter of the chance relations of individuals and of detached particular events, having significance as a series but never planned or controlled as a whole, or we may resort to the opposite way of thinking, and say that all of history, in every particular and detail, is divinely planned and prearranged, and each event fits into a rational whole. This, of course, is our final problem of history, we say, as it is the final problem of every question that considers life as concrete events having value precisely as the particular sequence that it is—when we view life historically, in a word, rather than by the methods of the quantitative sciences, or by the genetic methods such as are used mainly in the psychological sciences, and which we may say stand between history and the sciences of matter.

CHAPTER XI

THE SYNTHESIS OF CAUSES

It appears to be no very difficult matter to discover causes of war, and indeed a considerable number of causes. In fact the problem seems to yield an embarrassment of riches, especially if our chief interest happens to be a practical one, and we wish to find the causes of war in order to see how they may be controlled. We might even have discovered all the causes of war and still be as far as before from any real understanding of the cause of war. Unless one can know the relative importance of the causes, and the manner in which the causes combine to produce wars; unless the results give in some way a synthetic view of the causes of war, show *dominating* causes, or reveal a total cause which is not merely a summation of stimuli, but is both a necessary and a sufficient situation for the production of war; unless we have shown some fundamental cause and movement in the social order, we are still left in search of the cause of war.

We have, indeed, found a number of causes of war, but at the same time the causes have not appeared to exist as separate causes. We are always catching sight of a movement in the development of nations and of the world—of certain fundamental motives, the most basic of all, the most general, being the motive of power. These causes of war do not appear, however, to be of the nature of a *chain*, giving us the impression that in order to break the habit of war, all we need do is to discover the weakest link in the chain of causes, break the chain there, and so interrupt the whole mechanism of war-making in the world. Above all, although fortuitous events as causes of war must not be overlooked, war is not continually being made anew by the appearance again and again of accidental situations, which are thus to be regarded as the cause of war.

War is, first of all, a natural expression of the social life, resting primarily upon the fact of the existence, universally, of groups of individuals acting as units. But here cause and effect are lost in one another. Conflict cements the group, and the existence of the group, again, is the cause of conflict. War is an aspect of the social solidarity of the group acting under certain conditions, and these conditions are the presence of deep desires that can, in general, be satisfied only by the exertion of force on the part of communities acting as wholes.

These primitive motives and moods of war that we find in the nature of the social group itself, emerge finally in three aspects of the life of nations, and it is these aspects of the life of nations that appear to us as the causes of war. They are not separate and independent features of the social life, and it is in part only for the sake of convenience that they are sharply separated at all. They are all at bottom manifestations of the motive of power that runs through all history, and all the social and individual life. On one side this motive appears in moods and impulses that we called the "intoxication" moods and impulses. National honor was found to be another effect of it. The political motives of war are its concrete expression. These motives all together—all being but phases of a deep, powerful energy and purpose, are the source of the main movement in history out of which war comes. In this movement all the motives of the social life are always present and active at the same time. The good and the bad of national life are phases of a single purpose and are not two contrasted principles or moments. The past is always contained in the present.

War, then, is the result of certain motives which are fundamental to the group life. It is a natural form in which, given a certain degree of intelligence and of complexity of the social life, these motives express themselves. All the motives and forms of expression are present in germ at least from the beginning of the development of the social life. Considering the whole history of war we see that it is a part of a very complex movement in human society, and yet that no war appears to be the final term of a process of inexorable logic. Taking history as a whole, we see that the natural laws involved and the nature of the social consciousness make a state of war from time to time highly probable, but war is not a necessary consequence of any natural law. Nations are self-conscious personalities. Perhaps in the future they may change their ways, abandon voluntarily their desires, subject themselves to discipline, or deliberately invent a plan of international relations that will have the effect of eliminating war from their lives altogether.

It is always dangerous, but at the same time it is always tempting to try to explain national life, or all life and history, in terms of the individual and his experience. Once more, however, we may yield to that temptation and say that the world to-day is in a stage of development which has many traits that show its relation in some very significant ways to certain undeveloped conditions found in individuals, which in fact always appear as phases of the life of all individuals in some degree and form. Nations have acquired a high degree of subjectivism, partly on account of the geographical conditions under which they have lived, and the many barriers between nations due to difference of origin and of language, and the fundamental emotions of fear and jealousy which, as we have seen, play so large a part in the life and conduct of groups. Nations, however close to one another, have remained isolated in spirit; they have lacked both the initiative and the means for becoming definitely related to one another in purposive and sustained activities. Therefore all their relations have remained highly emotional, subjective, influenced by mysticism, filled with hatred and fear, hero worship and illusion. Nations have lacked both the power, and we might say, the organs, for externalizing their spirit. They have dreamed dreams and played plays, and followed their illusions of empire. Even their wars have not, until perhaps now, become wholly real and serious in a measure commensurate with their powers and resources. The present war more than any other, and more than any other event in history, represents an escape on the part of nations from their subjectivism, and a beginning, it may be, of the realization of a more mature, or shall we say more *normal* conception of the world. Nations have played at being great and have really produced but little true greatness. Now, let us say, their dream is over. We see that these nations can no longer play. Their wooden weapons have at last been turned to steel. They can fight no longer indeed without destroying one another. They must now *live* in practical and moral relations, give up their bright dreams of empire after the old heroic order, and be content to be imperial (if they are born to be imperial) by performing distinguished service in the world, by their own genius of leadership. There is work in the world for nations to do; there are empires of the spirit, it may be, greater than have yet been dreamed of in the nations' childish philosophies of life. The consciousness of nations contains, it may be, unsuspected powers, suppressed in the past by narrow nationalism, by fear, habit and convention. These powers may now, if ever, blossom forth; they have been wasted too long in patriotic feeling and in idle dreamery. They must now show what they can do in a practical world that will have no more of mere assertions.

The world stands to-day balanced between two ideals. Human spirit, the spirit of nations, is a free and plastic force; it is also a sum of motives and desires; but most fundamentally of all it is a growing, living, creative and personal spirit. It still clings to its luxuries of feeling, to its provincial life, it is still fascinated by its beautiful romance of empire. On the other hand we see the stirring of a new idea. A new world arises, less dramatic in its appeal than the old world, but a world appealing by its practical problems both to the will and to the intellect. Shall we yield to the fascination of the old romance and go back to our hero worship; or shall we be inspired now by this vision of a new and greater social order, create out of our own powers of imagination the forms this world must assume if it is to appeal to the deepest feelings of all peoples, and make this new world real by our own intelligence and determination?

We stand to-day at a dramatic moment in history; a more dramatic moment than when the victory itself hung in the balance. Perhaps our sense of responsibility for the future is an illusion; perhaps we are driven by an inexorable logic of history, and we do not after all choose what our world shall be. But certainly the sense of human power in the world has never been greater than now nor seemed better justified; nor, if we are deceived, has the reality ever been more out of harmony with the ambitions of man.

PART II
THE EDUCATIONAL FACTOR IN THE DEVELOPMENT OF NATIONS

CHAPTER I

EDUCATIONAL PROBLEMS OF THE DAY

Education, like all other institutions, has been charged, we know, with having contributed its share to the causes of the war. The Prussian school system, we have been told, was mainly a school of war; all the emotions and ideas necessary to produce morbid nationalism, distorted views of history, and a belief in and a love of war were there fostered and deliberately cultivated. There is, of course, some truth in this; it is a truth that is deceiving, however, if we regard it as at all indicating the true relation between education and practical affairs. If the school was a factor in the late war, such a creative effect of education appears to be rare in history. In general it is the negative effect of the school that is most conspicuous. It is what the school has not done to prevent war, what it has failed to do in not bringing nations out of their perverted nationalism into a life of more practical relationship with one another that really best characterizes the school.

It is difficult or impossible for us now, of course, to perceive what the war has done—in what way, all in all, the future will be different from the past. It is very easy and natural to look at everything dramatically now, see revolution everywhere and believe that all institutions are now to be radically changed. Or, going to the other extreme, we may become cynical, and say that, human nature being unchangeable, we shall soon settle down into the old routine and we shall see presently that nothing revolutionizing has transpired. Some will say, and indeed are saying that education must now be entirely remodeled; some will think that education had best go on as before—that nothing has happened certainly to require any new philosophy of the school, or any profound change in its form. We see these two tendencies in many phases of our present situation: in politics, in education, and in the business world.

It is impossible, we may repeat, to make wholly safe judgments now about the future, but still something must in the meantime be done. We must either stand still or go forward—or backward; we must act either with a theory or without one. The school is involved in this necessity. There is a new content of history that we cannot ignore, but must in some way *teach*. We must say something about the war; current events can hardly be kept out of the school, and to understand current events there must be a wider content of history than we have had in the past. There are new, or at least disturbed, conditions in the industrial and in all the social life, and these conditions cannot fail to have some effect upon the school. The school must adjust itself to them, and it must surely take into account new needs that have arisen. Patriotism may need to be taught now, or taught in a different manner. There is a problem of war and peace, the question of what ideals of national life we are to convey. Internationalism demands some recognition on the part of the school. It seems probable, therefore, and even necessary that a new interest in the function of education will be felt and must be aroused. Must we not indeed now examine once more all the foundations upon which our ideas about education rest? Certainly there will never be a more favorable time, or more reasons for such a task.

It is the impending internationalism, or the idea of internationalism now so vividly put before us all, that most incites new thought about education, and about all the means of controlling the ideas and feelings of the people. We hear much about *re*construction and *re*adjustment, and these terms obviously imply the old ways and the old institutions. But internationalism is something new, having many possibilities; it means new relations among peoples; it opens up new practical fields and new phases of sociology and economics. It is because of this new phase of the social life and social consciousness of man, we might suppose, that education is most likely to be affected in its foundations, so that no mere readjustment will be enough. A new politics and a new science of nations appear, and we cannot fail to see that there is at the present time something decidedly lacking in education; that there is a larger life perhaps for which our present ways of educating children would not sufficiently prepare, and that to prepare for this larger life something more would be needed than an added subject in the curriculum. This is because internationalism is not simply more of something we have already; it is a turn in the road, and a turn which, it can hardly be denied, will finally affect all institutions. If internationalism has come to stay, it will need, and it must have, powerful support from all educational forces. It will need something more than support; education must produce creative habits of mind, which shall make and nourish new relations in the world, and it must make people intelligent, so that they can understand what the new and larger relations mean and what must be accomplished by them.

A casual observation of the educational situation might indicate that education is limited in two ways, so far as being a means of meeting our present needs is concerned. *It is lacking in power*; it treats children and youths still in a fragmentary way, and the process of learning is somewhat detached from the totality of living. There is a lack of richness of content, and a lack of responsiveness in the school to the stirring life outside the school. If we may say that history now turns a new page, and that society stands at a change of tide, education is also in a peculiar and interesting position. The school may, from now on, if our view of it be at all just, be expected to do one of two things: it may settle down to a relatively successful work, in a limited sphere of usefulness, training children well, especially fitting them to enter into our present social order; or, on the other hand, the school may now become a much greater power, and may seize hold upon fundamental things in life and society under the stimulus of new conditions—find a way to a deeper philosophy, a more consistent theory, attain a more exalted mood and higher purpose, and become a far more potent factor in civilization.

That education will remain unaffected in profound ways by the war, is difficult to believe. One may very readily, as we say, see these impending changes in too dramatic a way, and begin to talk about profound upheavals and ideals that certainly will never be realized (and we ought to guard against this easy idealizing, which leaves human nature out of the reckoning); still we cannot but feel that in some way a new dimension has been added to the social life as a result of the war, and that education, in dealing with this greater society, must itself be raised to a higher power. If we think, educationally speaking, in terms of a world at all, rather than in terms of individuals, or communities, families and nations, we are quickly impressed by the sense of living in a new order of educational problems, and possessing, it may be, a new variety of self-consciousness. Nations in this new view are thought of as parts of a world, as having many external relations, whereas formerly almost all education has had reference at the most to the internal life of nations. Patriotism has been the expression of its most distant horizon.

If we believe that anything new is about to be realized in education, it might seem natural to begin to think about changes from the standpoint and in the terms of the old chapters and topics. We might ask what this or that subject of the curriculum means or must produce that it did not mean and did not produce before; or we might consider the old and the new requirements in the education of the feelings, the will, the intellect; or we might take any other of the educational categories as a basis for a discussion of the philosophy of the school. These programs, however, do not seem to be very inspiring. Would it not be better now to try to distinguish the main fields of life and the main interests in regard to which new questions and new needs have arisen, and see what changes in our educational thought are really demanded by them? On such a plan, internationalism itself would first demand attention, and indeed most of all. In a sense all questions about education must now be considered with reference to internationalism in some way. Then there are the problems already raised during the war and widely discussed, about the teaching of patriotism. Patriotism becomes a new educational problem, a chapter in our theory of education, in which we become conscious of ourselves in a new way, and are aware of our larger field and changed conditions. There are questions, too, about the teaching of the lessons of the war, what we shall think about war in general as a good or an evil, how we shall conceive peace and its values. Changes are taking place in government, and in our ideas of government, and governments are being put to new tests. Political education can hardly fail to be now one of our most serious concerns. Democracy appears to be our great word; the control and education of the democratic forces and the democratic spirit becomes an urgent need. Industry acquires new meanings; we must take up again all the theory of industrial education, for we have seen of late that industry contains possibilities of evil we did not before understand. Social problems arise in changed forms. The new world-idea or world-consciousness becomes an educational problem of the social life. Class difference can never again be ignored as it has been in the past in the schools. Moral, religious and æsthetic education seems to have a different place in the school, just to the extent that all life has become more serious on account of the war. These demands made upon the deepest elements of the psychic life suggest the need once more of a new philosophy of education, or, at the least, a greatly increased recognition and application of the philosophy we already have.

Before the war there was a sense of security and the feeling that our education was adequate to meet all demands. We were proud of our educational system. Our democratic ideals, people said, were safe in the hands of the public school. Industrial education was meeting fairly well the needs of the industrial life. There were no very pressing class problems. The troubles of capital and labor, although always threatening, seemed to demand no educational interference. The religious problem was temporarily not acute. Aesthetic forms had been attended to in the curriculum sufficiently to meet the demands of the day. Hygiene and physical education and individual attention seemed to be making rapid advances. All of these had been influenced by the scientific methods of treating educational questions. On the whole we seemed to have a good school. But now the question must be asked whether this school of yesterday will be adequate to meet the needs of to-morrow; whether new conditions do not call for new thought, new philosophy, new schools. These things of course cannot be had for the asking. We cannot give orders to genius to produce them for us. But a generation that does not hope for them, we might suspect of not having realized what the war has cost. For so great a price paid have we not a right to expect much in return, especially if we are willing to regard the war as a lesson rather than as a debt to us, and bend all our energies to make it count for a better civilization?

We may already see in a general way what the effect of the war is to be upon the mind of the educator. The journals begin to be filled with plans for the participation of the school in the work of reconstruction. There are many suggestions for the improvement of the school. Industrial education, the classics, history, military education, social education are all being discussed. Evidently many minds are at work. Some of them, indeed many of them, are apparently most concerned about what changes we shall make at once in the day's work of the school. Many wish to know what we are going to do now with Latin, or history, and how we can improve the method of teaching in this or that particular. But there are some deeper notes. Thinkers are asking elementary questions about the whole of human nature. They wish to know what the original nature of man is, and what the limits of our control over human nature are. Such books as Hocking's "Human Nature and its Re-making" and Russell's "Principles of Social Reconstruction," which grapple with the basic problems of human life, are signs of the times. No one can yet predict what the final result of the increased intellectual ardor that has come out of the war will be, but it seems certain that that striving of the mind which has made the literature of the war so remarkable a page in the history of the human spirit will continue, and in the field of education as elsewhere in the practical life there will be new vitality and earnestness.

CHAPTER II

INTERNATIONALISM AND THE SCHOOL

If we take a serious and an optimistic view of education as a social institution, and think of it at all as standing in functional relationships with the social life as a whole, we must conclude that internationalism as a new movement and idea, and the school as an institution in which changes in the social order are reflected (but in which also changes in the social order are created) are closely related. Adjustment is a relatively easy matter; it is the conception of the school as a creative factor that challenges our best efforts. Let us think of the school as a workshop in which there must be created the forces by which we must make a desired and an otherwise unrealizable future come to pass and we have a new and inspiring view of education. The school perhaps must do even more than educate the forces; it must help even to create the vision itself by which the future is to be directed. *The school becomes, so to speak, the working hypothesis of civilisation.* In it the ideas and the desires by which nations live must be made to take shape.

The idea of internationalism implies certain changes in the external relations of nations which, whatever the form internationalism will take on its political side, are not difficult to perceive. These in turn imply internal changes. We might readily outline or psychologically analyze what could be called the mood of internationalism, in order to see its relations to education. It contains a number of factors, more or less related to one another. *First,* there is a recognition of a world of growing, living historical entities which we call nations; and this recognition implies new understanding and an enrichment of knowledge. *Second,* there is a change in the consciousness of nations, slow but visible, by which they become more willing to investigate freely and fairly their own place in history, understand their own desires, functions, virtues, faults, the value of their culture and civilization. Without such an attitude all talk of internationalism in any real sense is idle. *Third,* there is a new and different practical interest. We begin to conceive our world as a world of complex practical relations, and this idea of a practical world is likely to become one of the leading thoughts of the future. *Fourth,* by extending, so to speak, this idea of a world of practical relations, we idealize a world in which there is a common interest in great international achievements,—a world devoted more than it is now to coördinated efforts to accelerate progress, more conscious of the needs of a distant future, perhaps, or even of an ideal of universal efficiency as a means of realizing some one world purpose or many good purposes. This is not now, as it once might have been called, merely an Utopian dream. In some slight degree it is already being accomplished. *Fifth,* social and moral feelings are widened in scope, and must be still further extended; it is in the form of the *democratic spirit,* that these feelings must find expression. And this democratic spirit is on one side practical, but it is also something more than the emergence of the common mind; it is the *aristocratic idea carried out universally* that we look forward to, an enthusiasm for all true values, a mood and activity in which all people participate. *Sixth,* there is a necessary attitude toward world organization or world government, according to which we think of world government or world organization as a means of accomplishing results which fulfill fundamental desires and purposes of the peoples of the earth; as a growing structure, something to be added to and improved. *Seventh,* if so general a tendency and demand may be made clear, there is a philosophical mood, which must be made a part of the ideal and the attitude of the future, *if that future is to realize even the practical hopes of the world.* This philosophical attitude is first of all a way of living comprehensively and more universally, in the world both of facts and of ideas. It means a less provincial and a more widely enriched life for all. It means also an ability to choose the good not according to preconceptions and narrow principles, but according to the wisdom contained in the experience and the selective powers of mankind as a whole. This means a life in which men live, so to speak, more collectively.

These factors of the idea of internationalism, whatever we may think of the possibility of their realization, make in their totality an educational problem: they are specifications, so to speak, laid before us for the making of a new educational product. If we say that it is useless to think of such things, we are saying merely that it is useless to hope to be a factor in conscious evolution, or that the world as a whole has no purpose and no goal. If we believe education has any function in the larger work of the world, educational philosophy must take these things into account, see how they may be created or sustained, and how they can be made to work together to help bring to pass the kind of future men are talking so much about.

I. The Essential World Idea

Our present situation has plainly made it necessary for us to understand the world in which we live far better than we have in the past, and to be willing to make more dispassionate judgments about it. For better or for worse we have entered upon a new stage of history, in which heavy responsibilities fall upon all peoples, and upon none more than upon ourselves. Enlightenment beyond all our present understanding is a necessity. We have been peculiarly isolated and separated from the world's affairs; now we are peculiarly involved. We have, however, one great and unusual advantage. In our case it is ignorance rather than prejudice that we must overcome in ourselves. The world feels this and recognizes the unusual place this gives us. We have no thousand years of continuous strife to distort our historical perspective. We out to be able to be just interpreters of the history of the world. Our universities ought to be the greatest centers of historical learning, and as a people we should feel ourselves called upon above all other people to know the world.

As a nation we pass out of a local into a broader political field. We become citizens of a world, but this world is no mere habitation of individuals who are to be affiliated with one another. It is a world of *national wills*. Internationalism is first of all a recognition of the legitimate desires of nations. But such a recognition of the legitimate desires of nations cannot be effected merely by spreading abroad good will. A widespread education in the meaning of history must first be made the foundation of international justice in the minds of the people. Current history and future events seen in the light of all history, of history as the science and story of all human experience, become our chief intellectual interest to-day. The war has taught us how little the people in the world know bout the world as a whole. All history thus far has been *local* history. Everywhere there tends to be the prejudice in some degree that comes from the private need of using history for political ends. Unless we can now put history, real history, at the head of our sciences, the war will have failed of a great result, whatever in particular, in a political way, it may have accomplished.

With such an understanding of what is to be meant by history we say, if that seems an adequate way of expressing it, that the teaching of history becomes one of the fundamental problems of the educational work of the day. It might be better to say that living in the historical spirit is demanded as a way of salvation of the world. However, adding geography and economics to history we have a content that must somehow be taught in the schools. History, as the most concrete science of the actual world in which we live, now seems to have become a new center for the curriculum. Hitherto we have tended to regard history too lightly, as the *story* of the world; now there must be a deeper view of it. We must have an understanding of the motives and the desires of peoples; history must not only be broader and more comprehensive but more penetrating and psychological. It is the purposes of nations, working themselves out in their history, that we must understand. There must no longer be great unknown places on the earth. Germany, Russia, Japan must not continue to be mysteries. National psychology must be made a part of historical interpretation. This new history must be the means of showing us our world in a more total view than we have thus far had of it, so that we may better discern the continuity, if there be one, behind the detached movements and multiplicity of facts presented by the world's story; for perhaps, in this way, we should better understand what the future is to produce, and what, more important still, it ought to be made to produce.

The need first of all is for a continuation of the interest inspired by the war—an interest showing itself in the form of an universal interest in all history, and an intensive investigation of history. We need now, indeed, the most comprehensive study of the world that has ever been conceived or dreamed of by man. This is the duty of the historians. This new history must show us what nations are at heart, what they desire, what they can do. Such an understanding of nations is, we say, the real beginning of internationalism. It is a necessary foundation for it, if internationalism is to be anything more than a merely practical, prudential or political arrangement among nations. In the school-room eventually, and indeed beginning now, there is demanded a readjustment of interest by which history takes a new and more central place. We must endeavor to give the new generation a *world-idea*. And upon the nature and clearness of this world-idea much, in the future, will depend.

Such a demand upon the school opens once more, of course, all the old problems of the teaching of history. All the dreary questions of the precise order in which history should be taught—whether backwards or forwards, local first or the reverse, may be brought up if one chooses to do so. But after all, these questions are not very fruitful. What we need most is the historical *spirit*. We want a dramatic presentation of the world's whole story, by which the true meaning of history is conveyed. The methods of art must be added to the methods of fact. A persuasive use of the materials of history must be made. This means a change finally, perhaps, not only in the methods of teaching history, but in the whole mood and spirit of the school. Methods are likely to adapt themselves to necessity. Certainly the slow methods of presenting facts, sometimes if not generally employed, the tedious lingering upon details, seems wholly out of place. We need a broader outlook in history. Even the young child must have a more comprehensive world-idea, some sense of the whole of the great world in which he lives. This is one of the instances, it may be, in which we must set about breaking up any recapitulatory order, natural to the child, which suggests an advance from the local to the more general and wider knowledge. The universal interests of the day so strongly affect the child, the social consciousness so dominates the individual consciousness that even the natural law of development must to some extent yield if necessary. This social consciousness, the interests and purposes expressed in the child's social environment, present the experience of the adult world dramatically and intensively, exerting as we might say, a creative power upon the mind. That indeed is precisely what the higher teaching, whether in the form of art, or in the form of vivid experience, conveyed though the practical life does everywhere in education.

We do not yet know what history, taught thus dramatically and intimately, under the stimulus of the greatest events of all time might do for the mind of the child or for all the future of the world. We have never had the most favorable conditions for the teaching of universal history. We have been obliged to create interest. History has been taught externally, from the standpoint of a far-away observer. Now history may and must be taught more as it is lived. The world has become more real to every one; this sense of reality of a world of historical entities must be made to persist. We must not go back to our unreal and intellectualized history. The spirit of the nations must be made to live again, so to speak, in the minds of the coming generation. What each nation stands for, its ethos, its personality, must be made clear. Powers says that all governments and all nations are *sincere*. It is the soul of nations, then, their own realization of themselves that must be made the real object of history. We must go back of the individual and the event at least, to the desires that have made history what it is; we must see why events have taken place, and while sacrificing nothing of our own principles and standards, understand and feel what the principles and the nature of these widely differing nations really are. For the actual teaching of history, it is likely that the story, carried to its highest point of art, will still be the chief method. But pictorial art must be heavily drawn upon, and all the resources of symbolic art, as we pass from the lower to the higher stages in education, or, we had perhaps better say, as we try more and more to convey moods and the spirit of nations and epochs and to appeal to the deep motives in the subconscious life of the individual. Plainly there is much work to do in the investigation and the teaching of history for every grade and department of the educational system, from the government and the higher universities to the teacher of the young child. It is an age of history, a day in which all sciences have as one of their tasks to aid in the understanding of history. In the broader world and the universal life which the idea and the reality of internationalism has opened up to us, all must live in some way, if only in imagination. History is a part of the necessary equipment for that life.

II. The Reëducation of National Desires

The second factor in internationalism is also, on its educational side, related to a knowledge of history. This is the attitude which peoples must take toward their own purposes and ambitions. We must begin to speak of the education of national consciousness. This process of the education of nations must be such as will teach peoples to surrender certain visions most of them have in regard to a future which cannot now be realized. The content of the desires of nations must now be changed. The future of many peoples will depend upon the extent to which they can remain progressive and enthusiastic without the stimulus of imperialistic ambitions.

Considering our own situation in America, it seems plain that we have confronting us a serious educational problem, that of imparting to the rising generation and of acquiring for ourselves, a better understanding of the meaning and place of our country in the world, and a more earnest interest in its functions and its welfare. This requires something more than a teaching of American history. It is time for us to take stock of all our material and all our spiritual possessions. We need perhaps to discover what our ideals really are and what the ideas and the forces are that have made our history what it has been; and what in the future we are likely to do and to be, and ought to do and be. We must question deeply at this time our own soul; we must look to our institutions, our literature and our art for an understanding of ourselves.

This more profound knowledge of ourselves must be made the basis of our especial educational philosophy. Here is the most urgent of all our educational problems. Education is, or should be, a process by which national character is constantly being molded. In the school the nation must learn much that cannot be read in books. It must learn to believe things that cannot be proved, or perhaps even definitely formulated as truth. The soul of the nation must be subjected, in a word, to some kind of *spiritual leadership*. Constructive statesmanship must be felt as an influence in the school. The problem is really nothing less than that of educating and forming national character. Now that we stand less alone as a nation our character cannot safely be left so much to chance and to the effects of our favorable environment and our original stock of virtues. We cannot continue to be so naïve and so unconscious of our country as we have been. What we are and what we must do as a people, we say, ought to be better understood. We should bring these ideals of ours out of the mists of partisan thinking and give them more definite shape, and at the same time translate them into the language of sincere living. National honor ought to be made a clearer idea. We ought at least to be sure it contains the idea of honesty. Such prejudices as our history has encouraged in us must be recognized, and computed in our personal equation. These prejudices we certainly harbor—in regard to our own particular type of government, our culture and education, our freedom and our democracy and our security. Every nation appears to have its own idols, its concealments and its self-deceptions, its belief in its own supremacy and divine mission, and its innocent faith in its own mores. To overcome such narrowness and perversion without introducing worse faults is a difficult problem of education. In either direction there appear to be real dangers. A nation steeped in provincial ways, plunged as we are now into the midst of world politics, has difficulties lying before it compared to which contributing a decisive military power is small. There are dangers in standing aloof from other peoples. But if we surrender too readily our prejudices and homespun ways, and too rapidly absorb influences from without, we shall be no safer, for carried too far, that would mean to lose our mission and our vision. There appears to be, moreover, no safe and easy middle course which we can follow. Our only course seems to be clearly to understand ourselves, rise above our limitations and difficulties, turn our faults into virtues, and make ourselves secure by our own inner worth and power.

Plainly there are difficult problems ahead of the teachers of American history. They must not inculcate suspicion and fear, but they must not present our security in a false light. They must not inspire the war-like spirit and imperialistic ambitions, but they must do nothing to lessen our seriousness of purpose and enthusiasm for the future. They must not teach national vanity, but they must not on the other hand encourage a spirit which is in any way over-critical and cynical or supercilious. There must be political wisdom on the part of the people but not a sophisticated state of mind. These teachers must inspire a wholesome pride, without creating an inflamed sense of honor such as has caused so many wars. They must make clear the virtue and the individuality of our own national life, but in doing this they must not disparage the foreign and give rise to prejudice and antagonism. How to establish us still more firmly in our own essential traits and philosophy of life without making us conceited and closed to good influences from without; how to give us a strong sense of solidarity without the attendant sense of opposition to everything outside the group is a part of our educational work which, in a broad sense, falls to the teacher of history.

The central problem of the education of national consciousness, in our view, is to make desires more conscious and to subject them to discipline and the influence of the best ideals of American life. MacCurdy says that by making instincts conscious we take a great step in advance. That we should say is true, if we make them conscious in the right way, and do not try to substitute rational principles for them. But we need to go further; we must not only understand and control the impulses of aggression, jealousy, fear and the like that have played such a sinister part in history, but we must know more about those complex and subtile things we call moods, which are really the main forces in modern life. These moods are accumulations and repositories of interests and desires, and they must be appreciated by all who as educators, undertake to direct the forces in our national life. These desires must be made more definitely conscious everywhere, and be subjected to influence and education. It is not simply institutions, organizations and factions that must be watched and controlled, just because these are the more obvious and most easily affected expressions of tendencies and desires, but all the subtile feelings or moods which are the raw materials, so to speak, of future conduct, ideals, and institutions.

Here comes to view, of course, our whole problem of assimilation of heterogeneous elements. Favored by our geographical position, and by the fortunate success and the great suggestive power of the ideal of liberty with which our history began, America has had, as we all realize, thus far an unusual career. We have been able to assimilate foreign elements with great rapidity. We may not be so fortunate in the future. Distances which have severed our new peoples from their old ties have become strangely shortened by the war. Our problems of adjustment have become more subtile and complex. The necessity of succeeding in unifying our population is more urgent. Therefore our future development, as a nation, becomes to a greater extent a process of conscious direction; what we have done naïvely and by sheer force of our powers of growth, we must do now, it is likely, more deliberately and efficiently.

We have before us in America the highly important and by no means easy task of harmonizing, under new conditions, all sorts of forces and desires by directing them in ways and toward ends which cannot now be wholly determined. There is both a psychological and a pedagogical aspect of the situation. Psychology must perform for American life something very much like a psycho-analysis; we should expect to see as a result of the war a greatly increased interest, on the part of the American people, in themselves; self-understanding and self-interpretation, we should suppose, would be advanced; all the sciences of human nature we should think would be called upon to help us to make a new American history and to formulate the purposes of our national life.

On the pedagogical side we might expect reasonably to see a deepened sincerity on the part of all who in any way stand in the position of teachers. We are dependent upon leaders in a democratic country, and all leaders in whatever place in society would now, one might hope, feel a heightened sense of duty, both to understand and to influence American life, to represent in their own persons and teachings the highest ideals, and indeed to become truly creative forces in society. Boutroux says that Germany is a product of an external phenomenon—*education*. America, we should say, must become more and more a product of an internal phenomenon—*education*. That is, the forces that will continue to shape our country must be in the form of leadership growing out of the best impulses and the true meaning of our civilization. No forces will make of us something we are not by nature; our strength must continue to come from within, but it is the aristocratic spirit, the aristocracy of genius in the fields of intellect, morality and art that must of course have the fullest opportunity to influence all our institutions, even the school room.

So to organize our educational system that it shall be thrown wide open to all new and good influences; so to conduct the school that it shall be immediately responsive to these influences, is one of the most urgent needs of the internal life of the nation. This, rather than the introduction of any new content into the school is now our chief need. Some of these influences must be personal, belonging to the present. Some belong to the past. We must make American history, poetry, oratory, science, art and philosophy serve more completely than they do now the ideals and the right ambitions of the nation. This is the way we must both bring the past to fuller realization and also create new life which shall make amends for the deficiencies of the past.

III. Practical Interests

The foundation of internationalism, in our view, is the recognition of the legitimate desires and needs of peoples. The desires of peoples when educated should become interests in the performance of all normal functions of national life. The functions are practical; they take the form of many commonplace and daily activities. The recognition of the legitimacy of the desires of nations implies, or at least naturally leads to, coöperation in their accomplishment. It is very probable, therefore, and it appears to be required in any internationalism that is more than a name, that there shall be in the future wide coöperation in the performance of various activities by international organizations and agreements. If this is to be the order of the future, new educational efforts will be demanded, and there must be different methods and different points of view in several phases of our educational system, for now all education is devised with reference to an autonomous state of the nation.

If practical coöperation becomes a part of our plan of international organization in the future, we shall see many problems in applied economics and industry taken up for far more serious consideration than has been possible hitherto. Some of these problems, attacked even on a national scale, have seemed hopeless, but when viewed in their international aspects and with a prospect of international interest and effort they seem very different. There are many such problems toward the solution of which education must contribute a large part. We might mention the food problem of the world as typical, and point to the present world-wide interest and coöperation as an indication of what may come in the future in regard to all the problems of production and distribution of necessities, *if* we really mean anything by our internationalism. Apparently we hold within our hands the means of alleviating most, if not all, the destitution of the world. Organization and education in efficiency are the necessary and the sufficient weapons.

So we may conclude that an efficient method of educating peoples in the work of food production, and in the habit of conserving necessities would make a wide change in the economic condition of the world. Organization which shall include in some way the service of all children, will add still more to efficiency, and will contribute an educational factor of great importance. In such ways we may to an unlimited extent increase the available energies of the world, and make possible, if we will, the further increase and expansion of the human race. Such a possibility and such an ideal give a totally new meaning to much of the fundamental work of education. All our departments and accessories of the educational system that have anything to do with the elemental occupations acquire a new interest and importance from this point of view.

The whole field of industry offers now, indeed, a broader educational opportunity. Children's hands are ready to do many things that will increase the happiness and the powers of the children themselves and at the same time add to the world's prosperity. Children must, of course, not be exploited in tasks that belong to the adult, but there is a proper place for practical organization of children in the world's work, and a potential helpfulness in children in the larger affairs of society that has not yet been drawn upon, although surely we have seen, during the years of the war, what children might accomplish. It is above all in its relations to universal social feeling that such practical education and use of childhood are most significant. Out of the practical activities, moral results could hardly fail to come. It is not too much to expect that the children of the world may sometime be so organized that the power of childish enthusiasm, raised to we know not what degree by the suggestive force of such world-wide relations as are now possible, may quickly be turned to the accomplishment of great tasks,—doing its part in the service, the conservation, the self denial, that any serious interest in internationalism will in the future with but little doubt make necessary.

Education that shall take into account the principles of efficiency and economy as applied to universal problems will be a great advance upon any teaching hitherto done in the interest of internationalism. It is through practical activity and interest, suggesting and requiring restraint and coöperation, arousing imagination and the dramatic impulses, that fruitful and permanent social affiliations of nations with one another will be likely to be made. We may safely assume, in fact, that firm affiliations can be made *only* in some such way. Internationalism, from this point of view, is at bottom not a political problem, but an educational problem. The world will be united only through the mediation of its daily practical needs. The motives for such union are themselves commonplace. Moral intentions are represented also, and world crises make the conditions ripe for such coördination of interests, but they do not alone produce the definite organization without which the world will continue to be, as Dickinson calls Europe, a society in the state of anarchy.

CHAPTER III

INTERNATIONALISM AND THE SCHOOL (CONTINUED)

IV. The Higher Industry

It is in the higher forms of practical coöperative activity and in the intellectual processes, the interests and social feelings accompanying them that we should expect to see elaborated and made more ideal the internationalism that has first been put to work in the service of the world at a lower level. There is work to do that appeals to profound motives and feelings. The great engineering projects that await us, the work of exploring, colonizing and the like in which universal interest and coöperation are necessary fascinate the mind. These things satisfy the dramatic instinct, and they may prove to be in the future an actual substitute for war, as James hoped. The educational opportunities of this theme, at least, are great. Any nation that expects to play a great part in the world's politics must expect to do much in the world's service. These nations must be prepared in every possible way to contribute greatly to the material improvement of the earth. To this end technical education, all along the line, must be kept at a high point of efficiency. Inventive thought in all mechanical fields will certainly be a large factor in the culture values of peoples in the future. When we see what four years of war have accomplished in the way of giving us control over material forces, we may realize what, with the continuation of a powerful incentive, might be done in the arts of peace. These great practical needs have also, as we say, their power of appeal to all the profound motives of the social life. We must make use of this appeal. All the power of the strong story of the day's work must be turned upon this educational problem. All industry, indeed, must be made more dramatic, as it can be under the inspiration of the larger industrial life which the idea of internationalism opens up before us. Industry must be made more satisfying to the fundamental motives of the individual, while at the same time it is made more efficient, and more social. The new generation must be filled with the romance of the world's work. Only by presenting to young and plastic minds the ideal features of work shall we be able to harmonize the individual and the social will. Only so, perhaps, in an industrial age shall we be able to escape from being destroyed by industrialism. Anything that will introduce art and imagination into work, anything that will even brighten a little the dull moods of toil will help both to prepare the way for the wider world relations we talk about, and to prevent the most destructive elements and moods of industrialism gaining the upper hand.

V. The Democratic Spirit

We must eventually think of internationalism on its educational side as most fundamentally a question of developing in the world the *international spirit*. We might quite naturally think of this as the education of social feeling or of the social instinct. This is, however, not the most productive attitude toward the situation, in our view, simply because when we think of the education of the feelings we are likely to be satisfied with the principles of an old static philosophy of life and of the school. Moral and social feelings, we believe, grow best in a practical medium. We cannot expand social feeling at will, or produce a democratic spirit by some simple process of education. When we try to extend social feeling too far we make the moral life insincere. To try to expand social feeling and moral interest so as to make it include the foreign, to try to love our enemies in advance of all æsthetic and practical relations with the foreign seems futile. Distance must first be eliminated by imagination. Social and moral codes must be founded upon intimate relations. External and distant relations among peoples make for diplomatic forms and a hypocritical morality. These are substitutes for social feeling. These purely social relations of nations (like those of individuals) always hide enmity and jealousy. We cannot expect, therefore, to create a moral spirit in the relations of peoples to one another by teaching alone. We cannot hope to change individualism to altruism merely by exciting feeling. Our main effort must be directed toward establishing ethical relations, rather than to stimulating moral sentiments.

It seems useless to preach universal brotherhood either to the child who lacks entirely the content of experience to make such sentiments real, or to the working masses who now lack enthusiasm in *all* the social relations. At least to depend upon such teaching to create international spirit is futile. Love for mankind is too ideal and too remote, as yet, to arouse deep and sincere impulses and feelings. All teaching, therefore, whether in the school or elsewhere that is directed exclusively or especially to the moral aspects of peace, altruistic behavior and internationalism, seems to-day, to say the least, peculiarly inadequate. Our spirit in education must be broadly humanistic, and must indeed lay deep foundations for all moral and social relations, but in so far as it ends in being cultural and hortatory it can have no deep and lasting effect.

The teaching of international morality and universal interests, and the development of a *world-consciousness* depend fundamentally, we may suppose, upon experiences which are perhaps not specifically moral in form at all. It is rather even by the aesthetic experience than the moral that the social consciousness will best be expanded and made to encircle the world. If we can make the world seem vividly real to the child we shall have the intellectual content for the making of moral feelings. The unmoral nature of international relations and of the feelings of peoples for one another are due in great part precisely to the lack of power of imagination and of that concrete knowledge and experience which would make the foreign seem real. That which is remote from us and different in appearance seems shadowy and ghost-like. The *internal meaning* of that which is thus far away in space cannot be perceived. Everything that is foreign tends to belong in our categories merely to the world of objects. Moral feeling towards objects is manifestly impossible. International law fails to have moral force because nations are in general aware of one another only in these external ways. The world of foreign objects must be changed to a world of persons having history and internal meaning. When we can interpret and understand international law in terms of relations within human experience and as affecting individuals, it will begin perhaps to seem real and hence morally obligatory.

There is another aspect of the work of creating and directing the wider social consciousness and giving it ethical purpose and form, which is still more fundamental, and at the same time, to casual thought, perhaps still more remote from definite moral improvement in the world and from all the immediately practical problems of internationalism. It is the mood of our social life which we call the democratic spirit, and which, made universal, is the substratum of internationalism that most of all needs to be controlled and educated. At the same time this democratic spirit is least of all susceptible to definite and routine discipline, of all the factors of internationalism. This democratic spirit contains possibilities of the greatest good and of the greatest evil. Out of it may grow international order, or international anarchy and internal disruption. How to keep this democratic spirit progressive and constructive in its temper, broad in sympathy and full of enthusiasm, how to free it from infection by all the poisons that are prone to attack the popular consciousness is one of our great problems of education.

This democratic spirit is the real power behind internationalism. It is as the mood of the city, the whole spirit of the modern urban life, that it is most significant. The mood of the city contains on one side the possibility of an internationalism which is nothing more than a surrender of all patriotism, and is at heart only a mass interest in rights and needs. On the other hand all the interests and impulses that make internationalism necessary and possible seem to have their origin in the city. The city represents, with all its evil, the higher life and the line of progress. Progress passes through the city. The city is the symbol of creativeness and achievement. Industrialism, the essential spirit of the city, is the condition, normal and necessary we must conclude, out of which the necessity of international order arises. It is a phase of the process by which nations become dependent upon one another by being specialized and becoming densely populated. It is also a factor in the cause of wars without and revolutions within.

The mood of the city is thus in a sense the essence of life, but it is also the source of disease and death in the national life. It is the price that is paid for civilization that the city tends to become the hardened artery of national life. The control of the city moods by educational forces we may believe is one of the most fundamental of all the problems of conscious evolution. It is the control at the fountain-head of the forces out of which internationalism is to be made that we undertake when we try to educate the life of the city, with reference to its good and its evil. The too rapid urbanizing of the life of nations, the production, in the cities, of powers too great and too rapidly growing to be controlled by the civilizing forces in a country is the great danger in modern life. So great indeed are the dangers in the accelerated growth of industrialism in all the great countries and the increased specialization in the industrial life, that something radical must be done, in our view, to counterbalance this movement, and especially to control and to raise to higher levels the psychic factors of city life.

Our educational work is serious. We are trying to save democracy from itself—from being destroyed by forces which accumulate in the cities. We must keep life from becoming sophisticated before its time. We must prevent enthusiasm from degenerating into mob spirit, and from becoming attached to wholly material interests. *There must be found, in some way, means of causing counter-currents to set in against the tide that flows so strongly from country to city.* Germany's fate should teach us the dangers of this city life, and show us how the forces that gather in the great cities can be turned in the direction either of fanatical nationalism or toward the lowest of all forms of internationalism, in which all form of government is thrown down. It must teach us also how to catch the note of new "dominants" that are concealed in the roar of city life, and to make these prevail.

The control of the formation of the city moods, and the direction and utilization of the great energies contained in them, now require, if ever anything were demanded of conscious creative effort, *more power on the part of all our educational factors*. The school appears now to be at the parting of the ways, we say, when it must either settle down to its routine and limited occupation of preparing children for life, or become a far greater power in the world than it has as yet been. We must decide whether the school is to control, or to be controlled by, the political and industrial forces of the day. We must see whether the school is going to reflect the culture and the moods of the environment, or whether the school shall exert a creative influence upon its surroundings.

It is plain that nothing less than a radical change in the school can now greatly alter its position, and release it from its bondage to politics and from the overwhelming influences of its environment, and prevent the leveling downward and the stereotyping process that is taking place in the school, both as regards its intellectual and moral product and the training and selection of teachers. Nothing less than a movement which shall break up some of the deepest and most firmly rooted habits and conventions of the school and throw the school back, so to speak, upon more generic and primitive motives than those that now control it will be sufficient. *The school needs more than anything else a change of scene*—a change of *venue*, if a legal term be allowed. The school everywhere, but especially the school of the city, is surrounded by influences that prejudice it to fixed habits of thought and keep it true to a type which has long since ceased to be necessary. The school is causing an in-breeding of the city spirit in all the great industrial countries.

No single change in any institution, in our view, could strike closer to the roots of our whole educational problem of the future than the bodily transfer of the city school far out into the open country. Such a move seems wholly practicable, economic from every point of view, even the financial, and it would place the school in a position in which profound changes in its whole plan and organization could hardly fail to follow almost automatically. With our present facilities for transportation, the daily exodus of children from the surroundings in which are being produced the elements of our civilization that are hardest to control would be entirely possible. The effects upon the whole of education, and upon all the future life of countries like our own could hardly fail to be profound. *The fundamental moods of childhood would be changed, and everything contained in child life would be more amenable to control.* Schools would become more variable and more experimental, and new selective influences would be exerted upon teachers presumably in the direction of raising the social and intellectual average of the profession. A much larger field would be opened up for all those methods of work in education that may be designated as æsthetic—that is, that contain qualities of freedom, activity and creativeness.

VI. Idea of World Organization

Some form of organization of nations having definite representation, constitution, and laws, and with a certain degree of centralization and embodiment in visible institutions and locations will exist, we may suppose, for all future time in the world. The existence, even in idea, of such organization presents to us inevitable educational problems. Instruction in a general way and universally in world politics, familiarizing all with the meaning of these laws and political bodies, is but a part, although a necessary part, of the work. Our democratic principle demands that more and more interest and participation in all forms of government be acquired by the people, that peoples and not merely governments shall be the units which are brought together, that there be more organizations of the people performing group functions. If the loyalty of nations to one another is to be secured, as seems necessary, by establishing practical relations among them, the education of the coming generations in these relations and organizations and in all practical affairs seems unavoidable. The people must have a proper appreciation of common interests as implying common work, and not be encouraged to believe that rights of representation are their chief concern. All must know the power of organization. All must see that the international structures of our own day, however complete in form, are but a beginning and basis of function, and that there must be put behind these forms all the energies of the people, young and old, made effective through organization for practical efforts.

It is through participation in activities that are international in scope that, in our opinion, the best education in the idea of internationalism will be obtained. This is the way to the good will without which political ideas will be likely to remain nationalistic in fact whatever political coördinations may exist among nations. It is as a practical idea that internationalism needs now to be impressed upon the minds of all. An international organization must be looked upon as something useful, which will remain only if it performs functions in which all are interested and in which all can in some way take part. *It is a sense of living in the world* rather than of belonging exclusively to one locality that must be taught. It is the idea of a world of nations in organic unity rather than a world of nations attached to one another by political bonds that we need to convey.

It is active participation in the business of a world that must be regarded as the necessary basis for education in the idea of internationalism. World government must be conceived in terms of world functions. But we must also provide for the most dramatic possible representation of everything contained in the idea of internationalism and represented in its laws and forms. The most vivid possible presentation must be made of everything that is done internationally, if we wish to keep alive the spirit which now prevails in the world. We must lose no opportunity to make current history impressive; we must bring out all its dramatic features in order to fixate once for all the idea of the organic unity of the race, and its necessary coördination in tangible forms. International law must be made intelligible to very young minds, and now that we are to have an international seat of congresses and courts the utmost must be made of its existence to give reality to the idea of internationalism.

Those who plan for the future of the international idea will do well to take into account these pedagogical aspects of it. *It is quite as important to make the international idea pedagogically persuasive as to make it politically sound.* Such an idea must have a place and an embodiment if it is to seize hold upon the popular mind. An international city seems indispensable, and the further the thought of it can be removed from that of existing countries the more readily will it aid the young mind in making the abstractions necessary to conceive the true interests of all nations or all humanity as distinct from the interests of one nation. In this we are making beginnings to be realized perhaps in a far distant future. We want no unnatural and sentimental internationalism, but there is every reason now for wishing to plant the seed of a higher and more organic life than at the present time exists in the world.

The question of the possibility of an universal language arises again. The invention of a new language, if we may judge at all by the past, is not practicable. But the extension universally of some living language seems possible. This seems to be demanded in the interest of the international idea. It is desirable and quite possible to make all civilized peoples bilingual, for of course we should not expect anywhere to see a foreign language supplant the native tongue. It is not alone to facilitate intercourse and give a sense of solidarity that the possession of an universal language is to be desired. We think quite as much of the impetus thus given to the production of an universal literature, in which there will be expressed not only ideas about the world, but moods which will not be found expressed in national literatures at all. This literature might be the beginning of a solidarity in the world which is not now definitely conceivable. Such an extension of language, however, we should hardly expect to take place except in the course of development of practical relations which first stimulate the desire for such common language.

VII. The Philosophical Attitude

There is an element in the idea and mood of internationalism which we can call nothing else but philosophic. The ideality and universality of internationalism itself are expressions of the philosophic spirit. Internationalism, we might say, is a philosophic idea, although this might mean to some that we place it among the unrealizable and Utopian plans. But this is not the case. The philosophic spirit is, in our view, the most practical of moods, since it is the creative, liberal, and progressive attitude and the source of the most profoundly right judgments even in practical affairs. The philosophic spirit is a background, we may say, for all the more specific moods, thoughts and activities that enter into the idea of internationalism.

And yet, real and important as the philosophic spirit is, we cannot readily discuss it as a definite aspect of education. The reason is that it involves the educational foundations themselves. The spirit, the method and the content of the school are all involved in it. We can, however, find some concrete manifestations of this philosophic attitude. In the first place we might say that it is a religious mood in education. It is demanded of any school that hopes to play a large part in the affairs of the world that, in a broad sense, its whole spirit be *religious*. The school must be deeply touched by the sense of a spiritual world. The history of the world must be felt to be real—that is, as an unfoldment of purpose in the world. The values and the meaning of everything are to be appreciated and understood, according to this view, through a process of enrichment of the mind under the influence of the highest social ideals expressed in the most persuasive forms. Education thus centers in the work of developing the power to appreciate values in all experience. Anything, too, that sustains optimistic moods helps to create the philosophical spirit, and one function of this philosophic spirit is to forestall the cynical moods and the narrow and prejudiced ways of thinking which are among the most dangerous tendencies of the times. The tendency to form judgments upon insufficient evidence and to act according to narrow and one-sided principles is incompatible with the philosophic attitude.

It is of course by no means the actual teaching of philosophy to every one, or the spreading broadcast of any particular philosophical principle that one would advocate as a preventive culture or to cure existing evils. It is rather a mode of living and of thinking throughout society and in all the educational process that is wanted. What we need is a better quality of mental product, more capacity to penetrate into the heart and substance of experience, greater responsiveness to good influences, greater ability to judge values, and a more plastic and more freely flowing mental life. These are of course large demands and imply faith and an interest in a remote future. *But a school which is religions through and through in its attitude toward life and is deeply touched by the influence of art in all its ways of dealing with the child will go a long way toward fulfilling the requirements of an education in the spirit of philosophy.*

Such conclusions as these might at least serve, we should suppose, as a working hypothesis, upon the basis of which we may consider in detail a variety of questions of the day. New problems have arisen before the eyes of the teacher, and indeed obtrude themselves upon all who must take part in the practical life of others. Some of these problems are due to changed external relations of countries to one another. Some are problems of internal adjustment and reconstruction. At least they may so be classified for purposes of discussion. In reality all changes are too closely bound up with one another to allow us to treat them practically as independent. No nation any longer stands alone. Internationalism is an idea that penetrates all other practical ideas. And no internal problems of any nation can be wholly local. The world is in a peculiar but also an inspiring way at the present time a single field of labor for the educational thinker and indeed the teacher in every field of human life.

CHAPTER IV

PEACE AND MILITARISM

Among the many pedagogical questions raised and given new significance by the war, is that of the teaching about war and about peace. This is a question of ideals, and of values and the teaching of history. There are practical and superficial questions to be considered. There are also more profound problems, since all our teaching of good and evil is implicated. Shall we continue, in one moment, to assume that war is the greatest glory in the world, and in the next to condemn it as the greatest of evils? Shall we as teachers take the standpoint of pacifism? Or shall we be still apostles of the heroic order? This is really no simple matter, and it is not one to be laid aside, directly it begins to disturb us, as unimportant. No one passing through the experiences of the past four years can have wholly escaped this dilemma, or can have kept himself entirely aloof from the doubts and perplexities that must always be attached to religious and philosophical problems of good and evil. These doubts and hesitations are necessarily increased when we try to become consistent teachers and wise counselors of the young.

It would be of psychological interest at least to collect all the arguments and opinions that have been put forth about the good and evil of war. There is a tendency for moralists to go to extremes. The writers on war are likely to be either ardent pacifists or strong militarists. They do not try to strike a balance between good and evil, but war is either a great blessing upon mankind or the greatest curse of the ages. In general they do not seek to base their conclusions upon ultimate philosophical principles, but rather upon moral or biological principles, or, again, upon preferences for the activities of war or the arts of peace. How very different the good and evil of war and peace may seem from different points of view is well shown by the following excerpt from a daily newspaper:

A DEADLY PARALLEL

THIS IS THE WAY GERMANY TALKS TO YOUNG BOYS OF SCOUT AGE

"War is the noblest and holiest expression of human activity. For us, too, the glad great hour of battle will strike. Still and deep in the German heart must live the joy of battle and the longing for it. Let us ridicule to the utmost the old women in breeches

THIS IS WHAT THE SCOUT ORGANIZATION TEACHES AMERICAN BOYS

From the "Handbook for Boys," 17th edition, page 454.

"The movement is one for efficiency and patriotism. It does not try to make soldiers of boy scouts, but to make boys who will turn out as men who fear war and deplore it as cruel and revolting. No; war is beautiful. Its august sublimity elevates the human heart beyond the earthly and the common. In the cloud palace above sit the heroes, Frederick the Great and Blucher and all the men of action—the Great Emperor, Moltke, Roon, Bismarck are there as well, but not the old women who would take away our joy in war. When here on earth a battle is won by German arms and the faithful dead ascend to Heaven, a Potsdam lance corporal will call the guard to the door and 'Old Fritz' (Frederick the Great), springing from his golden throne, will give the command to present arms. That is the Heaven of Young Germany.

"Because only in war all the virtues which militarism regards highly are given a chance to unfold, because only in war the truly heroic comes into play, for the realization of which on earth militarism is above all concerned; therefore, it seems to us who are filled with the spirit of militarism that war is a holy thing, the holiest on earth, and this high estimate of war in its turn makes an essential ingredient of the military spirit. There is nothing that trades-people complain of so much as that we regard it as holy."

to be fine citizens, and who will if their country needs them make better soldiers for having been scouts. No one can be a good American unless he is a good citizen, and every boy ought to train himself so that as a man he will be able to do his full duty to the community. I want to see the boy scouts not merely utter fine sentiments, but act on them, not merely sing 'My Country, 'Tis of Thee,' but act in a way that will give them a country to be proud of. No man is a good citizen unless he so acts as to show that he actually uses the Ten Commandments, and translates the Golden Rule into his life conduct—and I don't mean by this exceptional cases under spectacular circumstances, but I mean applying the Ten Commandments and the Golden Rule in the ordinary affairs of everyday life. I hope the boy scouts will practice truth and square dealing and courage and honesty, so that when as young men they begin taking a part not only in earning their own livelihood, but in governing the community, they may be able to show in practical fashion their insistence upon the great truth that the eighth and ninth commandments are directly related to everyday life, not only between men as such in their private relations, but between men and the government of which they are a part. Indeed, the boys, even while only boys, can have a very real effect upon the conduct of the grown-up members of the community, for decency and square dealing are just as contagious as vice and corruption."

The praise of war takes many forms, and invokes many fundamental principles—ethical, æsthetic, biological, sociological. From Leibnitz' saying that perpetual peace is a motto fit only for a graveyard to Moltke's that peace is only a dream and not even a beautiful dream, there is a long list of defenses of war. This philosophy of war is by no means peculiarly German, although German writers seem to have been the most ardent apologists of war in recent times. Treitschke, Schmitz (29), Scheler (77), Nusbaum (86), Arndt, Steinmetz, Lasson, Engelbrecht, Schoonmaker, all sing the praises of war as the most glorious work of man, or as performing for civilization some noble good. Even Hegel said that wars invigorate humanity just as the storm preserves the sea from putrescence.

But this praise of war, we say, is by no means exclusively German. Thucydides thought war a noble school of heroism, the exercise ground of the nations. To Mohammed and his Arabs war seemed not only in itself a heroism, we are told, but a divine act. This belief in war as divine is an idea that is very wide-spread among primitive peoples. Cramb, the English writer, says that it is very easy to demonstrate that the glory of battle is an illusion, but by the same argument you may demonstrate that all glory and life itself is an illusion and a mockery. Redier says that the war has brought us all the noble joys so necessary to stimulate mankind, and one no longer finds happiness, therefore, in sleeping comfortably, but only in living bravely.

There is no lack, indeed, of recognition of the heroic motive in war. Sometimes the argument appeals to religion, sometimes to art, sometimes to morality. Sometimes the advocates of war are thinking of war as the great adventure. War and the thought of war induce an ecstasy, a glow of the feelings. War is thought of as an expression of normal, healthy life, as making life more abundant and more beautiful. War brings out fundamental virtues in the individual; it also destroys the weaker and the meaner race and leaves the strong and the virtuous. Struggle, they say, is the method of civilization. Again, it is urged that war is always just in its issues. Like the old ordeal which always registered the decrees of heaven, war is the just arbiter of fate. The saving of the world through bloodshed, the uniting of the world through war, war as the great teacher of mankind, war as the creator of great personalities—all these are persistent themes in the literature of war. There is no place for the pacifist in the minds of these apologists of the heroic order. The crises of war are historic necessities; they come when it is time to release people from the bondage of the past and to bring individualistic generations back to the sense of duty and of loyalty to great causes. This is the belief of many, even now.

On the other side we find the great variety of pacifistic minds. War to the pacifists is wrong, unholy, morally sinful, biologically and economically and in every other way evil. The conscientious objector's point of view is very simple. War antagonizes some principle which is religiously or morally supreme for him. Therefore there can be no justification of war whatever, and it ought to be abolished at any price. When you ask the objector to go to war, you invite him to commit a flagrant sin. The English literature of pacifism is full of this moral and religious protestation against war which in the minds of the objectors becomes a finality beyond which it is futile to ask them to go.

The psychological and the biological pacifists are hardly less emphatic in their condemnation of war. The biological thinker undertakes to refute the theory that war is selective. He counts the cost of war in terms of human life and of racial vitality, and produces a condemning document. That war indeed selects but selects unfavorably and in an adverse direction is the conclusion of many, among them Savorgnan in his book "La Guerra e la Populazione," in which he calls war *dysgenic*. The psychologist tends to see in war a reversion, a lapse to barbarism. War is a product of the original savage in man, whom civilization has never tamed, as Freud would say. War lingers because of man's love of old institutions. We cling to old habits and customs, which take on a semblance of the æsthetic, because of their antiquity and old associations. This is the explanation by Nicolai. Russell thinks men fight because they are still ignorant and despotic. Patrick thinks of war as a slip in the psychic machinery. MacCurdy (37) and others think of war as a mental or a social disease.

Upon the hardships of war, its economic futility and its sheer senselessness, when looked at from the standpoint of any rational desire, many base their conclusion that war is evil. The working man and all the masses are likely to concur in this opinion. When they examine war they see that they themselves as they think are used in the interest of the few, that they shed their blood for a glory in which they do not share. They say, all men are brothers, and so why should they kill one another. Men seem more real to them than do boundaries of countries which they never see, and the interests of wealth that is also invisible.

Such thought as this has behind it some of the most powerful minds, as we know. It is Tolstoi's philosophy, and it is the argument of such men as Novicow. The professional economist and the student of history add their protests. They say that military peoples fade away, while the peaceful live and prosper, that "the country whose military power is irresistible is doomed." These are the words of Roberts. Some try to demonstrate that nothing is gained economically by war; that all the work of war is destructive, to every one engaged in it. It is argued that the nation that is suited to live will prevail without wars; and that without this inner superiority, war will avail nothing. War is bad business, in the opinion of these economic thinkers. War is like setting the dog on the customer at the door, the practical man in England complained at the beginning of the present war. As to war being associated with intelligence and with virtue in nations, or as to its ever producing either intellectual or moral qualities, many would flatly deny that war ever has such a result. The opposite would seem nearer the truth to them. Military nations are unintelligent nations, and militarism is always brutalizing.

Such pacifism and the dream of universal peace are no new ideas in the world. Like the philosophy of war pacifism has a long history. There have been pacifists everywhere and presumably at all times, since pacifism is quite as much a temperament as it is an idea or a philosophy. Cramb tells us that all recent centuries have had their doctrines of pacifism, each century having its own characteristic variety. In the time of the Marlborough wars, there appeared the book of Abbé de St. Pierre denouncing all wars. In the middle of the nineteenth century there is the doctrine of the Manchester school, maintaining that the peace of Europe must be secured not by religion, but by the coöperation of the industrial forces of the continent. Finally, says Cramb, we see the characteristic thought of the twentieth century in the position that war is bad because it is contrary to social well-being and is economically profitless, alike to the victor and the vanquished. This is the pacifism of the socialist who holds that the ties of common labor and economic state are fundamental, and divisions into nationality are secondary and unimportant; and that militarism belongs to the pernicious state of society which perpetuates capitalism and privilege and to government as a function of the favored classes.

This is certainly not the place to try to put order into this conflicting mass of opinion about war and peace by working out the principles of a philosophy of good and evil, since this would mean to attack one of the most fundamental of all problems of philosophy. It seems to be plain, however, that neither upon biological grounds nor by ethical principles, nor by finding any consensus in the desires and opinions of thinkers can we reach any hard and fast conclusions about the good and evil of war. It is rather by a broad interpretation of the world and of history and the nature of national consciousness, by some genetic view of national life, that we are most likely to see our way toward a practical view of the present good and evil of war. War is a phase of the whole process of social development of nations. We think of nations as living and growing, and of a world which is gradually maturing. War obtains a natural explanation on sociological and psychological principles, not as a disease, but as a natural consequence and condition of the formation of nations, or of any type of horde or group. In the course of the development of nations we see psychological factors coming more and more to the front. Desires which are more or less consciously avowed become the motives of history. It is in the play of these desires: their fixation, their generalization, and transformation, the manner in which they become attached to specific objects, that we seek the explanation of wars and of the especial psychology of nations. Nations have lived secluded and guarded lives, because of the nature of the desires which were most fundamental in their lives, and the objects upon which these desires have become directed. Now nations show some signs of emerging from their seclusion, of abandoning their ambitions of empire, and leading a more complex and more practical life.

In this progress we see the possibility of the final disappearance of war. But we have no right to pervert either history or education in the effort to eliminate war, or even to pass judgments upon war prematurely or upon the basis of personal preferences, or the moods of any moment. The whole world might, conceivably, be brought together and be made to declare solemnly that there should be no more war. Nations would thereby voluntarily relinquish their aggressive thoughts, put aside the love they have for the heroic and take justice and peace as their watchwords. And all this would seem ideal. But if the elimination of war should mean that we have no longer anything for which men are willing to die, if merely to escape from war we voluntarily sacrifice good that more than counterbalances the evil we overcome, we should say that peace had been bought at too high a price. *Terrible as war is, it cannot be judged by itself alone.* We have a right to look forward to a time when there shall be no more war, just as everywhere it seems to be instinctive for us to try to gain good without its attendant trouble and evil. In the meantime the world had best busy itself, mainly, in our view, with creating those things that are best, rather than in destroying those things that are worst. Nations, like individuals, must lead bravely hazardous lives, without too much thought of dangers. Peace as a sole program for the making of history appears to be too narrow, and especially too unproductive. Internationalism that is merely a combination of peoples to prevent war is not very inspiring, especially since it is doubtful whether it even leads to peace. A broad historical view that will enable us just now to make good come out of the evil of war will be a better organ of conscious evolution than a philosophy of peace can possibly be.

Such views as these give us at least some clews to the educational and pedagogical problems of war and peace. We can distinguish between an education which deals specifically with such problems, endeavoring to treat them sharply and with finality, making clear moral decisions, and an education which by enriching the mind and by educating all the selective faculties leads to an appreciation of all great practical and moral questions as aspects of the whole of history and of life.

Let us see what the specific teaching of peace may and may not include. First of all we cannot, for educational purposes, judge everything in the lives of nations by *moral* principles. The ideal of universal brotherhood and coöperation, of sacrifice and altruism, cannot be realized in the present stage of history. On the other hand, the stern picture of justice is one that fits into the present mood of the world. Justice is the natural link between individualism and altruism. A world determined upon seeing justice done, a world which, without setting absolute values upon peace and war, does distinguish between just and unjust wars, between the demands and the needs of peoples, leans toward the moral life. It has little to say about duties as yet, or comparatively little, but it has a strong conception of rights. A deep enough interest in justice, by its own momentum, introduces duties into the practical life. In time the world will perhaps not be satisfied with seeing and recognizing justice, and ensuring it in great crises; it will make justice as a matter of course.

This idea of justice seems, on the whole, to be the best basis for the teaching now of international morality. The teaching of pacifism, enlarging upon the biological waste of war, trying to present the realism of war in its worst light in order to overcome the warlike spirit and to assist the doctrines of internationalism to take effect upon the mind seems to be the wrong way of teaching peace. We seem to be obligated to teach war as it is. We cannot conceal its heroic side for fear of perpetuating war, and we must not conceal the brutality of war for fear of destroying morale and the fighting spirit. And it is to be much doubted whether it is *ever* necessary to teach history unfairly and one-sidedly in times either of war or of peace. We depend upon larger effects and deeper judgments than can be produced by selecting and distorting the facts. Nothing is meaner in national life than dishonest history.

Education in the ideal of peace, which we may hope to be the state of the world in the future, will be an adjustment of the mind to new and practical modes of life rather than the establishing of a principle. The educated attitude of mind which will best safeguard the peace of the world must include an intelligent knowledge of all the agencies proposed to aid in establishing this state of harmony toward which we look forward. We must all know about arbitration, leagues of nations, courts of honor, understand diplomacy better and the arguments for disarmament, understand the economic and the industrial situation, the possibilities of coöperation, reduction of the rights and privileges of classes, democratic movements. The inculcation of such knowledge is an education for peace. There is little that is abstruse in any of these ideas, and the very young child is not too young to know something of these wider aspects of the social life. All these may be presented in a concrete form as a part of the work of conveying a knowledge of current history.

We may think of various cures for war, and various efforts that might be made educationally to prevent war. Peace might effectually be cultivated by an educational propaganda. But after all it is not such cures of war as this that we are most concerned about in the work of education. We might even tend to establish in this way a peace which would be detrimental to the higher interests of civilization. *A true educational philosophy, at any rate, is not to be dislodged from its purpose of keeping education constructive rather than inhibitory.* This institution of education must not be too much influenced by the temporary moods of the day, by the present gloomy evidences of the devastation of war. We must teach and prepare for an abundant life in which there is glory and wide opportunity, and in which the motives of power may be satisfied. Then peace can take care of itself. But this abundant life must be a life of *activity*, not of mere patriotism and subjective glorification and nationalistic interest. Vanity, the low order of enthusiasms, the glory of display, can no longer have a place in this national life.

There appears to be a pedagogical lesson in the contrast between the heroic and the moral view of teaching war and peace illustrated by the German philosophy of war and the ideal of the Boy Scout organization. Deducting something for literary exaggeration, we may say that education cannot afford to neglect either of these attitudes, but must indeed in some way combine them. The exaggeration consists on one side in praising the specific act of war; but on the other side there is plainly lacking something of the dramatic appeal which any ideal life for the young must have. War is an evil, but the spirit that makes war is by no means an evil. The philosophy of war proves its failure by ignoring the moral ideal altogether, or regarding morality as something solely national, but the other, it may be, puts the moral ideal in a pedagogically impossible position. Both the content and the form must be taken into account in any educational plan that hopes to exert power or to be influential in any important way now, and it is the form which, more than anything else, is still lacking in our whole procedure of education.

Preparedness and Military Training

Military training has now of course become a practical question with us and with every nation. It is the military use of military education that must first of all be considered. For that reason it must primarily be a problem upon which political authorities and military experts must decide. These experts must be competent to tell us what military equipment is necessary at any time to meet the requirements of our political situation, and they must be able to advise about the amount and kind of actual military training necessary to make this physical equipment most effective. All this, plainly, must be provided whether it be good or bad from a general educational standpoint. But preparedness and national defense mean, of course, more than the possession of guns and more than military training as such. And there can be no hard and fast line between military preparedness and the wider technical preparedness in which all the equipment and skill of scientific and mechanical activities of the country are always ready to be mobilized in the defense of it; or between these and the still more general preparedness through the organization and control of the human factor in ways that are not specifically military or mechanically technical at all.

If preparation for defense is by no means exhausted by military training, on the other hand not all military training is intended for defense. Decision about the actual amount and kind of military training, we say, may be left to the expert, but it is for the psychologist and the educator to decide whether we need a mere minimum of such training or a general military training for educational purposes. After all, however, this is perhaps more a matter of taste in educational practices than of learning. There is plenty of opinion at least on both sides. Some maintain that military discipline is of very great benefit to the man and to society. From the German point of view it is the equivalent of hygiene for the individual. It is a national regimen for physical and mental health. It is also the symbol and the expression of social solidarity. Many believe that the discipline of soldiering would be especially good for all American boys. But there is no dearth of evidence on the other side—that military training in so far as it is really conducted in the military manner is brutalizing.

After all, we say this may be a matter of preference. Some like military discipline in the schools and everywhere; some do not. The present writer for one will confess that he does not. It is not the danger of making a people warlike that one sees in it, so much as the certainty of introducing into all the daily life a spirit that is inconsistent with our stage of civilization and with the most wholesome spirit of education. It savors of the unprogressive. It means, in our opinion, the introduction into the school, in a far too easy and simple way, and consequently at far too low a level, something that ought to be put into education in a different manner. The sense of solidarity and the idealism which the German has found in his military discipline we must express in some other way. It is especially the unproductiveness of military life, and the constant suggestion of that which is archaic without either the practical setting or the ornamental life to which such things belong, that are especially to be charged against militarism.

We ought to ask, rather, how peace morale, and the essentials of the warlike spirit may be maintained *without military training*. Is it not rather by way of the more general and untechnical processes of education which make for physical expertness, by fundamental social education, by giving attention to our foundations of religious education, that we shall be able to create and sustain the most efficient morale? The best foundation for all necessary military activities of a free people appears to be a by-product, so to speak, of peaceful life sustained at a high point of efficiency and enthusiasm. Military training disconnected from its immediate use and application in war must appear to some and indeed to many as a misfit in modern civilized life. This is not an argument for pacifism, however. The war has taught us that militarism and military capacity in high degree may spring up from very peaceful soil, and also that military training, however perfect, is no substitute for the generic virtues out of which courage and patriotism grow. In the long run will it not be the country that can do without military training that will have the advantage? Or the country in which military preparedness is so merged in everything else as to be indistinguishable from the rest of life? Is there not, in a word, a preparedness that will make a country superior and safe both in war and in peace?

CHAPTER V

THE TEACHING OF PATRIOTISM

It would be hard to find a word (unless it be democracy) about which so many questions gather as now cling to the word "patriotism." Patriotism is praised as the highest virtue; it is also cursed as the cause of war. Some think of it as the *sole* cause of war. Some would like to see it disappear for the reason that they believe it at best an old and out-lived social virtue, now having become merely ornamental and an obstacle to the true socialization of the world. Some think patriotism still the center of the moral and the social life.

This is not the place to attempt a psychological analysis of patriotism, but we may at least try to enumerate the principal factors in it, and say what we think patriotism as a virtue—or a vice—is. *Patriotism in our view is normally loyalty to country as a functioning unit in a world of nations. It is devotion to all the aspects and functions of a country as an historical entity.* We must think of these historical entities, moreover, as leading lives in which, although their own ambitions for honor and greatness are legitimate, there must be a practical recognition of the legitimacy of similar interests on the part of all other nations, and in which the recognition of the common interests of nations is also freely made. Since nations perform no one single function and have no single motive of life in their normal state, patriotism can be no devotion to a single purpose or cause. Such patriotism as this, we may say, does not antagonize internationalism. Loyalty to country is loyalty to the functions and interests that properly belong to country. The individual, the family, the country and all intervening groups and entities are natural formations. To each of these entities there is due a loyalty precisely measured by the character of the functions which these entities perform.

This view of patriotism is plainly, both in its theoretical aspect and its practical consequences, widely different from those that end in pure internationalism. Its essential feature is that it recognizes the validity of all entities and groups about which deep feeling has grown up. This means, of course, that as criteria of social values these feelings are placed ahead of certain logical or scientific considerations. Pure internationalism of the intellectual type recognizes the validity only of the whole world group. Nicolai, for example, says that there is a morality and there are rights pertaining to the individual and to the whole of humanity, but all intervening groups are temporary and artificial. That, certainly, we should not agree with. The coming greater coördination of the world we may suppose will deepen and intensify patriotism, rather than diminish it. The homogeneity toward which the biologists tell us we are tending and ought to approach is one in which, it is likely, still sharper national outlines may well appear. The ambitions, the functions, and the culture of nations ought to be made clearer rather than be lost in the coming internationalism. We shall still in the Hegelian sense find our reality in and through the state. An aroused sense of the function and worth of country will be the basis of patriotism. Advancement toward internationalism will be made by a generalized patriotism rather than by outgrowing patriotism. That is, it is by passing from a deepened loyalty to country through a sense of the validity and right of the patriotism of all peoples that international social consciousness will be developed.

So all those very numerous views of patriotism which assert that it is only through a decline of patriotism that a rational international order can ever be established, appear to be wrong. A fundamental question is at issue here. It concerns in part the criteria of valuation in the field of the social life. The kind of cosmopolitanism and internationalism that demands the final abrogation of the sentiment of patriotism is, as we have intimated, a rationalistic doctrine. It is an attempt to extend objective principles into the realm of social values. Reason tells us, they say, that we ought to organize universally and obliterate national lines. Reason tells us we should make no distinction between ourselves and strangers, between enemies and allies. But by the same rationalism we may break up any loyalty. Patriotism is an inner, a spiritual force, and it has its roots in moods and forms of appreciation which have a certain finality about them, for the reason that they are deposits from the whole course of human history. Veblen says it is a matter of habit to what particular nationality a man will become attached on arriving at years of discretion. That is true, and it is of course the whole secret of loyalty. But it is not a matter of unimportance whether a man shall become attached to any country. It is the dynamic power of loyalty that is in question, if we consider its practical value. Loyalty grows because it has a use, which is related to the most basic feelings. It is not a product of reason, and cannot justly be judged on purely rational grounds.

Any political ideal, or any plan for a world order, that would minimize patriotism is unnatural. The forms of socialism that do this and the *laissez faire* tendencies appear to have left out of the reckoning some of the modes of evaluating experience which are most basic. We may recognize all the excess of provincialism in the native patriotism of the peasant, and all the egoistic motives in the patriotism of the aristocrat and the militarist, but still we see no place in the world for the man without a country. It is not yet the workmen of the cities, who say that all men are brothers, who can lead us to a better social order. Patriotism must be educated, modernized, made more productive, but certainly its work is not yet done. It cannot be cast aside as something archaic and only a part of the ornamental and useless encumbrances of life. *It is not by weakening loyalty to country, but by strengthening it, that internationalism will be made secure.* If patriotism fits into modern life like sand in the machinery, as Veblen says, we must see how patriotism may be made to do better service.

Some views about patriotism which thus disparage it seem to be based upon a biological conception of it. Not a few writers apparently think of patriotism as a fixed trait of the human organism, even as a kind of mendelian character unrelated to other social qualities. This trait antagonizes social progress, but it is preserved because of secondary values which it represents, such as moral or æsthetic values. According to these views patriotism may be complex, but it acts like a unitary character. It is subject, theoretically, to selection, but as a matter of fact it remains a strong factor in the temperament of nearly all races.

But in our view patriotism is something less precise than all this would imply. It is a form in which the most fundamental and general of desires are expressed, in becoming fixated upon their most natural and necessary objects. It is an aspect of the whole process of development of the affective life. Leaving out patriotism (if such a thing were possible) would mean a break in the continuity of the social life. It would leave one group of functions without their natural support in desire. Economists sometimes seem to leave out of account the profound emotional forces and the irresistible tendencies which make social groups. They want organizations without the moods and impulses by which alone social bodies are formed or sustained; and they expect to see organization broken up or interest in it lost while all the conditions that keep alive the passion for it are intact. Patriotism and the existence of nations seem, however, to be the opposite sides of the same fact. And we may assume that so long as nations exist, at any rate, patriotism will exist, and one of the most necessary functions of public education will be the regulation of the motives and feelings which are contained in this sentiment.

Patriotism is first of all to be considered, then, as a phase of the social life as a whole, rather than as an unique emotion or a special variety of loyalty. It is a way in which the sum of tendencies that enter into the social life become fixated upon certain qualities of the environment, or upon certain objects. Patriotism will best be understood in a practical way by observing its objects. Patriotism is a total mood; country is a total object. But the mood of patriotism expresses varied desires, and the object of patriotism is a highly complex and variable object. In being loyal to or devoted to country in the sense which we usually mean when we say one is patriotic, we are devoted to at least the following objects: 1) physical country as home; 2) the ways, customs, standards and beliefs of the country; 3) the group of people constituting the nation; and here race, social solidarity, ideal constructions of an united people having common purposes and possessions enter; 4) leaders; 5) country as an historical entity having rights and interests—a living being having experiences, ideals and characteristics. The educational problem is of course the regulation of the attachment of the individuals of a nation to these objects. In one sense this educational problem of patriotism is nothing less than that of developing social consciousness itself. It is precisely the task of fostering or creating in the child the basis of all loyalty. Given a loyal mind in the child and a normal environment, we need to be concerned but little about the causes and the groups upon which that loyalty will expend itself, for the conditions are all present for forming an attachment to every natural group. Considered generically and psychologically there is no patriotism, we say, marked off from everything else, and there is no one object that excites patriotic loyalty. All educational influences that strengthen attachment to home, all social feeling, devotion to the ways of any group and obedience to its standards, respect for all law and authority, all appreciation of historic relations, help to develop patriotism, merely because country, in these aspects, is an omnipresent object to which the feelings thus engendered will automatically become to some extent attached.

The first task in the teaching of patriotism (first at least as regards the obviousness of the need) is to give all children a vivid sense of country as physical object, and a deep aesthetic appreciation of this object—although of course this idea of physical country cannot be detached from everything else. Each country has its different problem. Ours is to create a total country, in the imagination of the young. A German writer not long ago predicted that the future of America lay in the direction of breaking up into a little England, a little Ireland, and a little of the other nationalities here represented. That particular danger may seem remote enough, but in another way we do continue to be lacking in unity. Our patriotism has been too local, and America, even after the great war, is to some extent still a collection of geographical regions. New England, the South, the Coast are more real to many than country as a whole. Our great distances, and the impossibility of clearly imagining them have necessarily presented obstacles thus far to a unified image of country. The time may come, and perhaps soon, when such a divided consciousness of country will be a grave flaw in our national life.

It must be a serious function of some kind of geography to give reality to the idea of country, although of course we cannot separate entirely geographical from historical idea of country. The teaching of the geography of the native land must be different from other geography. Native land must have a warmth and home feeling about it that other countries do not have, but as yet the psychological conditions for this have apparently not been worked out. With our present facilities in pictorial art, the geographical element in the idea of country seems controllable. The minds of children are exceedingly impressionable in this direction. Intensity of feeling and vividness of imagination are at the disposal of the educator. The love of color, especially, must be used to make lasting impressions upon the mind. We need to notice also that the idea of physical country that enters most into patriotic feeling is not an idea of city streets but of the open country. It is the country that inspires the strongest home feeling, and it is the country that is the basis of the sense of changelessness and eternity of native land, that is a strong element in patriotic sentiment. This element of patriotism, it is plain, is something aesthetic. It is not so much a moral loyalty to country that is inspired by the everlasting hills, as an aesthetic love of it as the home land. This aesthetic love of the home land is a response to such stimuli as the beautiful arouses everywhere. It is susceptible, therefore, to all the influences of art—of music, picture, symbol; these must all be employed in teaching patriotism. The theme of home is especially sensitive to the effects of music. It is this idea of home, enlarged and enriched by pictorial representation of country, deeply impressed and influenced by music, and unified and imbued with the feeling of personal possession by the story of country that is the core of patriotic feeling. It is the function of art, especially of music, to help to make the home feeling of the child normal and enthusiastic—to raise it above the stage of being an "anxiety of animal life," as Nicolai terms the primitive love of home. Art must help to remove the fears and depressions that may lurk in the idea of home, which are great obstacles to the development of the higher devotions. It is the lack of normal love of home in the city, we should say, that makes socialism and all forms of internationalism that breed so rapidly there such dangerous moods in a democracy. Without true home love, we may conclude, the wider loyalties can never be quite wholesome, although they may be intense and fanatical.

The second element in patriotism we identify as the love of, or loyalty to, the sum of the customs, beliefs, and standards that make up the *mores* of a people. A peculiarly perplexing educational problem arises, since there are two opposite evils to be avoided We may too readily cultivate a spirit which either takes the form of a narcissistic love of one's own ways, or which, extraverted, so to speak, becomes a fanatical ambition to impose one's own culture upon the world; or, on the other hand we might become too self-critical, too cosmopolitan, and too receptive toward all foreign culture. National conceit, complacency and destinism face us in one direction, the danger of losing our identity and our individuality and our mission in the other. These problems of course confront all nations; they are especially urgent in America, because of the composite nature of our national life and the rapid changes that take place in it, and also because of the ideal nature of the bond that holds us together. We are still a somewhat inchoate and flowing mass of social elements, imperfectly coördinated, manifestly, yet deeply united by ideals which appeal to very deep emotions. Our work is to maintain social solidarity, preserve and educate certain fundamental qualities of our national life which are our real claims to individuality as a people. These essential traits, perhaps because of our newness as a form of civilization, appear to be less clearly defined, less definitely represented in institutions, and to be more abstract than the qualities that make up the essential character of other peoples.

Our educational problem is, naturally, different from all others. We are committed to an idea of liberty. We make this principle of freedom the dominant in all our national life. We have not tried, and cannot consistently attempt to centralize our educational institutions very much, or even allow our culture to become crystallized into a definite type, for this would be almost as bad as denying our principle of religious freedom. But we cannot, in the other direction, become too diversified intellectually, and still less in regard to more fundamental aspects of life, for this would break up our unity altogether, or determine it more and more in the direction of political coercion. Thus far, it appears, it has been our great virtue as a people that we have remained united by emotional forces, or by the suggestive power of an idea. Sooner or later we shall need to see whither our present tendencies lead, and education must in all probability be put to work to control and regulate the elements that make for unity and for disruption in our life. *Our work as educators will be to maintain a working harmony in the affective and instinctive life of the people.* We need now, and we shall need more and more, religious, moral and aesthetic unity in our life as a nation—not a forced and superficial agreement, but a deep harmony of ideals and moods. This purpose must never be lost sight of by the educator. It must be made to pervade all our educational philosophy and all our plans for the school. This educational problem exists of course everywhere in some degree, and in regard to all manner of social groups. But American life as a whole is peculiarly a growth in which diverse and even divergent elements must continue to be brought together and held together through the power of ideas which are subject to many influences. Diversity and differentiation are added as fast as the process of assimilation can be carried on. There can be no closing up of differences in a final perfection and security.

Must we not, then, make the education of instincts and feelings, and the control of the basic moods, rather than the development and stimulation of specialization and differentiation our first and chief concern? Must we not do this even at a loss of efficiency in some directions, if necessary? Certainly we must not go too fast nor too far towards industrialism. To control any tendency to over differentiation and industrialism that is now likely to occur we must have a broad humanitarianism and a humanistic ideal of culture (by which we do not mean classicism). *The sharing of all experiences that represent our spirit and purpose and American ideas, and equal opportunity to realize them, must be our thought in planning our educational work.* The future of America may well depend upon our power, or upon the power of our original idea, to hold people together by the essential moods in which our American ideas are represented. The production, out of these elemental moods, of common interests on a high level will be, we take it, the only preventive in the end of the growth of common interests on a low level, which is always threatened in democracies, and is the way democracies tend to destroy themselves by their democracy. Education in the fundamentals of industrial life, in social relations, in play and in art, in religion, is what we most need—the latter, we may conclude, most of all. We must have in some way a greater religious unity and more religion, not by attempting an impossible amalgamation of creeds as was promulgated by some of the founders of the New Japan, but by an education that includes and brings forth all that is common in religion. That at least is the only kind of unity that offers hope finally of making a world safe with democracy in it. This is not a plea for a back-to-nature movement, for the simple life, for a life which tends away from industrialism. Industrialism will go on, if for no other reason, because pastoral or agricultural peoples would soon be at a disadvantage in an industrial world as it is organized now, for want of rapid increase in population. But it is implied that industry itself must be made suitable for the democratic life. It means that we must go back of the identities of language and obedience to common laws, and take as our educational foundations that which American life is in truth based upon: physical power and motor freedom, the sense of liberty, the colonial spirit of comradeship and devotion to common cause, the ideal of an abundant and enthusiastic life. Merely becoming conscious of these and observing their meaning and their place in our national life is in itself a large contribution to the sources out of which patriotism may be drawn. *When our patriotism is sincere enough so that we shall be milling to sacrifice for country our religious intolerance and bigotry, our social antipathies, and our industrial advantages, we shall have a morale which for peace or for war will be wholly sufficient.*

Must our ambition be to teach American children that American ways are the best, and that these ways ought to be established in the world? There is both an evil and a good, both an absurdity and a sublime loyalty in the view which all nations have, that their own culture and life are the best. This conceit is in part a product of isolation, and is pure provincialism. But it is also of the very essence of the reality feeling and the sense of solidarity of peoples and of their loyalty to country. It must not be dealt with too ruthlessly. There is a primitive stratum of it that must remain in all peoples. Nations, however benighted, will not be dispossessed of this idea, but experience and education will make nations more discriminating so that they can at least see what is essential and what is superficial in their own characteristics. Certainly whatever is ethical in our foundations we, and all other peoples, will be expected to hold to. We feel it a duty to spread our moral truth abroad and our mores are necessarily right for us, and this idea of rightness of mores must imply a desire to make them prevail in the world. We may recognize, abstractly, other standards of conduct, but there is something in moral belief which, of course, cannot voluntarily be changed, and which must stand for the ultimately real in consciousness so long as it is held to be so by the mass of the people. This must extend also to æsthetic standards, and to all final judgments of values to some extent.

For these reasons we must suppose that the spirit of competition among nations, certainly so far as it concerns the ambition for empires of the spirit, must remain. Belief on the part of a people in the superiority of their own culture cannot and should not be eliminated. By this spirit the good, we may be sure, will prevail, but prevail only through opposition and competition. There can be no real compromise in the field of these moral possessions and appreciations. *We* must be Americans, and react with American ideas. True nationalists everywhere appear to recognize and to be guided by this truth. We cannot voluntarily lay aside our own beliefs nor help believing they are right, although we may see that were we differently situated we might change them.

There are three things at least, as regards our mores that cannot be accomplished. For this we may take our evidence and our warning from Germany. Culture cannot be spread by force, since force does not conquer spirit. Devotion to the basic principles of one's civilization cannot rationally nor safely be extended to include all customs and manners, so that we may assume that there is a right way in everything which is ours and a wrong way which is foreign. The mores of a people cannot be changed or manipulated by education and propaganda without uprooting the moral structures of society. When we begin to practice a Social-politik we enter upon dangerous ground.

Are we not, then, to take the attitude in education that *our culture is an experimental culture and represents an experimental civilization*? Although for us our ways and beliefs are final criteria of values in conduct, and we cannot hope or wish to free ourselves from them or to be guided by objective data, still we put them forward in the spirit of the enquirer, rather than as eternal principles. If this be right, we are not to guard our civilization jealously, hedge it about with national jealousy and bigotry but rather send our culture abroad on a mission. We are to understand and to teach the culture of every other nation sympathetically, trusting to our own foundations to hold firm. We must be so fortified in our own virtue that we shall not be afraid to send our spirit abroad to compete with whatever it shall meet in the old world or the new. This impulse to extend one's culture and philosophy is a deep one, and we believe it to be well-grounded. It has been said that the deepest impulse of British imperialism has been to extend English ways of thought throughout the world. There is truth in this. We may conclude also that unless a nation can feel sincerely that it is founded upon something that ought to endure and at least to have an opportunity to become universal, it lacks a growth principle and its civilization is not very secure. Certainly it lacks a great pedagogical advantage in all the internal work of education.

The work of the intellectual leaders of a people is to uncover this kernel of sincere belief and worth, and strip nationalism at the same time of its encrustations of vanity and deception. There are, we may suppose, at the bottom of every nation's consciousness such sincere principles which are entitled to a fair field in the competition of the civilizations and the cultures of the world. We may be sure that there is Americanism that needs to be taught both for the sake of the world and for our own sake; something which constitutes our best contribution to an experimental world in which the over-emphasis of all sincere principles can ultimately do no harm. Americanism, with all the errors it may contain, and all the limitations it may have as a universal principle is better for us and for all, we may believe, than any dispassionate and well considered intellectualism, or a cosmopolitanism that is based upon a fear of provincialism. Let us be prepared, therefore, to go forth not to conquer but to participate in the life of the world.

As regards materials by means of which we are to teach a patriotism that shall be a strong devotion to the mores of the nation, there appear to be three important elements. We have, first, a literature which contains in part at least the spirit of our national life, although it does so *only* in part. Secondly, we have a beginning at least of an interpretation of American life through an American history that is to be something more than a history of political events, and shall be a true history of the American people. This history must include the history of our ideas and our ideals, our literature, institutions, art, and be indeed a true social history. This history must be the main source book for teaching what our country has meant to those who have lived in it, and what these people have really been and done. This is national character study. Character study, a truly psychological and interpretative history, should teach us what we are likely to do and what we ought to do in all typical situations with which we are likely to be confronted. How far we are as yet from such a general knowledge in regard to ourselves needs hardly to be suggested. The third element in this aspect of the teaching of patriotism is something more tangible and more immediately practical. Our ideals have to some extent at least been crystallized in our institutions, where they will still further be elaborated. The participation on the part of all in some way in these institutions is a part of our required training for good American life. A book knowledge of institutions is, of course, better than none at all, but there is no reason why knowledge should end there. All people, especially those now being educated, ought to have more direct and more intimate part in all the representative institutions of our country, even in the political institutions, and perhaps in them most of all. Americanism, whatever else it may be, must be a practical Americanism. It must have ideals and clear visions, it goes without saying, but it is the making and shaping of institutions by living in and through them that must be the main feature of our social life and of our education. When the individual and the social form are molded and developed together, patriotism will be a natural phase of mental growth.

CHAPTER VI

THE TEACHING OF PATRIOTISM (CONTINUED)

Patriotism we thought to be, in the third place, devotion to the *group*. Here the problem of the teaching of patriotism becomes specifically a question of social education. The question arises as to precisely what the objects of the devotion we call loyalty to the group are, and what factors in group-consciousness need most to be emphasized or educated as patriotism. Is it race or manners or the pure fact of propinquity or herd contact or all together that are the objects of social desire and the feeling of solidarity?

Race has been emphasized as the prime interest in group loyalty, but there seems to be doubt about this. At least there are difficulties in isolating anything we can call love of race. We can never separate race from propinquity, for example, or from mores, or from the bonds due to common possession of causes. Race loyalty appears to be a primitive feeling. When races were pure, groups small and possession common, all the elements of loyalty to group were present at once and coextensive. As civilization progressed the bond of pure race lessened. All races have now become mixed, we are told, and kinship in a group has ceased to be a fact. Nicolai maintains that race patriotism has grown out of family instinct, as something quite separate from herd instinct, but it seems likely that common interests, organization under necessity, or the social attraction resulting from any common cause must have been stronger than any consciousness of kinship, or any herd instinct as such—which may indeed not have existed at all.

It is this more conscious bond of function and propinquity at least that must be taken into account in the education of patriotism—certainly American patriotism. We in America can hardly emphasize race patriotism, without producing internal disruption. It is common function that is the distinguishing mark of the individuals of a group, rather than common origin. Common function, especially subsumption under one ordered government, particularly if the purpose be that of securing common protection, can plainly overcome all loyalty to race. Common religion antagonizes race consciousness, and we see therefore within nations races splitting up along lines of religious difference. We see within races also greater antagonism and greater lack of common interest between classes than between the same classes as found in different races. Aristocrats everywhere, for example, appear to have greater mutual sympathy and sense of nearness than do the upper and lower classes of the same race.

One of our own urgent educational problems is that of overcoming race differences and of utilizing racial bonds for practical ends. We try to put loyalty to group first, and we assume that race patriotism can be supreme only among those who have no country worth being loyal to. Loyalty to race, however, has a pedagogical use. We see it being employed to extend social feeling beyond the point to which propinquity and common cause can carry it. It was used, we know, in the propaganda and educational campaign by which German statesmen and historians hoped to develop a wider German consciousness. The racial object in this case is apparently purely fictitious. We see the same concept being used now to create or expand social feeling throughout the Anglo-Saxon race. What we mean mainly by Anglo-Saxon race is really English speaking peoples, having common or similar mores and ideals. It is, of course, by emphasizing and participating in common functions that loyalty either to an Anglo-Saxon union or to the total group in our own nation will be developed. Our own type of patriotism, in which there can be little or no racial loyalty as such, must be built upon more ideal and abstract conceptions than that of race. It is loyalty to group having a common idea, we say, which must be the basis of American group loyalty. This we must regard as higher than any race patriotism. All nations are now, as Boutroux remarks, to a greater or less extent *psychological races*. The factors that have produced them are the factors that have caused men to become functioning units.

This gives us a clew at least to a practical principle for the education of social loyalty. We must secure participation on the part of the individual in every function that belongs to each group to which the individual himself is attached. Thus all degrees and kinds of loyalty may be made to exist in the same mind without conflict or confusion, precisely because the loyalty desired is loyalty to people as groups or organizations having causes, not to collections of individuals as such.

The teaching of loyalty to any cause appears to be a lesson in patriotism. So far as teaching of patriotism is centered directly upon the production of loyalty to the whole group which constitutes the nation, the first object must be to create a sense of reality of the group in the mind of the individual. We may expect to do this in part by the teaching of geography and history in an adequate way, but we must also instill such patriotism by inducing individuals to participate in nation-wide organizations, which are capable of realizing dramatic effects. The experiences of the war have taught us to see this. It is organization or coöperation for practical ends, under conditions in which deep feeling is aroused, that most quickly and effectually creates the sense of solidarity in great groups of individuals. We must study the psychological side of this matter, and see how the power and momentum that are so readily gained in time of need can be better controlled for all the routine purposes of education and the practical daily life. The organization of national activities by means of voluntary associations will be likely to be one of the main educational methods of the future. If we are far-seeing we shall try to utilize the powers of organization, coöperation and communication to overcome many antagonisms now existing in society. War temporarily suspends class distinctions and many other forms of social dualism. The reaction after the war may be in the direction of increasing all the former antagonisms. To attain a strong morale and unity in times less dramatic than those of war is an educational problem, in a wide sense, but it is also a problem of the practical organization of all the social life.

All nation-wide affiliations of children which in any way cross-section classes or antagonistic interests of any kind tend to create materials out of which patriotic sentiment is made. The school itself has tended to produce social unity, but it has also tended to level downward, and also to mediate associations which do not touch upon the activities and interests and differences of society. Our schools are democratic by default of social interest in them, so to speak. We need organizations that shall level upward and to a greater extent involve the home. Then we shall see how democratic and how unified our social life really is. These organizations must be both democratic and practical. They must engage the interests of all classes. We know little as yet about the potential power, both for practical accomplishment and for the building of a higher type of loyalty and patriotism, there may be in wide organization. Here we can best combine the initiative and spirit that usually come from the upper classes with the great powers of achieving aggregate results inherent in the people as a whole. If we are to have a nation which shall be a unit, the people as a whole must have practical interests that require daily exertion and attention. They must be not merely united in spirit as a people, but united in common tasks that are definite and real. Devotion to the functions of the people is loyalty to the nation. This we should say is but an elaboration of the old colonial spirit of coöperation, when merely living in a community meant a certain daily service to all the community. We must continue to do now more consciously and with more technique, so to speak, what was once done more spontaneously and in a more primitive way. It is thus that the idea of neighbor might extend throughout the country as a whole. All the materials are at hand for an unlimited development of the practical life. *The sense of solidarity and the comradeship and helpfulness that grow naturally in a small community, where conditions are hard and dangers imminent, we must still maintain in a great nation by organization.* This is at heart an educational problem. It is a work of national character building. It is training in patriotism.

In this, as in all other phases of education now, we must consider how the great energies hidden in the æsthetic experiences can be put to use. The æsthetic, especially in its dramatic form, is a power to be reckoned with. Interest, organization, moral obligation do not control or release all the energies contained in the social life. We need the high moods of dramatic situations to reach the most fundamental motives. The teacher must not only present ideas; he must generate power. And this is true of all efforts to employ for any end the interests of the people, old or young. The social life, if it is to be effective, must constantly be brought under the influence of dramatic stimuli. Dillon, a political writer, earnestly pleads for an extension and deepening of the sympathies of children, and says that patriotic sentiment must be engrafted upon the sensitive soul of the child. No one could refuse to admit this. The question, however, is of ways and means. In our view it is mainly through play, or better, art, that the soul of the child is thus made sensitive. A dramatic social life must be the main condition upon which we depend for thus extending and deepening the sympathies of the child.

Among these dramatic social effects we seek, the use of national holidays, all methods of symbolizing events, causes, or functions which are nationally significant are of course not to be ignored, but after all it is through practical activity made social and raised to dramatic expression or feeling, either by its own inherent idea and suggestive power, or by the addition of æsthetic elements, that loyalty to the greater group and its functions will best be educated. It is precisely the lack of these dramatic elements and these mass effects in the social life that now leaves the social sense in its national aspects weak, and allows the various dividing lines throughout society to make even the most necessary activities to a greater or less degree ineffectual.

The educational problem itself is plain. Unity of public interests, which can apparently now be obtained only under threat to national existence, must be maintained, not artificially, but voluntarily. We want the morale of war and the social solidarity of war in the times and activities of peace—in those activities that represent service to country and also those which consist of the service *of* country in the performance of its broader functions as a member of a family or society of nations.

A fourth factor in patriotism we recognize as loyalty to government, to state, or to leader. The place of such loyalty in a truly democratic country as contrasted with an autocratically governed country seems plain. It is not only sovereignty but statesmanship as well that must reside in the people. The people must not only have the power but the wisdom to rule. Even the ideals of the country must come out of the common life, or there at least be abundantly nourished. The German writers protest that the purely native ideals of the people do not represent the meaning and purpose of the State. The natural feelings of the people lack purpose and definiteness. The State is something very different from the sum of the people and the representation of their will. The native sense of solidarity is not at all like the organization that comes through the State. But this abstract conception of the State as a being different from the people is precisely, in the view of such writers as Dickinson, the cause of wars. Upon this point Dickinson sees now a wide parting of the ways. We must have either one kind of world or the other. We must continue our warlike habits, and make the God-state the object of our religion, or abandon all this for a thorough-going democracy. It is the special interest that is assumed to inhere in the God-state that is the menace to peace everywhere. The abstract theory of State inspires far-seeing policies, democracy lives more by its natural instincts and feelings. The theory of necessary expansion, the right to grow and to intrude, is a natural deduction from the conception of the God-state; loyalty to the State demands ever increasing lands and population in order to have more military power.

The democracy, of course, can harbor no such conception of State. Loyalty, in the democracy, must be to state and to statesmen rather as leaders of the people. The first and most necessary factor in patriotism as loyalty to authority is that authority *must* represent interests of country and people and must for that reason deserve loyalty. Educationally, the problem is quite the reverse of the educational problem of the autocracy. The people are not to be trained in obedience and subservience to the state, but we have mainly to create in the minds of all people the capacity to recognize true leaders. It is not loyalty to authority as such, we say, that is wanted, but loyalty to leader *who has no power at all except the power of the good and its forceful presentation*. A democracy is a society in which the aristocrats rule by persuasion, although we must think of this aristocracy as an aristocracy of intellect and morality rather than of birth and wealth. The ideal, we suppose, toward which our definition of democracy leads is a state in which authority as represented in the institutions of government, and leadership represented in natural superiority coincide. It is a State in which the good and the great shall govern. But in general, parliaments cannot now be the sources of moral and intellectual leadership of the people. They are subjected to too many conflicting interests. The time may come, we say, when authority and superiority will coincide, when laws will be made and executed by those who ought to do these things rather than by those who merely have the power to gain opportunity to do so. At any time and place we *may*, of course, behold great leadership combined with great authority. A true democracy is a state in which such coincidence will be inevitable.

The minds of men are now full of these themes. They ask how nations may become unified without injustice and autocracy. Trotter says that national unity is what is wanted most of all things now in England. England must become conscious of itself, he says, and infuse into public affairs a spirit that will carry leaders far beyond their own personal interests. England has survived until now in spite of a strong handicap of discord. He speaks of the imperfect morale of England, shown in the war, which arose from the preceding social discord, and shows that the only perfect morale is that which is based upon social unity in the nation. All this is true also of ourselves. We also have our problem of creating loyalty to government and a national unity upon which a perfect morale both for peace and for war may be assured, by inspiring an ideal of honor, honesty, and efficiency in all public service, and also by arousing an intense interest in public service and deep appreciation of what public service and leadership mean, on the part of all the people. This is plainly not merely a work of *cleaning politics*. It is a work of public education. The attitude of a people toward authority and leadership is something more than a *susceptibility* to leadership and influence. There is a desire for the experience of ecstatic social moods, the craving to be active and to be led. We make a great mistake if we think all that democracy means is an instinct of individual independence, a desire to take part in the government as an individual. It is also a social craving that is involved. The presence of the great leader, even in times of peace, stimulates social feeling, and raises it to a productive level. This social feeling, we say, is not a mere reaction. It is the expression of a desire and readiness on the part of the people to participate in social activities, and to attach themselves to worthy leaders, or to those now who appeal to the most dominant selective faculties.

It is precisely at this point that the educational problem comes into view. We are likely to think of the public education required in a democracy as too exclusively political education, education that will enable the individual to assert himself—to know, to criticize, to vote, to take an active part in politics. This spirit is especially prominent in English life. It is all very good in itself and necessary. But we need to educate ourselves also so that *we may have a capacity to be led, in the right di-*

rection. To increase sensitiveness to leadership, but also to make that sensitiveness selective of true values, is one of the great educational problems of a democracy.

It seems to be a part of the work of education to create popular heroes, to do upon a higher level what the public press does in its own way, but mainly partisanly and too often from wholly unworthy motives—make reputations. We must do more in the teaching of history and biography than to glorify the lives of dead heroes. We need to be quite as much concerned about coming heroes. We must excite the imagination of the young and prejudice the public mind through educational channels, in favor of sincere and true leaders. The opportunity of the story teller is large, in this work, and we need also to develop to a very high degree of excellence the educational newspaper. One of our great needs in education in this country is a daily newspaper for all schools—one that shall be both informing and influential, appealing by every art to the selective faculties, governed absolutely by ethical, or at least not by political and partisan motives. The power of such a press might be very great indeed. As an unifying influence and a ready means of communication, and an instrument of use in the organization of all children, the function of this press would be a highly important one.

All means of creating political ideals from within, of forging the links between leader and people in the plastic minds of children and youths, will be an education in one of the fundamental elements of patriotism. Such an education would be very different, however, from the state planned and authorized education that has been carried on under autocratic regimes. The difference is one of spirit and result, rather than of method. In one case the State becomes a kind of Nirvana, in the thought of which personality and individuality are negated. Patriotism produced in the minds of the young under the influence of a democratic spirit tends to become a creative force rather than a blind devotion to an accepted order. Institutions are made and advanced rather than merely obeyed and defended in this educational process. The widest scope and the freest opportunity are allowed for superior qualities of leaders and for right principles to have an effect upon society (and the result we invite indeed is a profound hero worship on the part of the young), but the conditions would be such that no other kind of authority would be able to exert a wide influence. To secure these conditions is, of course, one of the chief tasks of all the administrative branches of our educational service.

The final factor of patriotism, according to our analysis, is loyalty to country as an historical object. The ideas and the feelings centering about the conception of country as personal, as living, as having rights and experience, duties and individuality are likely to be vivid and intense. They are the inspirers of supreme devotion to country, and also at times, of morbid national pride and fanatical country-worship. The education of this idea of country we should suppose would be one of the fundamental problems of the development of patriotism. Presumably we are not to try to destroy this idea of country that all people seem to have, or to show it as one of the illusions of personification. Country is, of course, different from the mere sum of the people. It has continuity and it performs functions and it is an historic entity. Modernize and reform this idea, we must, but we cannot do away with it as something archaic and superstitious. Country is real, the concepts of honor and right belong to it, and country is something to which the mind must do homage.

Boutroux says that a nation is a *person,* and has a right to live and to have its personality recognized as its own. Granting this to be true, and that we must think of country as personal and active, the question arises whether this concept of country is something that *requires in any definite way educational interference.* We should say that if countries are essentially living historic entities having as such a high degree of reality, this reality-sense will be an important element in the practical life of peoples. There can be no thought in our historical era of breaking up these entities we call nations. It is a day of intensified rather than of diminished nationalism. The sense of reality of nations must, we might think, be made more intense; pride of country must remain; we may find some place even for the idea of the divine nature of country, which is an element in the patriotic spirit everywhere. That this conception of country is a very necessary element in the morale of a country in war seems clear; that the morale of peace must be founded upon the same personal and religious sentiments we can hardly doubt.

Ambition for country is a normal result of the acceptance of the idea of country as personal, and ambition for country appears to be the very essence of any patriotic sentiment that is sincere. Still ambition for country has been, in some of its forms, a cause of wars. What other conclusion can we come to, then, than that ambition for country must be subjected to radical educational influences? This is the reverse side of political progress. Ambition must be given new content and new direction. All the power and the sentiment of the old imperialistic motive must remain, but all peoples must now be educated to see that the maintenance of its position in the world on the part of any nation is now a far more difficult and far more complex task than ever before. The building of empire must be shown to have been far easier and far less heroic, and much less a test of the superiority of a nation than we have supposed. We can show that military virtues are much more nearly universal than has often been assumed, and that nations that are inherently superior must abandon voluntarily their ambitions of aggression, if they wish to remain superior and to have a place of honor in the world.

This implies no teaching of pure internationalism. We still recognize as fundamental the whole spirit of nationalism. Country must remain first after all. All must indeed learn to take in some way the statesman's point of view in regard to country—with its sense of the future, of wide relations and long periods of time, and its practical vision. It is futile to think of this future as one wholly without struggle and competition. We must teach history also far more with the forward view. History has dealt too exclusively even in America with the past. National ambition that has as its aim to realize, with independence and power, all the good that an enlightened nation contains, but at the same time to act with justice and with the thought of the nation as a part of a coördinated world must take this point of view.

It is a median course between merely naïve and day by day living, such as Lehmann (15) complains about as the natural tendency of uneducated patriotism, and the kind of program making that takes into account only the purposes of a single nation that we must follow in teaching this forward view of national history. There is a danger in either extreme. We may remain a nature people, without a true historic sense, and be conscious only of a dramatic past which appeals to sentiment and a still more ambiguously glorious future; or, on the other hand we may become too definitely ambitious and too conscious of some special mission in the world. A nation with a program, a nation that does not recognize the experimental nature of history, is a dangerous element in the society of nations, even though its ambitions be not purely selfish. Excessive rationalism in national consciousness is itself a menace. We must live by our historic sense, by some ideal of a future for our nation; the people must have *some* vision of a glorious future, and not be expected to see only an unending vista of problems and labors, but this history must be understood and taught intimately and appreciatively and not merely objectively and logically. We must take an interest in the careers of all nations, and understand history psychologically and be willing to judge it ethically. So far we have had the opposite view in most of our teaching and writing of history. We must take a fair and tolerant view of the power motive that exists in all nations, and try to understand what it means to be of another nationality and to have ambitions like our own. Without such an attitude, we should argue, no one can be truly patriotic, if patriotism means having at heart the true interests of one's own country.

It is not only possible and fair, therefore, but necessary that patriotism be enlightened. It is possible to be devoted each one first of all to his own country, to have few illusions about its values, and at the same time to have tolerance for all other nations. What other spirit is there, in fact, in which our history can now be taught? It seems absurd to say that such a spirit is weak. It implies consciousness of strength, of being able to hold one's own in a fair field, to have the dignity and sense of maturity that come from contact with a real world. With such a spirit it would not be necessary to accept as inevitable the brutality of all national development, to use the words of Mach, a recent writer. We need no longer believe that war is the only thing that can prevent national disintegration, as many maintain. National consciousness certainly makes progress even without such dramatic and tragic events as have recently taken place. Boutroux says that in France, after the Dreyfus affair, although strong nationalistic feeling was stirred, there was also a new vision of the destiny of the French people as not only defenders of their own country but as champions of the rights of all nationalities. German writers have not failed to notice this, and have been inclined to regard this spirit of France as a sign of degeneration and decay of the national life. We see now that generosity and justice are far from being evidences of weakness, and also that in the larger logic of history these weaknesses generate strength; at least they bring powerful friends in time of need.

Once Germany herself was affected by such ideals of history. In the time of Goethe, Cramb reminds us, mankind, culture and humanity were the great words. But upon this love of humanity and culture and love of the homeland a political spirit was engrafted, and this new spirit of Germany has manifestly now led to her downfall. No! there is no threat to national existence and no disloyalty to country in the form of internationalism that now is before us. As social consciousness widens and social relations become more intricate and more practical, national lines are not lost, but indeed become clearer. These national boundaries are not temporary or artificial or imaginary lines, for they represent and define activities and interests that engage the most fundamental and the most persistent of human motives.

It is in this spirit that loyalty to country as historic object should, we believe, be taught. This idea we teach of course through history, in part, but history alone in any ordinary sense, as we might think of it as a subject in the curriculum of a school, is not enough. These ideas must be made persuasive and dynamic. For this as we see over and over again, art is the true method. The object to be presented and which must inspire devotion is an ideal object. It is complex and it performs practical functions, but it is through and through such an object as appeals most deeply to the æsthetic feelings. The image of this object must be made impressive. Since the ideal of our country is more abstract than that of most countries, as an object still less vivid and less personal, since it lacks some of the means of appeal to the feelings that imperialistic countries have, there is all the more need of art to make the figure of ideal country stand out sharply before us. As we pass beyond the patriotism which is only a love of home, or a devotion to a political unit, to a patriotism that is a loyalty to a more abstract and more intangible idea, the art by which the idea of country is conveyed would, we should suppose, also become more abstract. Hocking says that it is through symbols that the mind best gropes its way to the realization of ideas. Feeling and imagery, we know, are very susceptible to the influences of the symbol, and also to the phrase which is a lower order of symbol. Dramatic representation, all pageantry, pictorial art, music, even the art of the poster artist and the cartoonist have a place in the work of portraying country as an ideal object, and inspiring devotion to it and its causes. A far-seeking educational policy will scorn none of these in its effort to crystallize the concept of country and give it power and reality.

Finally this idea of country must be put to work in every mind and in every life. Otherwise all education of patriotism will tend toward inevitable jingoism, and arouse all the violent and introverted feelings that have made history a long story of wars without end. This idea of country has been too aristocratic. It must now become accustomed to a life of daily toil, and not merely expend itself in enthusiasm and in self-sacrifice in crises such as war. Country as an idol of the aristocratic patriotism has always been too far removed from practical affairs. This patriotism has been too personal and too exclusive. Glory, honor and fame have played too large a part in it. On the other hand, the common idea of country needs to be made more vivid and more glorious. This spirit is accustomed to toil but not to have enthusiasm. It certainly needs more of art in its patriotism as well as in its daily life. We all need historical perspective. We must have through education what tradition has failed to give us. It is just by lacking the patriotism that a vivid sense of country as historic personage gives, by lacking imagination and the ability to detach themselves from the reality and the surroundings of the daily life that the working classes are so likely to be affected by influences that tend to break down *all* patriotism.

We shall have a true patriotism, we should say, only when country is an idea that is worked for by all classes; when it is an idea that is woven into the daily lives of the people; when it makes the daily toil lighter and touches it with glory, and when it enters into all the enthusiasm of the more favored classes and inspires it with the spirit of daily service.

CHAPTER VII

POLITICAL EDUCATION IN A DEMOCRACY

One of the results of the war has been to raise in the minds of all peoples, to an extraordinary degree, the most earnest questions about the nature and validity of government. The political sense of all peoples has been stimulated. We see on every hand new conceptions of government and demands for more and better government, but also the most radical criticism and the denial of all government. The determination in very fundamental ways of what government is, and must be, what ideas must prevail, what must be suppressed, what an ideal government is, if such an ideal can be formed, the question of evils inherent in the idea of government itself (if such evils there be), the laws of development of government in all their practical aspects—all these questions now come up for examination, and will not be repressed. If we do not take them at one level we must upon another. Naively or scientifically, philosophically or radically, the nature of government must be dealt with.

Government is now being examined, we all see, from points of view not hitherto taken. The conscientious objector raises the question of the ultimate basis of the right of the many to control the lives of individuals, and he asks especially whether there is any ground for the assumption that in this sphere, more than in any other, might makes right. Conscription, in fact, has driven us to consider the meaning of liberty and the foundations upon which the right to it rests. This stern fact of conscription, the realization that in a moment the most democratic governments in the world are capable of bringing to bear, quite constitutionally, absolute control over the most basic possessions of the individual, has led many to ask seriously whether government is after all a good in itself, or is merely a necessity having many attendant evils. They wish to know whether there is in the principle of government something that takes precedence over all the assumed rights of the individual. Does government, they inquire, have a *right* to the individual; or is it only in *serving* the individual that it is entitled to exercise authority that limits the individual?

These are questions, manifestly, that involve the whole foundation of sociology, but we need not be unduly dismayed at that. This is a time when naïve thinking and exact science must make compromises with one another. For better or for worse we must find some working hypothesis upon which a fair adjustment may be made in the practical life of the present moment. This *working hypothesis* must also serve—and perhaps that is after all its main function—as something to guide us, something having solidity upon which we can stand, in performing our work as educators.

What we need, what we believe all feel now the need of, is a conception of government satisfying to the multitude of common people. We wish to know whether we live for the state, we say, or whether the state lives for us. We wish to understand what the basic rights and duties of the individual are. As average individuals, willing to give service in any cause that seems good, we do not ask so much to have determined for us precisely what type of government best satisfies the requirements of science or philosophy, but what the best working basis for harmonious adjustment in the social life of the future is to be. These enquiring moods on the part of the people are a part of the temperament that has issued from the war. We shall make a mistake if we regard it as a mere passing effect, however; *it means a deep stirring of the political consciousness of people throughout the world.*

Significant differences may be observed in the general attitude toward government among the people in the great nations of the world. Each nation appears to have its own political temperament, and this quite apart from the views represented especially by political parties and the like, and quite independently of the scientific and philosophical conceptions of government and its functions of which there are a great number, and among them certainly no agreement upon the main issues and values.

Taking public opinion as a whole, Germany, England, France and America seem to represent distinctly different attitudes toward government. The State in the German philosophy of life, as every one is now aware, is all; the individual derives his reality and his value, so to speak, from the idea of the supreme state. Individuality and freedom in this philosophy of life do not refer to *political* individuality and freedom at all. In England, and perhaps to some extent in all democratic countries, the prevailing thought seems to be that the government that governs the least is, on the whole, the best government. The English government is supposed to be the servant of the people, and the individual has been in the habit of looking to the government for many services. The individual, free and self-determined, is the unit of value and of society, and the regulation of his conduct by government is at best a necessary evil. It came as a surprise to the Englishman when he realized that the state could command the most personal service and the most complete surrender of the property rights of the individual.

Le Bon says that the Frenchman, too, thinks of the state as something to be kept at a minimum and to a certain extent to be opposed. Opposition to the government is a part of the Frenchman's plan of life. Boutroux says the same—that in France the habit of thinking of the government and of society as two rivals has not been overcome.

Our own idea of government is certainly somewhat different from these. We are watchful of individual right, but we do not tend to think of government either as opponent or as servant. We do not ask the government to take care of us as individuals, and we do not feel in the public attitude the resistance to government that the French writers observe in France. The American expects on the whole to look out for his own interests and he has never felt the pressure and over-powering force of government—until perhaps now. Mabie says that the American has conceived of his government as existing to keep the house in order while the family lived its life freely, every individual following the bent of his own genius.

These temperamental attitudes toward government, we said, seem quite apart from scientific and philosophic conceptions of state. We see, however, something of the temperament reflected in the philosophies. Philosophers do not wholly detach themselves from the mores of their race. The monarchy of Germany, Munsterberg says, appeals to the *moral personality and the æsthetic imagination*. Its main function, however, is to safeguard the German people. Its faults are the faults of its virtues. Other German writers praise the German government especially for its efficiency, for its incomparable body of officials—indeed for its very clock-work perfection that Bergson hates in Prussian life. Lehmann goes so far as to say that the German state had reached the *perfect balance* between individualism and communism. These writers see plenty of self-realization in German society, and quite enough of participation, on the part of the individual, in the government. Schmoller (51) denies that Germany ever lacked the spirit of free institutions, and even compares Germany with ancient Attica, which he thinks was great not because of the rule of the *demos*, but because the people followed their aristocratic leaders. Troeltsch tries to show that the German idea of freedom is different from, and indeed superior to, that of all other peoples. The French, he says, rest their idea of freedom upon the doctrine of the equality of all citizens, but in reality lawyers and plutocrats prevail. The English idea of freedom comes from Puritanic ideas; the individual's independence of the state is based upon the idea of natural rights, and upon the theory of the creation of the state by the individual. But German freedom is something entirely different. Here freedom is in education, and in the spiritual content of individuality. German freedom is the freedom that comes from the spontaneous recognition of rights and duties. Parliaments are good in their place, but after all they are not the essence of freedom.

Totally different conceptions of state are easily found. Consider, for example, the views of Russell. Through every page of his book there shines the determined belief in the inalienable rights of the individual. Self-expression of the individual through creative activity is the basic value, or at least the fundamental means of realizing values. Russell sees nothing sacred or final in any form of existing government. He would like to see government expanded in some directions and contracted in others, for the functions of government cannot all be vested in one body or organization. For defense the nation is *not large enough*. For all civic government the nation is *too large*. In its internal control it treats the individual too ruthlessly. Wasteful and in large part even unnecessary, it antagonizes the free development of the individual. Government should cease its oppression, it should no longer support unnatural property rights, or interfere with the personal affairs of individuals. At the present time, however, we should not expect a radical cure for all the evils of government. If only we can find the right direction in which to make advance, we should be satisfied with something less perfect than an ideal.

The state in Russell's view, instead of being an ideal institution, is even harmful in many ways and terribly destructive. It promotes war. It makes the individual helpless, and crushes him with a sense of his unimportance. It abets the injustice of capitalism. It excludes citizens from any participation in foreign affairs. We must indeed not let this incubus of state overwhelm us. We must keep it in its proper place, even in performing its necessary functions, such as preserving public health. It is better to take some risk, even in such matters, than to override too much the individual's personal rights. All the functions of the state must be made to center more about the welfare of the individual, and in doing this the state must plainly regard as fundamental the right of the individual to free growth and the development of all his powers. We must learn to think more in terms of individual welfare and less in terms of national pride.

In syndicalism in some form Russell sees the most promise for reform of government. Some type of government at least which does not make the geographical unit the basis of everything must be the government of the future. This would lead in the end to a higher state than that based primarily upon law, for it would be a government in which free organization would be the first principle.

Plainly we are to-day in a time of flux in which ideas and institutions are unsettled, and there is a great variety of political theories of all kinds. We can hope to find no agreement among theorists and certainly no common ground for the reconciliation of conflicting parties. Still, even for the most practical daily life we must find some guiding principles. We must look for some means of bringing order out of the present diversity and conflict. Some valuation of government, some idea of the ultimate purpose of government ought to be agreed upon, if for no other reason that we may have some principle which will give us continuity in our educational work.

Consider the varieties of political creed now offered us, and there can be little doubt both of the difficulty and the necessity of finding guiding principles for the practical life and to preserve sanity of mind. The monarchical idea still lingers; there is a variety of conceptions of democracy, differing widely; there are socialists—state socialists, Marxian socialists of the old line, Bolshevists, regionalists, syndicalists, and others—and anarchists of pure blood. Of internal and party differences, policies, and plans there is no end. Through all these we have to thread our way, and reach what conclusions we can.

No American can of course be expected to see the question of government otherwise than through American eyes. He is to some extent prejudiced and bound to the ideas of liberty, individualism, and democracy, whatever his variety of party politics be. Democracy he may regard as an assumption, but it will seem now even more than ever a necessary assumption upon which to build a working conception of government.

We have to look somewhere in actual life for the elements and principles of government. Why should we not look for them in American life, where government has grown up comparatively free from traditions and prejudices and where it has been by all the ordinary tests *successful*? There has been something both ideal and generic in American life. Whatever personal equation may be involved in saying this, the point of view has some objective justification. It is a genetic method, at least. In early American life society was simple, and life was earnest, and we see government and the individual in their essential relations to one another.

In this primitive and yet modern society we see the individual as a collection of functions, so to speak, existing in a group. The individual also has various desires, which do not appear to be wholly in agreement with his social functions. Some of these desires of individuals are strongly antagonistic to society. In this society, government is plainly the means of protecting the individual or the group, by the suggestion or the exertion of lawful force, from the threat of lawless force. Law is a means of enabling and also compelling the individual *to perform the various functions which* belong to him as an individual or as a member of the group. To some extent the law also *aids* the individual in performing his functions. But this simple social order already shows certain basic disharmonies. It is an experimental regulation of the individual. Every restriction the individual helps to put upon other individuals by participating in or acquiescing in the establishment of government and law reacts to limit his own freedom, in ways which he cannot wholly predict. Freedom of the individual, even in the simplest social order, becomes greatly limited, if not necessarily, at least naturally—and indeed necessarily, since the only choice appears to be between lawful and lawless limitation of freedom. From the beginning, therefore, there can be no perfect satisfaction of individual desires or of either general or individual needs, in the ordered social life. Society as a whole regulates the conduct of the individual both by aiding and by inhibiting his activities, and must do so. In doing this, it is plain, it promotes all or most of the functions of the individual. Ordered society widens the total sphere of action of the individual. The individual left to himself tends to become an end-in-himself. Law makes him to a greater extent a means. In doing this it serves him and it also uses him, and there can never be any guarantee, in any individual case, of what the sum of these services and restraints shall be. Society uses the individual in part, but not exclusively, in his own service. The good and the evil, the necessity and the dilemma of all government are outgrowths of this primitive service of the social organization and this original disharmony among the wills of individuals and the will of the group to serve the individual and also at the same time certain general purposes which may not in any given case coincide with either the desire or the need of the individual. For this reason we conclude that there can be no *perfect* government. All government is experimental and exists by compromise.

What, then, in the most general way, can we say is the legitimate function or purpose of government? Hocking says that government is the means of assuring the individual that his achievements will be permanent. To this end it puts order into the structure of society. In our view something similar, but not identical with this, is true. We can say that in its complex forms it is in principle only what we found it to be in its primitive or simple forms. *Government is ideally a means of aiding all the functions of every individual. Functions,* let us observe and not primarily desires are served. These functions are such functions as the individual has as a member of every group to which he naturally belongs. Government, then, so to speak, has no standing of its own. Its proper function is to facilitate all other functions. Neither individuals nor governments have any rights as abstracted from the sum of functions which they essentially are.

If this be true, we can certainly define no one best and eternal type of government, any more than a fixed and perfect plan of life for an individual can be defined. Government might be supposed properly to change according to the functions which from time to time were most important for the society in question. Social life, under government, differs from a free and unorganized social life mainly in that a certain *objectivity* is acquired in regard to the functions of the individual. The individual becomes a creature of functions rather than of desires and needs. Common interests, or the interests of the group are served, we say; in doing this the individual is made to serve his own interests, perhaps, but the most outstanding fact is that in this organized life the *immediate desires of the individual are likely to be thwarted.* Regularity is put into conduct, and conduct is made to serve multiple and distant ends. The functions of the individual, left to the desire of the individual, will seldom be harmoniously performed. They will lack precisely objective consideration. But in the organized social life there will also be no perfect order and harmony, no final balance of functions. Everything is still relative and experimental. Government is a system in which any one individual at any moment may gain or may lose. But *on the whole*, under the good government, both more freedom for the individual and better conditions and better life for the individual will presumably be obtained than in any possible disordered or unorganized society. But government will really add nothing that does not already belong to the functions that naturally develop in any social group.

The actual functions of governments are, therefore, highly complex, because it is in some way involved in all the functions of the individuals themselves. Governments will be judged good or bad in two particulars: according to the completeness with which they include all the social functions, and as regards their efficiency in facilitating these functions. We must not make the mistake of judging a government merely by its form. Under the same constitution and holding the same ideals, there is room for widely different forms of activity on the part of the government, and great differences in efficiency and in the functions performed. The same functions may be performed and the same degree of efficiency reached apparently with different organizations. Cleveland shows, for example, how our own government might become much more efficient and make radical changes in the mechanism of the legislative and executive functions without sacrificing any principle we hold to, and perhaps without any change in our constitution.

It is this idea of the proper functions of government and the relative adequacy of existing governments to perform them that seems to be deeply questioned. Life has suddenly grown more complex. The individual is brought face to face with new demands upon him. He becomes, it may be, a member of new groups, having new functions. Government also, and correspondingly, expands. The question is not now of the efficiency of government in doing what it has hitherto undertaken; we wish to feel sure that government is adequate to meet the requirements of a rapidly changing social order. That just now is indeed a very vital question. Governments, we say, may be obliged to adapt themselves to entirely new tasks. Society assumes new external relations, and therefore we should expect that new organs would be needed for performing these new functions.

In all this we have been making *objective* valuations of government. An ideal or a definition of government in terms of its functions and the degree of efficiency in the performance of them might still, we ought to observe, leave a wide scope for preference in regard to forms, and other subjective valuations. Even between aristocratic and democratic forms, there may be still room for valid appreciations on æsthetic or moral grounds. Our objective valuations of government must in fact in various ways impinge upon fundamental questions in which no purely scientific considerations will be wholly decisive.

We can certainly find no precise way of valuing in detail or in their totality existing or proposed forms of government. Our most valid method, however, appears to be to refer at every step the functions of government back to the functions of the individuals who make up society. Every phase of legitimate government must thus go back to the individual, and his desires and functions. If we do this we shall see again why in national life we have the same kind of experimental problem that we have in the life of the individual. There can be no perfect adjustment among the acts of an individual, and no final valuation of them. There is no perfect balance between present use and future good, between individual and social values, between desires or needs and functions. The reason for this, we say, is that life is so complicated and made up of so many functions and of so many conflicting desires that it cannot be conducted according to any single principle or combination of principles. If we think of government as only a phase of the widest social living, and so as being through and through of the nature of the life of the individual, we ought to have the right point of view for all practical consideration of it. We must not expect consistency or perfection in government, and we can have no hope of passing absolute and final judgments upon it. Radical politics, in our present situation, must be regarded as one of our greatest dangers.

Democracy has become the "great idea of the age." It is our own fundamental principle, so we of all people ought to be able to understand and to defend it—and to *define it*. Yet many writers complain and more imply that the idea of democracy has never been very clear, and perhaps not even very sincere. Sumner says that democracy is one of the many words of ambiguous meaning that have played such a large part in politics. Democracy, he says, is not used as a parallel word to aristocracy, theocracy, autocracy, and the like, but is invoked as a power from some outside origin which brings into human affairs a peculiar inspiration and an energy of its own.

Democracy has apparently meant quite different things to different people. To some it is essentially a form of government in which control is represented as in the hands of the majority of the people. Some seem to have no further interest in democracy, if only they see that the democratic form in government is preserved and jealously guarded and the majority by its ballot rules. To some it is the aspect of democracy as individualism that has appealed most—freedom of the individual even from the restraint of law and custom—or again equality of opportunity. These perhaps think of freedom as a supreme value in itself. Some think of democracy more in terms of its internal conditions or its results. They think of freedom as a means of *accomplishing* good, not as merely *being* a good. They believe that the good of the individual is not necessarily represented by the satisfaction of his desires, and so perhaps think of the law and order of the democratic community, the control and regulation of the individual in his daily life by the will of all, as the essential feature of a democracy.

Here in America, taking our history and our life as a whole, it seems certain that the dominating mood has been the love of *individual freedom*. Our democracy is founded upon the idea of the *rights of the man*. But these rights and privileges of the man can be secured only by social organization that immediately takes away some of them. So our national life, just because of the strong individualism with which it began, also began with a firm principle of law and order modifying the idea of freedom. Some would say it began thus in a paradox or a delusion. Even to be morally free was not allowed. The group, in the Puritan society at least, exercised strict supervision over the moral life of the individual. Giddings says, in fact, that this experiment in moral control on the part of the people over all individuals is one of the chief characteristics of American life.

Our history is the story of an experiment in freedom, in which according to some we have more and more suppressed the individual. Grabo says that the history of democracy here is the story of a dream rather than an accomplishment. Such views, however, do not appear to be true representations of the case. They assume that the independence of the individual is more real or more realizable than it can be in any society. Is it not rather true that *our apparent relinquishment of the idea of freedom is the reverse side, so to speak, of the persistence throughout our history of an impossible ideal of independence of the individual*? It is individualism, rather than control, that has increased. The original freedom was a freedom such as comes from the willing participation of the individual in an order in which the control was immediate and vested in the whole. Control has become more definite and precise as the individual has become further removed from the direct influence of the social environment. We have developed relatively too much our original idea of independence, and from time to time elements have been added to our national life that represent an ideal of radical individualism, as for example Jacksonian democracy. Willingness to participate freely in the functions of society, and desire on the part of the individual to perform all his functions, have been relatively too slight. Even in politics it is not so much by the desire to participate in government that we have shown our democratic spirit as by the desire not to be individually governed. The old colonial spirit of coöperation and neighborliness with which we started has been (speaking relatively again) neglected. We have developed toward individualism and control rather than toward free association under leadership. We have lacked ability as individuals to see ourselves from the standpoint of the whole of society. Now, therefore, we are faced by the apparent still further decline of our principle of freedom, because we see that we may have *efficiency* only by increasing *authority*.

The question may fairly be asked whether we are not at a parting of the ways, when our democratic idea must be more clearly defined, and we must decide whether we shall change toward autocracy; or now, at the end of our stage of primitive democracy, enter upon a plane of higher democracy. Sumner says that always in a democracy it is a question what class shall rule, that the control in a democracy always tends to remain either in the hands of the upper class or the lower class, and that the great middle class, the seat of vast powers, is never organized to rule. Such conditions show, again, the effects of the individualism that prevails—national unity and the capacity for free organization without individual or special motives are wanting.

Cramb has stated a fundamental truth, from our point of view, in saying that hitherto *democracy has been more interested in its rights than in its duties*. It is very true that the *subjective state of freedom* has been the real attraction and appeal in our social life. It has brought to our shores vast numbers of people who would otherwise never have crossed the seas. Perhaps it has brought us too many, and those with too keen a love of freedom. At any rate, the question is now whether as a people we shall be able to take a more advanced view of the individual, a more functional view, so to speak, a new and enlarged conception of the meaning and place of the individual man in society. Democracy, in a word, must henceforth, certainly if it is to be a world state or order and not a condition of world-wide anarchy, go beyond the negative idea of *freedom, justice and equality*, to a more positive idea of service, in which we think of individuals as having more complex, more free and more internal relations among themselves.

In this idea of democracy, freedom is seen to mean first of all freedom to perform all the functions which belong to an individual as a part of a highly organized society. It does not include, however, freedom not to perform these functions. It is freedom to lead a normal life, in a word, not freedom to lead an abnormal life. Whether, in this democracy, the performance of these functions will be more or less under compulsion, whether the individual will voluntarily surrender certain *rights* assumed to be inherent in the principle of *freedom*, or whether these rights will be taken away by the show of force on the part of authority, seems to depend now mainly upon two things: whether in this society superior leadership will have an opportunity and be strong enough to exert deep influence upon the people; and whether, in general, such an educational program can be carried on as will make men susceptible to such leadership, capable of judging its values and able also to organize freely for the accomplishment of the purpose and functions of the social life. In such a democratic society as this, it is plain, the evils of individualism and also the evils of control will *tend* to disappear. Perfect identity of individual and social will we should not expect to be attained anywhere.

The evils of our present democratic society—the individualism, party politics and class rule—appear in sharp relief when we compare existing institutions and the present spirit with what is required in a true democracy. The old idea that the will of the majority must prevail is seen to be inadequate, if we mean by will of the majority the average or the sum of the desires and opinions of the majority. These do not necessarily represent the good, and indeed under existing conditions, they cannot. We want the will of the superior man to prevail, but to prevail not by force, but by the power of influence. The politicians talk about the soundness of the instincts of the people Something more than instinct is wanted in a democracy. Instincts are not progressive. Individualism, the pleasure of the moment, and mediocrity are represented too much by instincts and in every expression of the mere will of the majority. People in the mass are governed too much by impulse. Conduct and purpose are too discontinuous and fragmentary; or perhaps we had better say that the stimuli of the moment are too likely to control conduct. Whereas social life under the influence of the highest type of leadership is governed by more complex states of consciousness, by moods, which are more original and creative, and in which desires and impulses are no longer the controlling factors in conduct.

This view of democracy shows that democracy is something still to come. It is not an achieved social order or a well-founded doctrine that must merely be exploited and spread abroad over the world. Democracy is experimental civilization. We do not know whether it represents the ultimate good in government and society or not, and whether it is destined to continue and to prevail. That will depend, we suppose, upon what we make it. We have our evidences of history, but after all democracy is still based upon assumptions. It is an experimental order, we say, in which we try to realize many desires and to harmonize many functions. The final justification of democracy must be in the far future. It must be judged then by its fruits, rather than by rationally testing the validity of its principle. Thus far it is a working hypothesis.

The precise form which government in a democracy ought to take is, from our present point of view, of secondary importance. Democracy is a spirit, an idea, a social quality, first of all. A monarchial government, though it might be otherwise out of date, might be entirely democratic in spirit; and republics, we know, may be anything but democratic. Where control is in the hands of the people and not of a class, but of the people subject to the best leadership—a leadership that is based upon influence rather than upon any excess of authority or show of force, there is democracy, and of this, of course, the ballot itself is by no means the only test. But where thus far shall we find any democratic society that is so sound that it can offer itself as a model to the rest of the world?

Most of the political questions of the day appear to be relative and conditioned questions. The question of governmental control of industry is an example. This seems to be a question of expediency, and to be conditional upon local needs and the status of particular governments. It is certainly no fundamental question of the social order. Those who make socialism a supreme and universal principle also appear to be too radical. Sellars says that socialism is a democratic movement, the purpose of which is to secure an economic organization of society that will give a maximum of justice, liberty and efficiency. Drake, in "Democracy Made Safe," says that socialism implies equality everywhere; more than that, it means social, political, economic and legal equality throughout the earth. One cannot but feel that these enthusiastic writers are making the mistake of undertaking to do by political mutation, so to speak, that which can be accomplished, we may suppose, only by a slow process of experimentation in government, and the still slower but more certain method of education, in which all people are trained in fundamental social relations. Radical and venturesome change in so great and complex an organism as a great nation is now dangerous, because only a part of the conditions can be taken into account, and the result, therefore, must be conjectural.

Radical socialism that threatens to throw political power into the hands of a political class, or of any social or economic class, bolshevism which Dillon (speaking of Russia especially) says is doomed to failure because of its sheer economic impossibility, any plan which tends to concentrate authority in any class is threatening to our future. The democratic spirit must hold fast against the rising tide from the lower classes, just as it has been obliged to contend against autocracy. Democracy has on one side to assimilate aristocracy, and not overturn it. So it resists the rise of the proletariat, not to turn this force back, even if this were possible, but to control it. It is precisely because of the deep movement of the people—the world revelation and the world revolution, as Weyl calls it—that we must make all political institutions flexible and adjustible, and also throw into the balance all the powers of education and thus save democracy from itself.

These dangers to democracy are not to be taken too lightly. Democracy indeed faces two dangers. Hobson in "Democracy After the War" has stated one of them. He says that the war will result in no easy victory for democracy, for the system of caste and bureaucracy is very likely to become fixed. Democracy therefore must be worked for, and to that end there must be a union of all types of reformers. We must play off the special interests against one another, says Hobson, work for industrial democracy, educate the people. On the other hand there is that danger from the rising of the masses which Weyl heralds. This war underneath and after the war is as Weyl sees it, the war of the poor and exploited against all the exploiters. These elements are at heart antagonistic to government. Democracy, if all this be true, is neither well defined as an idea nor well established in the world. An unjust and privileged class above and an unwise and uneducated class beneath threaten it. But the case seems by no means hopeless. Indeed the remedies and the way of escape seem in a general way plain. Political changes on one side and political education on the other must become, we should suppose, the order of the day.

Of the actual political changes impending and those that ought to be advocated this is not the place to speak, except to say that they must by their nature be tentative and experimental. The radical mind is to-day one of the most dangerous elements in society, just because all the world over men are very ready to be influenced and are eager for change and are uncritical. Cleveland in an essay entitled *Can Democracy be Efficient?* exhibits a type of thinking about political questions that ought to appeal to all practical thinkers. It is his method rather than, in this connection, his conclusions that one should notice. Cleveland would study all countries with reference to the efficiency of their governments in fulfilling what seem to him to be the proper and essential functions of a government, working under our present conditions. Germany, France, England and America, he observes, have all adopted different ways of conducting the work of government. These essentials of government he reduces to five: 1) Strong executive leadership; 2) a well disciplined line organization; 3) a highly specialized staff organization; 4) adequate facilities for inquiry, criticism, and publicity by a responsible personnel independent of the executive; 5) means of effective control in the hands of the people and their representatives. Of these principles, Germany used only the first three, England left out the second and the third, France used all (but was late in seeing the need), America has left out all of them.

This is the type of thought, we suggest, that seems best adapted to meet present requirements for a practical theory of government. Analysis of the functions of government, critical examination of the needs of the present time, and a plan of modifying what already exists, rather than of making revolutionary changes, seem to be the right direction of progress.

If the source of power in the future is to be vested in the people, the education of the people with reference to their function as rulers will naturally be one of the most vital and permanent of the requirements of the social life. Dickinson says that the time has gone by for entrusting the destinies of nations to the wisdom of experts. If this be true, and popular opinion is to supersede the wisdom of the experts, if the people are really to have power, and be competent critics of good government, or merely to become good material in the hands of constructive statesmanship, education must include or be essentially *political education*. The people must be educated *for* democracy, but also made competent to *create* democracy.

Of course everything we do in the school, the intention of the school to represent what is best in civilization, and to be a center in which creative forces come together has some reference to education for the democratic life, but there are also more definite and more specifically political things to be taught. And yet, if what we have said before has any truth in it, it seems certain that no educational policy at the present time can include the teaching of specific political *doctrines*, or try to prejudice the minds of children or the people to any political creed. We are in a position in regard to political teaching very similar to that in which we stand about religion: we must not teach creed, but we may and must teach natural religion. We cannot teach politics as such, but we must teach natural democracy, or at least the fundamental social habits and functions.

There are two essential educational problems of democracy that have especial reference to the political aspects of it. The first is to teach universally in as practical a manner as possible the materials out of which political wisdom may be derived. We maintain that the lack of political education and experience is one of the most serious defects of the German people. These people are at first submissive to an extraordinary degree and then they become dangerously revolutionary. The lack of political competence is shown in both cases. We wish, of course, neither of these excesses in our own country. And yet we do have to cope at the present time with both a tendency to fanaticism, radicalism and intense partisanship, and with indifference and ignorance of the nature and purpose of our institutions and government. Both the indifference and the partisanship play into the hands of party politics, and no advantages gained by the balance of parties in opposition to one another can compensate for the loss of energy and the encouragement of inefficient service the system fosters.

To help offset these tendencies it must be possible to give to all youths, and of course we mean both sexes, through our educational system and otherwise an education in politics, and besides this some practical experience in public service in institutions and in organizations. This is a vital spot in education in a democracy; we have tried too much to reform or make progress in government from within the political system itself, and too little by going back to the ultimate sources of social life and educating the people as a whole with reference to playing their part in political life.

The work of education in the field of politics is not merely to give information, but to establish what we may best call *morale*. We need an attitude and spirit throughout the public life of the nation in which there shall be constantly displayed the same qualities which we see so quickly coming to light in time of war. Enthusiasm, seriousness of purpose, devotion of the individual to common purpose are the essential elements of this war spirit. To produce and sustain this in the activities of peace is an *educational* problem. The first task is presumably to establish the causes and the organizations through which they may be served, but *political education itself consists largely in the production of public spirit*. The correction of evils in the political system is of course but a small part of the work of political reform. Dowd says that it is the low personal idealism of mankind that creates our multitudinous social problems and strews the path of history with wreck and ruin. That is of course true. Raising the quality of the personal idealism of the people is the real work of political education. Political thought which is most concerned as it is now with securing advantage for party, class and individual must be superseded by a wider interest in government as a means of aiding the performance of the functions of the individual and the group. It is the purpose to be accomplished by government, not its form, and certainly not the interest of the few or of any class that must be emphasized, until partisan politics no longer dominates our political life. To accomplish this change means, we say, raising the quality of the personal idealism of the people. This may seem an ideal and impossible task, but we have some of our experiences of the war at least to give us encouragement.

If we wish to consider details, we may notice that in an educational process having such ends as we have suggested, the teaching of civics, for example, becomes more functional, the teaching of what an individual in a community and what all governments do, rather than analyzing the structure of government. Such civics teaches the meaning of individuals as having functions which are represented and fulfilled in the institutions and organizations of society, including every department of government. It is not the intention to enter here into the special problems in regard to the content and method of teaching civics in the schools, although it is evident that this subject must have an increased place in the future. We already see advances both in the purpose and the plan of civics teaching and in the literature prepared for the schools. Dunn, for example, makes fundamental in all the teaching of civics the question, What are the common interests which people in communities are seeking? Tufts also tries to deal with the fundamental ideas upon which government is based.

Presentation of facts is surely a necessary part of all education, for it is an indispensable means of giving the content of experience upon which wisdom as a selective appreciation of experience is based. But erudition is only a part of education. We must hold firmly now to the principle which is indeed an aspect of the democratic ideal itself, that participation is also a necessary part of education. Institutions become real to the child through the child's association with them in some active way. We shall probably see the idea of free organization carried far, and in every organization and every institution, private and public, there must, we believe, be some place for the services and the interest of all. Let us take the position that there is nothing in government, in any of its branches, that is outside the sphere of the practical life of the individual and we shall have the right point of view even for the work of the school room. Government, in a word, is not a specialization of function in which the few are involved, but it is a generic function, the means, we assert, of carrying to completion all the projects of individuals in all their social relations. Therefore all, not merely those who just now are included among voters, but all women and children, must have a part in the general education for democracy and also have a part in some way in the institutions of government. From first to last government must be thought of and understood in terms of what it does, as a phase of the total social life of the nation, not as something outside the social order. Government is a collective activity. It is as an aspect of the day's work of the nation, that government must be impressed upon all—both legal citizens and citizens in the making.

The second phase of the educational problem in regard to government is perhaps after all only the first in another form. If we hope to have a democratic civilization in any real sense anywhere, we must secure efficiency and superiority both in individual and in social conduct, not mainly by the exertion of authority (except as a temporary make-shift) but by making all the people of a nation susceptible to the influences of the best life and thought the nation contains. This means the voluntary and intentional development of leadership. This we have spoken of as a general need; it is also a phase of political education. The genius, the leader, must of course himself be produced in part by education. We must have such conditions as shall allow natural leadership to come to the surface, and every spark of genius must be carefully nourished. But there must be also opportunity for what the genius produces to work its effect upon all, as a stimulating and directing force, in turn arousing the creative activities of the people. Democracy seems to be wholly dependent upon what seems now the accident of genius for raising it above the mediocrity of the average, or even preventing a decline in its civilization. It is this idea of the relation of the best to the average that James evidently thought to be the fundamental point in education. Education consists in his view in the development of ability to recognize the good in every department of life, the ability to recognize all sham and inferiority and the habit of responding to and choosing the best. Applied to the problems of government, this means such a method of educating the young as will make all susceptible to and appreciative of the superior qualities of mind and character that may be exhibited in public life. Such responsiveness being itself creative and a powerful factor in producing and bringing to the front the superior man, it must be regarded as one of the most necessary and fundamental qualities of a democracy.

We might single out the teaching of history and biography as the best means of educating the appreciative powers in regard to values in human life, and the best means of facilitating the emergence of the best individuals and the best principles, and of making their influence powerful, but after all it is something more than any or all teaching that is required. Most fundamentally, no one can refuse to admit it is such an organization of the whole educational situation as will allow, or rather cause and encourage, precisely the total of the good and progressive life of the world to play upon the mood and the spirit of the school. Assuredly the school is not to-day so fortunately situated. It is too much removed from some influences and far too closely joined to others. Much of the good of society is walled out from the school by barriers that arise in politics, City ways, all the bad life of the streets, the trivial interests of the day, affect the school too much. We are greatly at fault in all this, because we do not take education as yet seriously enough. There must be now a decision. Either the school must be content to remain what it is now, a local institution performing a very limited service, or it must arise to quite new heights, and mean far more as a civilizing and creative force than it has thus far. The school must occupy more hours of the day and more days in the year. It must claim the child more completely. It must extend its influences further, and draw its life from a deeper soil. We certainly shall never allow the school to become a great evil in society, but it is almost as bad morally to leave it but a feeble good. Let no one speak any longer of good schools. Our schools were good for yesterday, perhaps. But of to-morrow's needs they are not yet even fully aware. The school has yet to learn with certainty to lay hold upon the fundamental things in the nature of the child, and to appreciate the child's real and greatest needs. Continuity and creativeness are still for the most part beyond the powers of the school.

But perhaps after all we are asking the impossible. Perhaps the forces needed cannot be brought to bear upon the child. Perhaps conditions are too unfavorable, and an educational situation cannot be devised that will be greatly superior to what we have already. Perhaps the time is too short. Perhaps worst of all the nature of the child himself is too trivial and unpromising. But if we believe this, we certainly at the same time conclude that democracy is a failure and is not in any true sense possible at all. Democracy cannot be created by forces from without, for this would be indeed a negation of its nature. Democracy is self-creative. It grows from within. But how can it grow from within unless the new life which enters into it be creative; and how can this life be creative and progressive unless it be so lived that it shall absorb all the good the old life has in it, and also be inspired to go beyond it in every possible way? Unless democracy is merely a product and natural direction of growth in society, democracy and education are not unrelated to one another. If democracy is a good that can be obtained only by conscious effort, we may suppose that one of the greatest factors in producing it will be education.

CHAPTER VIII

INDUSTRY AND EDUCATION

We have as yet no deep philosophy of industry. For better or for worse work came into the world as a result of desire. Men did not desire work, but they desired that which could be obtained only by work. These desires multiplied and the modern industrial world is the result. When material objects alone were desired, the motive of work was relatively simple; but as we pass from the desire for goods to the desire for wealth, and to the desire for wealth as a means of gaining power and prestige, the industrial movement becomes more complex. We go on and on, producing ever greater wealth and generating more and more power, and we do this we say with no deep purpose and with no philosophy of life. For the justification of it all, if it be under our control at all, we can only say that through industry we realize an abundant and enriched life.

The good and evil of work put upon us some of the most perplexing of our problems. Industry, we say, is the way to the rich and the abundant life. It makes life more complex. The relations of life are multiplied by it. It represents and it achieves man's conquest over nature. It puts force into his hands. It has its ideal side and its romance. It gives scope to pure motives of creativeness. But the industrial life has also its dark side. It has created the city with all its good and its evil. It has created great nations, but see what the added populations consist of. It brings on the old age of nations. It stands for struggle that is often fruitless and unproductive. It engenders moods and arouses interests and powers that lead to wars and revolutions. It fosters sordid interests, and has made almost universal the necessity of an excess of toil in order barely to live. The great majority of workers do not live in their work, because they produce nothing that is in itself satisfying. The spirit remains outside their daily life. Life is divided into a period of toil without deep interest and motive, and play which may be only a narcotic to kill the sense of monotony and fatigue. Individuals have specialized at the expense of a whole life. Men have been exploited and used like material things. Bergson says that by industry man has increased his physical capacities, but now it is likely that his soul will become mechanized rather than that his soul will become great like his new body. Industry, worst of all, has become an end in itself, rather than a means to higher ends. To live, on the one hand, to gain wealth on the other, men give all there is in them to toil.

We saw all this before the war, but one important result of the war has been that we now see that this industrial life which has so rapidly created new institutions, and which grips the world almost like a physical law, is not in all its ways so fixed and inevitable as we had perhaps thought. In regard to the industrial life, more than in any other department of life, we see new and radical thought, and the possibility of conscious effects, although it must be admitted that some of the proposed changes may well cause apprehension.

We had hoped, even before the war, to see industry and art become gradually more closely related, and to see industry become more socialized. Its physical hardships were to some extent already being ameliorated. We hoped to separate the great industrial interests from politics, and to curb the powers industry has that make it a trouble producer in the world. But now, after the war, we see possibilities of more fundamental changes in the industrial order than these improvements implied. Our thoughts now touch upon the whole theory of the industrial life. We see that by a coördinated effort and common understanding which it is no longer chimerical to hope for, the conditions of the industrial life might be very different. In the first place we are convinced that the world could produce vastly more and could use its products with far greater economy than now. We see that much greater return for less labor could be gained. Even the desires themselves upon which many of the evils of industrialism are based have shown themselves to be controllable. It is no longer idle to believe that the restraint and coöperation necessary to eliminate most of the poverty from the world are possible to be attained. The isolation of the individual worker, which has made his struggle so hard, seems about to be relieved to some extent at least. We even hope for permanently better relations between the capitalist and the laborer, and to see some of the evils of competition, even the industrial competition among nations, lessened.

Although the interest here is in the relations of industry to education, rather than in the practical changes pending in the industrial world, we must think of the two as related. Changes that take place in political and industrial conditions will be likely to be temporary and ineffectual unless they are supported by changes in the field of education. The reformer and the educator must work together.

Noyes says that the most fundamental change that has occurred during the war has been the world-wide assertion of public control of industry by the government. Perkins says that centralization is the order of the day, and that the government now properly takes on many functions that once belonged to the states, and that this process of centralization naturally extends to international relations. Smith speaks of the growing interdependence of government and industry which will especially give security to investment in productive enterprises. Hesse says that there must be national team work in all industries, and that in a democracy everything that autocracy can accomplish must be repeated, but upon a basis of voluntary coöperation. In France it has been proposed by Alfassa that there shall be established a department of national economy, to bring about a closer coöperation than there has been in the past among private interests, and to centralize industry. Wehle thinks that in America, even before the war, industrial concentration was leading to political concentration and that the states were losing their relative political importance. The grappling of states individually with large industrial problems is now, he says, at an end. Dillon has expressed the view that England ought to adopt industrial compulsion. Clementel, the French minister of commerce, thinks France ought to substitute for liberty without restraint in the industrial field, liberty organized and restricted.

There can be no doubt that the world is thoroughly awake to the need of more effectual coöperation in industry, and it is natural that the first thoughts should turn to government control as the simplest and readiest method of securing it. When we examine these suggestions about the coördination and centralization of industries it becomes evident that most writers have been strongly influenced by Germany's remarkable success, both in peace and war, under the system of governmental control of industries. The manner in which the German government turned all the country into one great industrial plant has appealed to the imagination, and many writers see in centralization under the control of government the means of curing most of the evils of industrialism. There are many proposals, all the way from the plan to introduce cabinet ministers with limited power to have oversight over industry to the total abolishment of the capitalistic system and all the rights of property. Many of course, while still believing in concentration and coöperation, cling to the system of private and individual ownership, and believe that the best results will be obtained in the end without any radical change in the relations between government and industry, and without resorting to any socialistic reform.

Another phase of the problem of industry in which we may expect to see great changes in the future concerns the status of labor and its relation to capital. The rising of the laboring class is certainly the greatest internal result of the war. Here again the question is whether the changes will take place by coöperation or by compulsion—either on the part of government or of some organized class. Will labor and capital continue to be antagonistic, or will they find common interest; or will the only solution be again some radical change involving change of government or abrogation entirely of our present system of ownership? That the position of labor has become stronger as a result of the war no one can doubt. Perkins says we are just entering upon a period of copartnership, when the tool-user will be part tool-owner, and capital and labor will share more equally in the profits. Increase in wages will not be the remedy, but only profit sharing. Others think the same; they see that the laborer's discontent is not all a protest against his hard physical conditions. He wants more social equality, more equality of status in the industrial world. He objects not so much to what the capitalist has as to what he is.

There has no more illuminating document come out of the war than the report on reconstruction made by a subcommittee of the British Labor Party. This report calls for a universal minimum wage; complete state insurance of the workers against unemployment; democratic control of industries; thorough participation by the workers in such control on the basis of common ownership of the means of production; equitable sharing of the proceeds by all who engage in production; state ownership of the nation's land; immediate nationalization of railroads, mines, electric power, canals, harbors, roads and telegraph; continued governmental control of shipping, woolen, leather, clothing, boots and shoes, milling, baking, butchering, and other industries; a system of taxation on incomes to pay off the national debt, without affecting the living of those who labor.

Although such a document as this could hardly up to the present time have been produced by American workmen, since here political doctrines of socialism have never obtained a strong hold upon the laboring classes, in England these radical demands are nothing surprising. They have the support at many points of so keen a thinker as Russell. Russell does not, it is true, believe that Marxian socialism is the solution of the problem of capital and labor, but he does believe in the state ownership of all land, that the state therefore should be the primary recipient of all rents, that a trade or industry must be recognized as a unity for the purposes of government, with some kind of home rule such as syndicalism aims at securing. Industrial democracy, as planned in the coöperative movement, or some form of syndicalism, appears to him to be the most promising line of advance.

That such demands and proposals as these are significant signs of the times can hardly be doubted. That from now the status of the workman will be changed and changed in directions more satisfactory to the workman we may accept as one of the chief results of the war. Politically the laborer is prepared to assert his independence. Both his social and his industrial status are likely to be improved. He will be better safeguarded against unemployment. Wages in the old form and the old tradition that the worker has no contract with his employer will, in all probability, be less generally acceptable. Work, if these new conditions are realized, will mean more to the worker. His own interests and the purposes of his work will be more harmoniously related. The individual made more secure in his work, protected more by law and participating more in the affairs of business and government, will have a sense of playing a more dignified part in the social economy. Conceal as we may the inferiority of the laborer's position under the pretenses of democracy and liberty and equality, this inferiority of position exists and the inequality that prevails in democratic society is certainly one of the fertile sources of evil in the world to-day. We have still to see to what extent the workman, his lot ameliorated in many ways, and his position changed, will himself become a new and different man, and thus make the world itself a different place in which to live. All that is thus suggested we have a right at least to hope for now. If it is also worked for with intelligence and good will, why should it not come to pass?

The third idea which is beginning to make great changes in the whole field of the industrial life and throughout all the practical life is the *idea of economy*. This means that in many ways questions of the values, the purposes, and the ways and means of what is done in the world are being sharply examined. Labor has been uncritical of its purposes, and lavish and wasteful of its energies, however watchful it may have been of its rights. Production has been governed too much by desire, too little by careful consideration of need. Distribution has been carelessly conducted, allowing large losses of time and material. Consumption has been quite as careless as the rest, and has been thoroughly selfish as well. The war has changed many of our ideas. Thrift has become a word with a new meaning. We see what industry at its worst might do in the world, and on the other hand what wise control of all the motives and processes that enter into labor and all the economic life might accomplish.

Some of these changes are coming from readjustment in the coördination of industrial processes themselves. We hear much of standardization and stabilization. An economic technique and the control of fluctuating conditions might do much to increase the efficiency of industry in every way. This idea of the application of scientific procedure to life we see extending to the control of the energies of the human factor. We have already spoken of guarantees that affect the spirit and the morale of labor. We hear of the prevention of unemployment, the removal of the bugbear of "losing the job." Most advance of all is being made in the application of the principles of mental and physical hygiene and of scientific management to the actual details of movement and the whole process of expenditure of energy, counting costs in terms of time and energy, in much the same way as all the items of value that enter into production are estimated. Some writers, for example Gilbreth, see in this movement a great advance. It is a way of giving equal opportunity to all. Economy becomes a factor in freedom, since it helps to eliminate the drudgery and depression of toil.

Plainly, then, economy or thrift has a much wider meaning than mere saving. It is many-sided, and the study of economy in the use of essentials is but a part of it. The war has, of course, emphasized this, and this idea of saving has served the purpose of awakening an interest in the whole theory and purpose of work. There is a better understanding of values, and of the difference between the essential and the unessential, and we see that not all labor that commands pay is useful labor. Many things that the public knew but little about before are becoming better understood. Industry, finance, business, taxes, transportation, have all to some extent become popular subjects. The present high cost of living raises questions in the theory of the economic aspect of life that have compelled the attention of the public. The theory of money, interest, savings, foreign investments, the place of gold in the world's economy is carried a step further and is popularly more extended. We hear all sorts of proposals about the production, the distribution and the consumption of goods, which are intended to make living easier and less expensive. Increased production of staples and more direct route from producer to consumer are urged upon all, and the economists have many suggestions for increasing our prosperity: while financiers try to direct to the best purpose our investments at home and abroad. Fisher attacks the whole theory of costs at what he believes its root, suggesting a plan of "stabilizing the dollar itself" by using the index numbers of standard articles as units of value, and regulating the weight of gold in the dollar according to the fluctuations of these. All these plans, hasty and narrowly conceived as many of them seem to be, are of interest and have value, for they indicate a serious determination to solve the fundamental problems of the practical life.

Any educational theory that could hope to deal adequately with the needs and the impending changes in the industrial situation of to-day must take into consideration the basic facts both of the individual and the social life. Teaching of industry and all attempts to teach vocation must be seen by all now to be but a small part of education with reference to the industrial life. We must do much more fundamental things than these. We must plan far ahead and seek to lay a firm foundation for the idea of coöperation which appears to be the leading thought of industrialism to-day. Every individual, we should say, ought to be educated in the fundamentals of labor, so that he may understand for himself what labor means. Finally the idea of thrift in all its implications must be made a part of the educational program. All this may seem too ideal and impracticable to think of in connection with industrial education, but if we consider industry and industrialism as the center of our whole civilization, as it appears to be now, what less ideal educational foundation will be sufficient as preparation for and control of the industrial life? No teaching of trades, we assert, will be enough. We shall need to apply, in industrial education or in an educational plan that takes industry into account, all the methods of teaching: those that employ industry itself, but also art, erudition, and play.

It is first with industrialism as a world condition that education is concerned. Industrialism has been, as all must recognize, too individualistic. It has motives and moods and products, and it grows in social conditions, that are full of danger for society. Industrialism lacks a soul, as Bergson would say. Yet it is a movement that sweeps on with almost irresistible force. Its most characteristic product is not what it turns out in shops, but city life itself. Many would agree with Russell in saying that all the great cities are centers of deterioration in the life of their nations. Education, then, must undertake to control industrialism. This does not mean, necessarily, that it must try to check it, but that the motives in individual and social life that produce industrialism must in some way be under the control of educational forces.

First of all it seems certain that no political arrangement, and no change taking place entirely within the industrial system itself, and no simple and direct educational procedure will give us control over the forces of industrialism. It is mainly by preventing the city spirit or mood from developing too fast and thus engulfing the children of the nation that we can introduce a conscious factor strong enough to hold industrial development within bounds. This means, we must earnestly demand, turning back the flow of life from country to city by educating all children in the environment of the country. This would have a double effect upon the industrialism of the day. *It would break up the present inevitable inheritance by the city child of all the ideals and moods of the city, and it would give opportunity for training in the activities that are basic to all industry, which alone, in our view, can give to industry a solid and normal foundation.* By such effects, in such a general way, upon the children of an industrial nation, we might reasonably hope to prevent the evil effects upon our national life from the fatigue, the routine, and the deadening of the spirit which even under improved conditions cannot be overcome in an industrial life that is left to its monotonous grind and its morbid excitements and exaggerations.

Another work that education must in the end do for the industrial life is to infuse into it an ideal and a purpose. Industry is too individualistic, we say. It works for a living, for power, from necessity. It lacks through and through as yet the spirit of free and intelligent coöperation for common and remote ends. Coöperation in the industrial world, we have seen reason to believe, is likely to be the great word of the future. It is precisely the work of education to make the future of industry an expression of free activity, to make it democratic, and to such an extent, we might hope, that socialism, whether as a governmental interference or as a class system, would not be necessary—or possible. In trying to give industrialism an ideal, we must presumably go back to elemental mental processes. We must, in the beginning, present the world's work dramatically to the child. We must give work interest, and it is certainly one of the chief purposes of that nondescript subject we call geography thus to give the child a deep appreciation of the world as a world of men and women engaged in work. We must show industry as a world-wide purpose, not as something essentially individual and competitive. We must show it as an adventure on the part of man in which he goes forth to seek conquest over the physical world; we must think of it as a means to an end, of fulfilling purposes not all of which perhaps can as yet be foreseen, but which certainly can be no mere satisfaction of the individual's desires of the day. This is what we mean by putting a soul into industry. Soul means purpose—purpose which includes more than the desires of the individual, and in which the interests of the world as a whole are involved. Industry that has thus a purpose, and that is imbued with a spirit of freedom takes its place among the psychic forces and becomes a part of the mechanism of mental evolution. It is this idealism of industry, toward the production of which we must turn every educational resource, that must offset its materialism. This is, in part, the work of the æsthetic experiences, the dramatic presentation of the day's work to the child; but art can of course work only upon the soil of experience; the child must see the world teeming with human activity, but he must observe it in a detached way, rather than as a participant in its realism and its dull and its unwholesome moods. Then we shall have a content upon which the æsthetic motives can work. In this idealized industrial experience, we try to make visible the real motives which in the future must dominate the world's work.

All this may seem too general and too ideal, but if we do not begin with broad plans, and if we do not take a far look ahead, we shall fail now at a vital point of the social development of man. The result at which we aim is *the socialisation of the motives of industry*. We make work voluntary by bringing into it persuasively and insidiously deep motives and interests which represent social purposes and ideals. Given these motives and the beginning of a change from the relatively more individualistic to the relatively more social spirit in industry, the actual means of coöperation would not be far to seek. Work would become by its own inner development under such conditions, something different from an unwilling service of the individual, a compulsory service to family or state. Everything we can do to give to children and to all workers an intelligent appreciation of the social meaning and purpose of work is both industrial training and an education in basic social relations. This socialization of the moods of work and the founding of them upon the necessary experiences, is as important as anything education is at the present time called upon to do. Given this foundation, precisely the form industrial education, in the ordinary sense, shall take, seems to be of secondary importance.

Turning now to another phase of the industrial problem on its educational side, one cannot escape the conviction that the rising tide of the powers of labor presents urgent problems to the educator. The common man, as we call him, is to take a greater part in the affairs of business and state, and the education of the common man with reference to the especial capacity, as worker, in which he seeks this new position, becomes highly important. This education of the people with specific reference to work is of course something more than teaching vocation. Education, indeed, with any explicit attention to labor itself, whether in its industrial or its political implications, is but a part of the educational problem. All education for the democratic life is involved in it. The whole problem of specialization comes up, and indeed all questions of social education in one form or another.

Specialization, in particular, can no longer be treated with the indifference that has so far characterized our industrial education. The ideal of fitting the boy for work is as naïve in one way as that of our generalized education is in another. *If the war has taught us anything beyond a doubt, it is that specialization must never be such a differentiation as shall infringe upon the common ground of human nature.* We must take this into consideration in all our vocational training. We must preserve an identity in all the fundamental experiences. In a democracy this appears to be wholly necessary, and to outweigh all considerations of efficiency. The individual must be kept whole and generic, so that each individual is an epitome, so to speak, of the virtues and the ideals of the nation. The humanity of the man must be first, and his special function secondary. This does not imply that we must not give to all children individual and vocational training. All must be directed towards life work. We may even carry vocational training further than it has been extended anywhere as yet, but we must see that industry occupies the right place in the school, and in all educational processes. It is neither the whole method and purpose of the school, nor something simply added to the curriculum. It is a phase of the life of the school, both in its active and its receptive states. The child must live in an atmosphere in which both present and future usefulness are assumed and provided for. The idea of a life of work must be made early an accepted plan of the child, and it must be one of the entirely general tasks of the school to see that the tendency of the child in the school is toward occupation. Occupation must in fact be made to grow naturally out of the life the child leads in the school.

All those disharmonies in our industrial countries such as the prevalent discord between working and capitalistic classes seem, we have said, to be social rather than economic in nature. Social education, then, is the main cure for them, if we wish to attack them at their root. The motives of pride and the sense of inferiority have to be dealt with in a practical manner. We sometimes quite overlook the importance of habitual moods or states of feeling in society and in the school. These moods are powers which motivate conduct. Any form of education in which the poorer and less favored are given an opportunity to acquire the experiences, and through these the moods, that especially distinguish the more favored class, strikes at the general disparity in society which takes form in such antagonisms as that between capital and labor. It is not difference in degree but difference in kind of experience that appears to separate the classes from one another. The difference seems to lie in those parts of life which are sometimes believed to be the unessentials and which indeed our whole educational policy assumes apparently to be trivial. *The fundamental differences between the poor and the rich, the favored and the common people, is in the sphere of the æsthetic.* Distinction of manner and an environment rich in æsthetic qualities are the main advantages of the few, as compared with the many. Social experience is what is most needed by the many, but of course this experience can never be gained by making the educational institutions merely democratic, and especially social experience cannot be gained in a school in which all situations are studiously avoided in which really significant social relations are likely to be experienced. We gain no social experience in the naïve and the highly special activities of the school which for the most part is arranged in such a way as to exclude organized social relations. This is a process in which such leveling as there is tends to be downward, whereas what we need is for all the truly aristocratic elements in our national life to have an opportunity to propagate themselves and to extend to the many. Leaving aside the need of a differently organized social life in the school, we might say that there is hardly a greater need in democratic countries now than that of recruiting the rank and file of teachers from a socially superior class. These socially favored individuals have given themselves loyally to the service of country in a time of war, for two if no more of their deepest motives have been appealed to—the dramatic interest and the spirit of *noblesse oblige*. There are duties in times of peace which are quite as important, but which as yet appeal to no strong motive, and have not even been presented in the form of obligation. Once these common tasks were made to appear a part of the fulfillment of duty to country, the way to finding deep satisfaction in them might be opened. Social and dramatic elements would be introduced as a matter of course.

Another need throughout our whole effort to educate all in and for a life of work, one which has appealed to many writers in recent years, is the need of making all the experience of work more creative or more free and animated or joyous in mood. *This means, again, that in all industrial education the mood must be social and the form æsthetic or dramatic.* Social values must be felt through social activity, and the sense of worth in labor and of value of the product which is felt in the social mood must be enhanced by the dramatic form of the activity and the artistic quality of the product. This is also the condition for creative activity. Some writers apparently now see in this need of making the activity of all those who work more creative, more free and more joyous the crucial problem of education and of social adjustment. This is Russell's constant theme. Helen Marot in "Creative Industry" says that our problem is to develop an industrial system that shall stimulate and satisfy the native impulse for creative production. It is difficult to see how, by any other educational process than one which is essentially æsthetic and social, we can make much headway toward changing the conception of work from the now prevalent one of a means of making a living, more or less under compulsion, to that of a voluntary social act done both for its utility from the standpoint of the individual and also because of its social value, and performed to some extent, however humble the work, in the spirit of the creative artist.

For the adult generation that now works (and for how many generations to come we do not know), we cannot hope to make ideal conditions. Work will still be work, with its evil implications, as toil without complete inner satisfaction, and without sufficiently free motives. But the direction in which practical changes should be made seems clear. There must still be a lessening of the hours of routine labor, until there are perhaps no longer more than six or five devoted to vocation. The remainder of life is not for idleness but must be in part productive or the lessened hours of routine will not be possible. There must be possibility of both practical and recreational activities outside the regular day's work, as well as for educational work, all of these in part at least publicly provided for. This activity may serve many purposes and accomplish a variety of results. As educational it ought to open up new opportunities; it must fulfill the desire for creative activity; it must be a socializing power; it must lead to an appreciation of the nature and value of skill and efficiency; it must introduce all to the higher world of art and the intellectual life. Above all it must impress deeply the truth that growth in the normal life is never ended.

The third phase of industrial education which is to be emphasized now is the teaching of what we have called *thrift*. This idea of thrift, for pedagogical purposes, is equivalent to the broad principle that purposes in this world are achieved by the expenditure of force—by the control of energies which are not unlimited in amount as now controlled and which are subject to definite laws. Since objects which are to be secured by the expenditure of energy differ in value it is a part of this education in thrift, indeed an important and necessary part, to give to all such knowledge and powers of appreciation as will enable them to recognize that which is essential, and to give the essential and the unessential their proper places in the whole economy of life.

It will never be right of course to inspire a parsimonious spirit in regard either to goods or to energies. Life itself and all its energies must be given freely; material goods must not be evaluated too minutely. The miserly life is not what we wish to teach. Still there is a wise attitude toward all material things and toward all values which recognizes goods as means to ends, which places true values high and demands economy in the use of all things that must be conserved in order to attain them.

It must be a part of the work of physiology, which thus branches out into psychology, to teach to all the efficient use of human energies. These energies are the precious things in the world; they must be valued and respected as the source of all efficiency. The idea of economy of movement, from this standpoint, has an important place in all motor or industrial or manual training. Processes must be regarded as definite series of acts in which we may approach perfection. Technique in motor operations is not to be regarded lightly as a mere finish applied to useful acts. It is the expression of an ideal of efficiency and economy. Children recognize the value of technique in games; its wider and more practical application needs to be impressed.

In the same way knowledge of the precise values and uses of material things ought to be imparted. The war has had the effect of showing all of us the values of materials and the relations of materials to one another. It has given us a sense of the great powers of natural wealth, and also of its limitations and the weak points that exist now in our economy. The war has proved to us how closely related the things we use lavishly and wastefully may be to the most ideal possessions. It has shown that the production, the distribution and the use of wealth of all kinds are parts of the accomplishment of the main purposes of life and that all these things belong to the sphere of *duty;* and that no individual can escape obligations in regard to economy.

Education, therefore, must lay foundations both for an understanding of economy and for the practice of it. First of all, every individual, we may assume, ought to have some experience in the production of the elementary forms of material goods, and in the conversion of them into higher values and in their conservation. We looked carefully to some of these activities as a war measure. It is hardly less necessary in times of peace. We should teach these things, not simply because the practice of them is educational, but because the practice of them is useful, and is a necessary service, on the part of every individual, to the world. Adding to the world's store of goods and consciousness of the need of doing this directly or indirectly should be regarded as a fundamental duty and habit. To establish both the habit and the sense of duty, we may suppose, a stage is necessary in which the individual's contribution shall be direct and tangible. Hence the value of those educational activities that deal with foods and their conservation.

On a little higher plane, and in a little different way we can apply the same thoughts to the whole cycle of material things. The distribution of wealth is of course in part a technical and a theoretical problem. It is also a practical and a general one. All at least ought to be judges of the waste that now goes on in the industrial life because the "middleman" has occupied such a place of vantage in the economic order. In teaching occupation and in all preparation for vocation ought we not to take this into consideration? Occupations that are purely distributive and which involve a great waste of human energies and of materials have been unduly emphasized, at least by default of more positive preparation, by the school. Because they are easy and untechnical and have a little elegance about them, in some cases, they fit in very well with the generality and bookishness and detachment from real life that the school sometimes represents.

The occupations that are more creative, both in the field of material things and of ideas, have, relatively speaking, been neglected. Inventiveness especially seems to be a quality that we have supposed to be a gift of the gods, and we have given but little attention to producing it, or even giving it an opportunity to display itself. Have we not gained from the war new impressions both about the powers of the human mind in producing new thoughts and in controlling both material and psychic forces, and also about the necessity for developing originality and independence? Is it too much to expect now that greater ingenuity be displayed in education itself to the end of producing more originality? This is a hackneyed request to make of the school, but it seems certain that we do not succeed in obtaining through our educational processes the highest possible degree of productiveness of mind, as regards either quantity or quality. It is because indeed we seem to be very far from our limit in these respects, and because better results might perhaps so easily be gained that it seems necessary to make this plea so often. More activity, more art, greater enrichment of the mind, ought to have the desired result, especially if the environment of the school could be so changed that its moods would be more joyous and intense. These changes are at any rate demanded for so many other reasons that if they fail to make the intellect more productive, they will not be completely a failure.

Education in the use of wealth must now be regarded as a part of *moral* education. In America we have ignored the necessity of thrift, and the idea of thrift has certainly had no part in education. The proper use of everything we produce or own is a fundamental part of conduct, and it ought to be a persistent theme in education. We have now the interest and incentive that have come from the war, we say, for we have felt, if only remotely, what poverty means, and we have seen that no amount of natural wealth and no degree of civilization can wholly insure us against famine and disaster. We need throughout our national life now, again, something like the old New England conscience in the uses of things, applied in a different way, of course, and now made more effectual by our broader science. The encouragement of this spirit will perhaps make the difference in the end between having a world seriously engaged in progressive tasks with its material forces well in hand, and a world which in all its practical affairs, large and small, is operated according to the principle or the lack of principle of a *laissez faire* attitude throughout life. Saving in a good cause, and with a clear conscience and determined purpose, is one of the elements of the higher life and is far removed from miserliness. It is a principle of *adaptation of means to ends,* and that any school which trains this power is reaching fundamental principles of the practical life needs hardly to be said.

The higher uses and appreciation of wealth which we are wont to call plain living and high thinking, the moral idea of philanthropy, the æsthetic values and hygienic implications of the right kind of simplicity must not be omitted from the educational idea of thrift. To impart something of the spirit of restraint and generosity, and to make the child feel what living simply, and with definite purpose, and making means serve one's real ends in life imply, to teach the joys of the higher uses of common things, is no mean achievement. But can we indeed do these things which after all have their main virtue in being general and social, and a part of a program? All we can say is that if we are to have a better order, and if we think education has any place in it, economy in its broadest sense, but economy also as applied to the details of daily life must also have a place in it. It is both fatuous and insincere to talk about good things to come, and not be willing to pay the price in labor and in sacrifice necessary to obtain them honestly. Especially when the price of these things is in itself no demand for the sacrificing of any real good, but quite to the contrary is a summons to a more joyous life, we should be glad to pay it.

CHAPTER IX

NEW SOCIAL PROBLEMS

The social problems of education that have arisen because of our new world relations and new internal conditions in our own country are of course only special phases of social education as a whole, and social education cannot indeed be separated sharply from other educational questions. There are, however, new demands and new evidences, and new points of view from which we see social education (or better, education in its social aspects), in a somewhat new and different light, as compared with our ideas of the school in the days before the war. We have discussed some of these social problems. Now we must consider them both in their general significance, and also in their more specifically pedagogical aspects.

There appear to be two things that social education needs especially to do now: create and sustain a firmer unity at home—a wider and deeper loyalty on the part of the individual to all the causes and to all the groups to which he is attached; and to make our *world-consciousness* a more productive state of mind. It is perhaps because such educational proposals as these are generally left in the form of ideals and things hoped for in a distant future, and are not examined to see whether they may be made definite programs, and are legitimate demands to be made now, that we are likely to regard all suggestions of this nature as impracticable. And yet the production of *morale* at home and a social consciousness adequate for our new relations abroad seems to be a proper demand to make even upon the school. In part, of course, and perhaps largely, the need is first of all for practical relations, but we must consider educationally also the fundamental and creative factors of the psychic process itself which must in the end sustain the relations that we have established at such cost and shall now begin to elaborate as practical functions.

The greatest work of social education to-day is to infuse into all the social relations a new and more ardent spirit. It is the elevation of the social moods to a more productive level, we might say, that is wanted. Æsthetic elements, imagination, and the harmonizing of individual and social motives are needed. War has shown us the possibilities of exalted social moods; what we ought to do now is to consider how we may make our morale of peace equal in efficiency and in power to our war morale. This is in great part a problem of social education.

Every nation has its own especial social problems which must become educational problems, and be dealt with in some way according to the methods available in schools. In England the social questions seem to be more in mind and to be better understood than here. They are more conscious there of social disharmony and of living a socially divided life than we are. They have seen at close range the dangers of class interests and individual interests. Individualism, class distinction and party politics and the independence of labor came near proving the ruin of England. The Bishop of Oxford has expressed himself as believing that the blank stupid conservatism of his country, as he calls it, is really broken and that a new sense of service is actually dawning in all directions. Trotter says (and he too is thinking of England) that a very small amount of conscious and authoritative direction, a little sacrifice of privilege, a slight relaxation in the vast inhumanity of the social machine might at the right moment have made a profound effect in the national spirit. Generalizing, and now thinking of social phenomena in terms of the psychology of the herd, he says that the trouble in modern society is that capacity for individual reaction—that is for making different reactions to the same stimulus—has far outstripped the capacity for intercommunication. Society has grown in complexity and strength, but it has also grown in disorder.

Such disharmony of the social life of course exists also in America. We have not the sharp division of classes and interests and the demonstrative and protesting individualism that are to be found in England (our individual rights are taken more for granted perhaps) but for that very reason, it may well be, our disharmonies are all the more dangerous and difficult to overcome. The tension of the individual and the social will (using MacCurdy's expression) is great. We are highly individualistic in our mode of life, as is shown both in domestic and in public affairs. Specialization and an intense interest in occupations that bring individual distinction and large financial returns have certainly taken precedence over the more fundamental and common activities and interests.

It is these fundamental and common activities and interests and sympathies that ought to be the chief concern of social education, or perhaps we had better say that all our educational processes ought so to be socialized as to broaden sympathies and make activities common. Education must constantly strive to make the common background of our national life more firm and strong. More important to-day than any further education in the direction of specialization of life in America is the securing of a strong cohesion throughout society by means of common interests and moods. It is true that specialization carried out in some ideal way may provide just the conditions needed for the best social order, but this can be only in so far as individuals become specialized within the whole of society, so to speak, in which individuals continue to have a common life. Individuals as wholes must not be differentiated and left to find their own means of coördination and association, or be brought together artificially by law or convention. Specialization must be made the reverse side, as it were, of a social process in which at every point coördination is also provided for. At the present time, it is the latter rather than the former that is of most importance to us.

Social education in a democratic country must always be a matter of the greatest concern. In autocratic societies the cohesive force exists in traditions or can at any moment be generated executively. The autocratic country can be held together in spite of social antagonism. In a democracy this cannot be. We voluntarily accept some degree of incoördination and confusion for the sake of our ideals of freedom. We do not wish cohesion based upon any form of pessimism or fear—fear of enemies without or of powers within. To secure unity in our own national life we must work for it incessantly, and we ought to be willing to, for unity means so much to us. It is not cohesion at any price that we want, but voluntary and natural union, and to secure that we should not hesitate to make our educational institutions broad enough to include the education of the most fundamental relations of the individual to society. We want neither a "healthy egoism" nor a morbid self-denying spirit that is only a step removed from slavery—neither instinctive independence nor an artificial and enforced social organization. We must not be deceived either by a vague and false idea of liberty or by the equally vicious ideal of militarism with its superficiality of social relations and its pedagogical simplicity. Both these ideas represent social life on a low plane. Healthy individualism, even with its strong sense of tolerance and comradeship and its respect for law and order, is not the kind of social ideal that we should now cultivate, for it is too primitive a state to fit into our already complex social life, or to be a basis for the firm solidarity we need for the future. As for militarism, it may become a mere shell, giving the appearance of social unity when its bonds are mere shreds and the last drop of moral vitality has gone out of it.

Our need and problem are plain enough. We wish to develop social cohesion and unity upon a natural and permanent basis of social feeling expressed in, and in turn produced by, social organization, voluntarily entered into for practical and for ideal purposes. Such solidarity can neither be made nor unmade by external forces. We must form and sustain it by creating internal bonds. We live, in any great society, always over smoldering fires, however highly civilized the society, and we are always threatened with the eruption of volcanic forces. It is fatuous to ignore this, and to make a fool's paradise of our democracy. Our problem is to produce such a social life as shall keep us safe through all dangers—dangers from enemies without, and within, and underneath. A democracy, or indeed any society after all and at its best, contains the makings of the crowd and the mob. Organized as it is, it is always an order made of material units which *may* enter into disorder. Society is based upon social consciousness, upon the consciousness of kind, but it also has *collective force*. The crowd and the collective force are always contained in society. However far human nature is removed from its primitive form, the social order is always fragile. Mental operations that are not intelligent and are not emotional in the ordinary sense, but which consist, so to speak, of common factors among primitive feelings, may gain and for a time hold the ascendancy. Eruptions in the social consciousness are of the nature of morbid phenomena, and are rare and exceptional expressions of the collective life, but we are never free entirely from the menace of them. Social order, we say, is always fragile. We must not overlook that fact. It is this characteristic of the social life, the potentiality of mob spirit and the forces of primitive anger and fear, that lead some writers to think, wrongly we believe, that this is the psychological basis of wars in general. War comes out of the order of society. The higher ecstatic states and the ideals of man enter into them. These things we speak of are of the nature of disorder, or are only the order of pure momentum. But whatever the truth may be about the relation of instinct to war and however remote the dangers to ourselves from the forces which in society make for disorder, it is the work of social education to control, transform and utilize all social and collective forces, the primitive emotions and instincts, the moods of intoxication and all the higher ecstasies of the social life, and it is only, we suppose, by thus consciously and with premeditation controlling these forces that in any real sense we can "make democracy safe for the world."

It is the idea of society coördinated by intelligence and by common interests and moods that we must always hold before us. Trotter says that civilization has never brought a well-coördinated society, and that a gregarious unit consciously directed would be a new type of biological organism. If this be so, the time seems peculiarly ripe to make advance toward this better social solidarity. Both the promise and the need seem greatest in the great English speaking countries now. There is waiting, we may truly think, a larger sphere of life for all democratic countries. If it be conscious direction alone that can bring about the change, education has a long and a hard task before it, to make the democratic peoples capable of such conscious direction. This must come in part by the development of the idea of leadership, and by the production of all the conditions that make leadership possible. In part it must come by the clear perception of definite tasks to be performed by nations and by all organizations within nations—tasks which have all grown out of the relations existing within society. In part it means cultivating intelligent appreciation of social values, and developing in every possible way all the social powers.

What we appear to need most in our social education just now is a conception of what the individual is and what the social life is in terms of the desires and the functions they embody. These are the raw materials with which we work. We should then treat all our social problems in a somewhat different way from that in which they are mainly dealt with now. We should try especially to make harmony in society not by maneuvering so that we might have peace and good feeling for their own sakes, but by coordinating the functions which are expressed in the life of the individual and in all social relations. That is precisely what is not being done now, in our present stage of society, either in the life of the individual, or in the wider life of society. People live without deep continuity in their lives, and we are not conscious enough of the ideal relationships individuals should have with one another, in order to make the social life productive. In a word we do not sufficiently take account of the purposes to be achieved, but are too conscious of states of feeling. We do not yet appear to see all the possibilities contained in the social life, what voluntary unions are necessary, and what kind of community life must be developed before we can have a really democratic order.

We must not be content, certainly, with a merely superficial and external solidarity or the purely practical gregariousness of the shops or the artificial forms of the conventional social life. Society must more and more accomplish results by the social life. Coordination in the performance of a few obvious functions, and enthusiasm for a few partisan causes, will not be enough. Nor will such order as militarism represents suffice. Is it not plain, indeed, that democracy must rest upon deeper and far more complex coördinations than we have now, and that social feelings or moods must be made more creative? It is the desire to accomplish ends through social organization, rather than the desire to possess and enjoy, that must be made to dominate it. To effect such changes in the social life must be in great part the work of education.

Social education in our present time and conditions might very well be considered in terms of the antinomies which exist in society. These antinomies represent the obstacles to national unity. They stand for inhibitions which are expressed in feelings that are wholly unproductive. Each one of them is a measure of so much waste, so much failure and lack of momentum, so much disorder and disorganization. A program of social education, we say, might be based upon a consideration of these antinomies. It would consider mainly how the waste and obstruction of these conflicting purposes of the social life might be overcome by giving desires more harmonious and more positive direction. A complete account of social education from this standpoint would need to take notice of many disharmonies now very evident in our life as a nation. Among them would be found sectional antagonisms, party opposition, frictions of social classes and industrial classes, religious differences, disharmony between the sexes, racial antipathies. Some of these we have already touched upon briefly. Some others seem to require further mention in the present connection.

The lack of understanding and sympathy between lower and upper classes in society plays a larger part in democratic America than we are usually inclined to admit. There are divided interests, divergent mores, lack of unity and coördination in some of the most urgent duties because of the antagonism of classes and the lack of understanding, on the part of one, of the ways of another. Especially in civic life the unproductiveness of the situation is very apparent. What money and advantage on one side combined with willing hands on the other might do is left undone.

In part this antagonism of classes is merely the result of difference in manners. There are manners and forms that constitute a common bond among the members of a class everywhere. Ought we not to take advantage of this example and use the suggestion it offers for bridging over the differences that we complain of? We have seen during the war, also, how well common tasks can unite all classes. Does not our educational institution afford us opportunity to continue this advantage, and make common service lead more directly to understanding and appreciation, not for the sake of the sympathy alone, but because of all the practical consequences and the opportunities for the future that are thus opened up? We assume that social feeling may be created through social organization. Mabie says that America is distinguished by its capacities for forming helpful organizations. We must make the most of this habit, which presumably is derived from the neighborliness and comradeship of our original colonial life. We need many group causes, not artificially planned as trellises upon which to grow social feelings, but, first of all certainly, in order to accomplish those things that can be done effectively only socially.

The secret of harmony among classes is presumably not to allow any class to have vital interests which are exclusively its own, since to have an exclusive vital interest means of course to live defensively or to carry on offensive strategy. The chief interest of the great working class at the present time is plainly to secure a living, and it is the sense of isolation in this struggle which in part at least is the cause of many unfavorable conditions in our present social order. Ought not education to prepare the way for a different attitude in which all should become vitally interested in the economic problems of all? This does not mean an education directed toward enlarging the spirit of philanthropy; it means mainly organization to serve common purposes.

These social problems are very numerous. They are both national and local. Any city which will undertake to solve in its civic relations this problem of securing greater social unity in social causes will provide an object lesson which will be of the greatest value. It is in these local groups perhaps that some of the best experimental social work may be done. Here the educational and the political modes of attack can best be coördinated, results can be made most tangible, and the primitive and simple forms of solidarity most nearly realized. It is indeed by going back to these simpler forms of social life and seeking means of coordinating the group in fundamental activities that the greatest headway will be made in the solution of wider social problems.

Another of the disharmonies which social education must from now on undertake to control is the disharmony and the inequality of the sexes, not so much as this appears in the domestic life as in the broader relations of the social life. Brinton says that the ethnic psychologist has no sounder maxim than that uttered by Steinthal, that the position of women is the cardinal point of all social relations. Every one, of course, now recognizes the fact that the position of women is to-day in a transitional and experimental stage. Conflicting motives are at work, and on the part of neither sex do the highest motives seem to prevail, nor is there a full realization anywhere of the values that are at stake. Men are thinking of the question of the position of women too much from the standpoint of expediency, and are scrutinizing too closely the immediate future. Women perhaps are thinking too much just now of their *rights*. There is a decadent form of chivalry or at least a sexuality that perpetuates conventions and interests that on the whole seem to interfere with progress. Jealousy and in general the tense emotional relations between the sexes obscure larger issues. Thus misunderstanding or antagonism, or at least disharmony, prevails in relations in which there should be perfect harmony of ideals and purposes, and productive activities of the highest nature. The education of women, whether for the domestic life or for the life outside the home is plainly but a part of the educational problem. The sexes have different desires, and it is precisely the work of harmonizing these desires, and regulating and coordinating activities and functions, that is the most important part of social education in regard to the sexes.

It is not at all difficult to see what the basic need is. It is not so easy to find practical means of applying the remedy in the form of education, because the whole system of living of the sexes must in some way be affected. The generalized principle on the practical side seems clear. All classes or groups in society must learn to think and to act not in terms of and with reference to the desires of their class alone, but with regard to wider tasks and values that are not fully realized by the most natural and the conventional activities of the class. The question is not one of making a moral change—converting individuals or classes from a spirit of selfishness to that of altruism. What we need is an educational process and a social life in which the nature of the individual and of the class is revealed as social, as best represented and satisfied in situations in which both the individual and the wider social idea work together.

Practically, we should say, the problem of education of the sexes with reference to one another and to a wider social life consists first of all in actually educating them together not merely in juxtaposition but in relations of a practical character. The relations of the sexes have evidently been mainly domestic and emotional, or in cases where they are practical the position of women has been little better than servitude. Of social coördination there has been little. *Education of the sexes through situations in which the special abilities of each sex are brought into action*, doing for the wider social life what the natural and instinctive differentiation of activities has accomplished in its way for the domestic life seems to be the main principle now to be employed in the education of the sexes. Women must be made to see that the ideal of independence which is uppermost at the present time is only the mark of a transitional stage, and that coördination in which of course competition of various kinds cannot be entirely eliminated will be the final adjustment. We should have no fear of placing the sexes, in their educational situations, in positions where competition is necessary, since through competition fundamental desires may be brought to the surface and regulated. Provided we admit at all that a new social adjustment is needed between the sexes, we can hardly fail to see that it is primarily in a practical life lived together that both education for the new order will best be conducted and the new order itself realized.

The details of method of what we have called social education for democracy we can only suggest here and of course in a very imperfect and tentative way. All aspects of education and every department of the school are involved; and every available method employed in education must in some way be turned to the purpose of developing social relations. In a very general way we think of these specific processes of the school as methods of learning, methods of art, and methods of activity, although of course in reality there can be no such sharp separation of them as this might imply.

There must be some place in the school now for a subject which in a general way might be designated as social history. We must teach the whole story of the social life of our country in such a way as to reveal the motives of classes, parties, sections, and of all organizations, institutions and principles. Such teaching should have the effect of bringing to light the causes of the disharmonies of society, and it should also be a means of conveying the feelings and moods as well as the ideas that govern the conduct of all groups that make up our national life. We must teach *sympathetically* what the desires and intentions of all are, on the assumption that behind all conduct there are natural causes and essentially sound instincts. By showing the desires of groups in their relation to one another, their disharmony and their possible harmony, we indicate what society as a functioning whole may be, and we may say that it is the chief end to be gained by the intellectual treatment of the social life to make clear what the ideal of social unity for practical life is, and what the main obstacles are that now stand in the way of it. By this social history we do not mean, moreover, something abstruse and academic suited for the college alone. Wherever the social antagonism is experienced, at whatever age, there is the opportunity to begin to set the mind at work about it, and to prevent the formation of prejudice and resentment. These states of mind begin very early indeed, and they are hard to eradicate.

A very large part in the work of social education is played by methods of education that we may call æsthetic. This must mean not only the inclusion of the methods of art in presenting facts, but we must bring to bear all kinds of æsthetic influences upon the social life. Social life in which there is introduced the dramatic moment is one of the main objectives of all education. It is in the recreational life that some of the best conditions for the realization of social moods in dramatic or æsthetic form are obtained. In the recreational experience the social states must be made productive of social harmony, as they themselves tend to be. In these experiences the conflicting motives of the individual and society, and of individual with individual, and the opposing desires of the individual are harmonized by means of ideal experiences in which the desires are exploited. Since we here touch upon the whole theory of the æsthetic in its practical application, we cannot be very explicit and clear, but the main service of the æsthetic social life experienced typically in the form of recreational activities, ought to be plain. Recreation is a means of giving the common experience so much needed in democratic countries like our own—common feelings, common activities and interests. This store of common life, containing exalted social feelings, expressed in play and art—languages which all nationalities can understand—must constantly be increased. All institutions that control the leisure hours of the people must be made educational as means of raising the social life to a higher level and making it more harmonious and productive of common interests. It is indeed one of the functions of the recreational activities and institutions to create and sustain public morale.

In the recreational experiences under control of the school we have the opportunity to educate the deepest and most powerful of motives. Play and art we should suppose, therefore, ought to have a greater part and more serious recognition in the school. We cannot of course accomplish much merely by crowding more arts and plays and games into the curriculum. It is something larger and more transforming that is wanted. We need to make the school take a greater place in the life of the child; it must reach a deeper level of human nature, in which the motives of play and art lie, and there must be a broader exposure of all young life to those influences of the social life everywhere which contain our highest social ideals. The place of art and to some extent of play as the methods and the spirit of the school is to convey persuasively to the child this larger and better life in which we expect him to take part.

Neither erudition nor art nor both together can, of course, fulfill all the requirements for a social education suited to our present needs. It is presumably in the social life itself, in the form of a practical activity, that social education will in great part be gained. This educational social life, which is also practical, will, however, be one in which every opportunity is taken to show the social life in its historical perspective, and to make clear its purposes and meaning; and in which sympathetic moods and intense social states are realized by conducting this social life, so far as possible, so that it will be subjected to the influences of what we may call in a broad way *art*.

CHAPTER X

RELIGION AND EDUCATION AFTER THE WAR

The war, which has left no field of human interest untouched, has raised many questions about religion that must be dealt with in new ways—about its validity, its power, its future. The impression the whole experience of the war seems to convey is that religion has failed to be either a great creative force or a great restraining power, although to express this as a failure of religion may imply more than we have a right to expect of it. Religion did not cause the war, but it certainly did not prevent it. It had no power to make peace. Yet we see that now religion is needed more than ever, and that if the social life be not deeply infused with the religious spirit, and if we do not live as a world more in the religious spirit, something fundamental and necessary will be wanting which may be the most essential factor of progress and civilization. The war leaves us with the feeling, perhaps, that until now the world has had far too many religions and too little religion. There has been too much of creed and too little of deep and sustaining religious moods. Perhaps, as Russell says, we are to be convinced that religion has been too professional; there has been too much paid service, and too little voluntary service.

Such conclusions of course have in them all the reservation that personal reactions must have, but it is easy to believe that in the life of such a nation as our own, and indeed in the world, no practical unity will ever be permanently reached unless there be a firm basis in a common religious foundation. This we might say is made probable by the truth that religion is the most fundamental thing in life, and if there be no unity and common understanding in that sphere, there can be none in reality anywhere in life. Differences in creed mean little, except in so far as they conceal basic agreement and make artificial barriers; differences in the way of understanding and valuing the world mean everything. We want a common religious faith—common in the possession at least of the moods which make a harmonious social life possible, and of the spirit in which the world's work can, we may believe, alone be done.

Upon such grounds one might maintain that a very important part of the work of education everywhere is to teach now more *natural religion,* or rather perhaps *that the school must be everywhere conducted to a greater extent in the spirit of religion.* Then we might hope to see religion becoming actually a power in the social life, helping to transform the crude forces and purposes of the day into higher ones. With such a religious basis we might begin to see the working of God in history and in the world as a whole, and we should feel in the history of the world and in the world that is before us the presence of reality. Then we should have a common ground for the sympathy and understanding without which not even the most practical affairs can be conducted efficiently. That ideal in education, often expressed by the educator, which holds that the purpose of all teaching is to convey the meaning of the world to the child, to make the world live in epitome, so to speak, in the soul of every child, is religious and nothing else, and quite satisfies the demands of our present day.

If such a standpoint be the right one, certainly the ambition of any nation (or indeed of any group) to have a religion peculiar to itself and an outgrowth of its own culture is unfortunate, and indeed comes from the very essence of morbid nationalism. In such desires there is thinly veiled the hope that through religion the old claim of nations to the right to temporal supremacy may be vindicated. Lagarde, in about 1874, was probably the first to say that Germany must have a national religion, but during the war this hope has been expressed again and again—Germany must have a new religion, befitting a great independent people, and must no longer be dependent for its religion upon an old and inferior race. Whether this longing for a new religion has not been in reality a longing to be upheld again by the old pagan faith, which was a fitting cult for the nationalistic temper, with its ideal of force, may justly be asked. It is interesting to remember that in Japan also, in recent times, there has been a demand for a national religion that should unite all the creeds in one. That this idea of a national religion, as contrasted with an universal religion, is opposed to the spirit of Christianity is plain, and the claim that Germany has not been able to understand the key-note of Christianity, as it is revealed in humanity and justice, may therefore be said to have some foundation in truth.

Can we say that the work of education, in the religious life, is that of inculcating and extending Christianity? It might indeed so be interpreted, and with a liberal enough understanding of Christianity we should say that this is true. But after all, it is Christianity as the vehicle of certain fundamental religious moods and ideals that, from an educational point of view at least, is of the greatest concern. It is the optimistic mood, the ideal of justice and humanity, the recognition of the worth of the soul of the individual, the ideal of service—it is these qualities of Christianity rather than its specific doctrines that we must now emphasize in our wider social life, and such religion is natural religion, or philosophy or Christianity as we may choose to call it. Any experience, indeed, that fosters such moods and ideals has a place in religious education. Who can doubt that such religion must henceforth have a large place in the world? It will be the test in the end of the possibility of sincere internationalism. Unless we can have common religious moods we can have no universal morality that is founded upon secure feeling and principles, and unless we can include the whole world in our religion, we shall certainly not be able to include it in any sincere way in our politics.

No religion, finally, will be profound enough and have great enough power to be thus a support of a future world-consciousness unless it be a religion of feeling rather than primarily of ideas—*a religion in fact capable of inspiring ecstatic moods*. And this ecstasy of feeling can never in our modern world be a prevailing quality of the religious life unless religion be something that extends over all life and draws its power from all the energies and capacities of the psychic life. The religion of our new era, we may be sure, if it be in any real sense a religion of the world, will not be something apart from and above other experiences. It will be a secular religion and a democratic religion, a quality and spirit of life as a whole. Experience referred to what we believe is real and universal, and subjected sincerely to all the capacities and criteria of appreciation that we possess is religious experience. Religion, educationally considered, is a means of giving to life a sense of reality and of value. That spirit should pervade and inspire all we do in the work of education.

CHAPTER XI
HUMANISM

There has much been said during the war to the effect that the great struggle was essentially a conflict between the spirit of humanism and some principle or other which was conceived to be the opposite of humanism. Humanism is said to be opposed to rationalism, or to nationalism, or specialization, or paganism, or Germanism as a whole, humanism often being thought of as the spirit of Greek or Christian thought and philosophy.

There is truth, we should say, in these views. Humanism in a broad sense emerged from all the purposes of the war as the principle of the greater part of the world, as opposed to the idea of Germanism. This spirit of humanism, however, is no single motive or feeling. It is a complex mood, so to speak, and it is not to be regarded as strange that it has been felt and described in various ways, and that it is not yet clearly understood. *Humanism appears to be most deeply felt as the appreciation of the common and fundamental things in human nature.* It inclines toward the employment of feeling, or at least to subjective rather than to purely objective principles in the determination of fundamental values in life. Humanism includes an interest in personality, which is of course the most basic of the common possessions of man, and it is therefore interested in justice and in freedom. Humanism as thus an appreciation of fundamental values in life by feeling rather than by principle, belongs to the deeper currents of life, those that flow in the subconscious—it is close to instinct, to moods, and the religious and the aesthetic experiences.

The later German philosophy of life we might mention as a denial of much that humanism asserts. Here we see a doctrine of force, an ideal of life based upon the elevation of conscious will to its first principle. If we seek concrete contrasts to this anti-humanism we might mention our own national life, governed by an idea of free living, which has made possible the assimilation of many stocks, in a life in which common human nature is regarded as the supreme value. Extreme specialization, rational principles, objective standards are watchwords of the plan of life that is most opposed to humanism. In this life instincts and values determined by feelings are brought out into the clear light of consciousness and are there judged with reference to their fitness to serve ends determined by reason. It is all noonday glare in this rational consciousness. Collectivism is based upon coercion and upon calculation of the value of order in serving practical purposes, themselves determined by a theory of society, instead of upon social feeling or upon a natural process of assimilation of the different and the individual into a common life. Specialization also, in this philosophy, is a result of calculation rather than of a belief in the value of the individual, and is gained by the sacrifice of those experiences which, if we hold to the humanistic ideal, we regard as essential to the life of the individual and to society. This calculus of values extends, of course, into the field of international life. Here too conduct is based upon estimation of effects, freedom is relative to and subordinate to economic values. A theory of the state takes precedence over all subjective ethical principles, and there must be a disavowal of all native sentiments and judgments as regards justice which issue from an appreciation of the worth of personality and other fundamental human values and possessions; and all common human sentiments which would stand in the way of carrying out the decisions of reason and state-theory or any political policy must of course also be denied.

This contrast, however inadequate our analysis of the spirit of humanism and its opposite may be, will at least show that the idea of justice, which in the humanistic ideal grows directly out of the appreciation of the value of personality is the central practical principle of humanism, and it is exactly as an opponent of the idea of justice on the ground of its alleged weakness, that the rationalistic or the nationalistic philosophy is best conceived.

It is upon this question of justice that we must take our stand for or against humanism. If we are humanists we believe in the rights of individuals, whether men or nations, to their own life and independence, which they are entitled to preserve through all forms of social processes. Justice means recognition of the right of individuals to perform all their functions as individuals, and humanism is precisely an appreciation of the values of the individual as such a functioning whole. If we are humanists we believe that this principle of justice, and this feeling of justice ought to be cultivated and made world-wide. This is the ideal of equal rights to all human values. Hence it is the mortal enemy of all philosophies of life which place any principle above that of justice and its moral implications, Whether in the narrower or the wider social life. This is humanism.

There are various ways of interpreting humanism as a practical philosophy or principle of education. Burnet says, perhaps not very completely expressing what he means, that the humanistic ideal of education, as contrasted with the merely formal, is that the pupils should above all be led to feel the meaning and worth of what they are studying. We should say that the meaning of humanism in education is that *the child should understand and appreciate the meaning and worth of all human life*. This requires that education should so be conducted that the child may learn to see—rather to feel and appreciate—the inner rather than the merely external nature of all life that is presented to him, and in which he participates. Not language, but thought; not history, but experience, is his field. Justice depends wholly upon an ability to come upon reality in the realm of human nature. This implies not only intellectual penetration, but a form of sympathy which consists of putting oneself as completely as possible into the life of that which is studied.

All this means, it is plain, a power in the educational process, a spirit and a mood in all education which we have not yet in any very large measure attained. What is required is indeed that children should live more intimately with reality, so to speak, and that we should not be satisfied when they have merely learned about it. We shall not be content, however, with an educational process which, in fulfilling these requirements for more life, becomes merely *active*. Life must also be dramatic and intense and abundant. All the mental processes—the feelings, the intellectual functions and not the will alone must participate in this active life.

We shall soon see, no doubt, and in fact we are beginning already to see a renewed interest in all the arguments for and against a humanistic as opposed to a scientific culture and curriculum for our schools. It is the humanistic side from which, it is likely, we shall now hear the most pleas, for the war has ended, they say, in victory for humanity and for humanism—hence for the humanities. It is the Christian and the Græco-Roman civilization that has prevailed. Victorious France, whose culture is founded upon that of the Greek and the Roman, has vindicated the supreme value of that culture. On the other hand we hear that our present age has become an age of science. If science has been a factor in causing the war, science has also won it. If industrialism involved the world in disaster, the world will be saved by more and better work, more practical living, wider organization for the production of goods and of wealth. Therefore our curriculum must become more practical. We must have more of business and industry, more vocational training, more training that sharpens the intelligence.

There is a truth which cannot be overlooked in the claim of the humanists, but the acceptance of it as it stands as a philosophy of education is not without its serious dangers. What we may well apprehend is a reactionary philosophy of education, and of all culture. We begin to hear very strong pleas, for example, for a school in which language, literature, and perhaps history become the center. West[1] asks for a wider recognition of the humanities after the war. Moore[2] says that the war is a victory of the civilization finally established by the Romans on the basis of law, over the barbaric ideas of power. Seeing this he is led to plead for a closer union now between Latin and modern studies, binding civilization of to-day with the thought and feeling of old Rome. Butler[3] says that we are surely coming back to the classical languages and literature.

Such conclusions as these raise many questions and perhaps doubts and apprehension. The ideal they express of penetrating the heart of civilization and experiencing in the educational process the inner life rather than the outer form of life, must indeed appeal to all, and we should all as humanists agree that this ideal expresses what humanism means and is the center of a true philosophy of education—but whether this ideal can be realized by any school that clings to the old classical learning, even in spirit, is quite another matter. To-day, if ever, we need to go forward in education. Our spirit must be that of the searcher for new truth, and for a better life. The old will not satisfy us either as a model and ideal or as a method. No already accumulated culture material will be adequate for our new school.

Our schools of to-morrow, we should conclude, must still be inspired by the scientific spirit, but what we need is science humanised, and science in the service of moral principles. One may well ask whether it is not now the most opportune time to leave

[1] *Educational Review,* February, 1919.

[2] *Educational Review,* February, 1919.

[3] *Teachers College Record,* January, 1919.

our classical learning behind, and try to find a more adequate culture in which to convey the spirit of our new humanism. If we have won a victory for humanity, as we think, and have kept alive the Christian spirit by means of a meager culture, we need not still cling to that culture if we can find something better. Even if modern Germany has misused science and brought it to reproach, we need not be prejudiced against science. We need more science but we need to bring science into closer relation to the whole of human life. We need more of all the psychological sciences as an aid to our appreciation of history as the story and a revelation of the meaning of spirit in the world—and it is this way rather than through *language* that we must undertake to know and to explain life. On the other hand, it is for the business of practical, social living that the material sciences should have most significance in education. There is no science, not even mathematics, that cannot be taught as a phase of the adventure of spirit in the world, and none that cannot in some way be made to aid spirit in finding and keeping its true course in the future. Such use of all culture is what we mean by humanism. The secret of the difference in the educational ideals of those whom we may call the old humanists and the new is that to one education means predominantly *learning*, and to the other it means mainly *living*. Living, for the child, means growing into the life of the world by participating in spirit and in body, according to the child's needs and capacities, in the activities of the world. To gain a consciousness of the meaning of those activities through a knowledge of their history and by an appreciation of their purpose is indeed the main purpose of learning.

CHAPTER XII

AESTHETIC EXPERIENCE IN EDUCATION

Throughout this study we have again and again been led to consider the relations of the aesthetic experiences to the practical life. It is as the repository of deep desires and as the appreciation of values that the aesthetic may be most readily seen to be practical, but it performs other functions. As ecstatic experience it is the source of *power* in the conscious life, and it was indeed the belief in art as a means of attaining power that has given art its place in the world. The aesthetic experience is the form also in which desires are brought into relation to one another, harmonized and transformed, or transferred to new objects. So the aesthetic is the type of adaptation in the inner life.

We have asserted that all life, and certainly the educational process, must have its dramatic moments, since the dramatic experience, as ecstasy of the social life, is the expression of social feeling in its highest form. The aesthetic experience is the central point of experience, so to speak, at which social ideals impinge upon and influence and mold pure nature. Art is the form in which play, representing biological forces, is carried to a higher stage, and made a factor in conscious evolution. The aesthetic experience is a practical attitude in another way. It is by our aesthetic appreciation, more than we commonly understand, that we judge life as a totality, that we estimate the fitness of its parts to belong to the whole, and that indeed we guide life when we judge it not according to principles which so often are seen to be inadequate, but when we try to bring to bear our utmost of powers of appreciation and to find ultimate values.

Such a recognition of the relation of art or the aesthetic to life we see often expressed in the literature of the day. It is a sign of the times—of an effort to attain higher powers, to take more comprehensive views of life, and to gain deeper insight into it. It is a phase of the seriousness of purpose which the war has aroused in us. Dide speaks of a deep but obscure need that drives all human beings to put themselves in harmony with the universal, and says that this is the end and purpose of the aesthetic tendencies. This phase of the place of the aesthetic is seen and expressed in various ways. Some think of it as a significant change in the attitude of life which is to bring about an era of peace. Clutton-Brook, an English writer, says that unless we attain to some kind of beauty and art, we shall have no lasting peace. We shall never have freedom from war until we have a peace that is worth living. Some see in the humanistic spirit an essentially aesthetic principle. The fairness and justice of the French, the spirit of the English that expresses itself in their ideal of sportsmanship, some attribute to the aesthetic spirit.

All this is in keeping with our new experiences of life in all its dynamic expressions. It becomes easier for us to see the truth about the nature of the aesthetic and of all other powers of consciousness, since consciousness has revealed itself to us as itself so great a power. The aesthetic experience may no longer appear to be only a joy, something subjective, but, indeed, as a practical force in the world. The aesthetic is a feeling of power, but it is also an experience in which mental power is generated, and it must be employed to such an end. The aesthetic mood is a mood of happiness, but it is also a mood of persuasion, in which something is being done to the will, and in which desires are being turned continually toward new objects, and composite feelings are being formed which will direct the course of future experience. So art and the aesthetic experience are not things apart from life, but may even be thought of as the method and the quality of life in some of its most dynamic forms. They are not added to life as an ornament or a luxury, but are the spirit in which life is lived when it is indeed most productive.

When we make specific analyses of aesthetic experience we find represented in it all the deep motives and tendencies, of life. This gives us our clew to the practical application of the aesthetic in the business of life. All it contains, all the art and the play of the world must be put to work, although this is a conclusion that might readily be misunderstood. We do not expect to harness the powers of childhood to the world's tasks, or expect industry to become fine art, but we do expect art and play to be something more than passive and unproductive states. We expect them to sustain and to create the energies by which the world's work is to be carried on. We would utilize them to give more power to life at every point, and to make all activities of the practical life more free and creative. And was there ever a time when power was more greatly needed—in industry, in political life and in every phase of life both of the individual and of society?

But it is not only in creating and doing that the world needs art to-day, in the sense in which we mean to define it. An aroused world is called upon to feel to the depths of reality, and to draw from these depths new and more profound valuations. We stand at a point where many things in life must be tested and judged anew, where the danger of perverting and misjudging many things is great. It is by the powers of appreciation gained in dynamic states of consciousness, we may believe, rather than by discoveries and an accumulation of data that we shall be most certain of finding true values, and the way of extrication from our present grave doubts.

Can one hesitate to conclude, then, that in all our educational experiences, we must try not only to train these powers that we call aesthetic, but to give opportunity at every point for the exercise of them as selective functions, and as a means of creating and expressing power in the mental life?

CHAPTER XIII

MOODS AND EDUCATION: A REVIEW

In the philosophy of education it is with moods that in our view, we have most of all to deal. Man, we have a right to say, is a creature of *feeling*, not of instinct or of reason. It is not the instinct as a definite reaction to stimulus or as an inner necessity, nor emotion as a subjective response to this stimulus that is the driving force of conduct, but rather the more lasting and deeper and more complex states or processes that we can call by no other name than moods. Since it is in the moods that the most profound longing or tendency or desire is represented, we say that moods are the object of chief concern in a practical philosophy of life. These moods are the repositories, so to speak, of instinct, impulse, tendency, desire, and it is therefore by the control and education of moods that the individual in all his social and in all his personal aspects will be most fundamentally educable if he is educable at all.

It is as the seat of the will to power, we might say, that the moods which are the main sources of human energy are to be conceived. The craving for power, as a generalization of more primitive desires, comes to take the position of the main motive in life. The craving for power is a desire, as we see when we analyze it, that expresses itself as a longing for ecstatic or intense states of consciousness, and an abundant life. It is a craving to be possessed by strong desire and also for the satisfaction of many desires—often vicariously, since the objects desired may be confused and general. So this motive of power and the ecstatic states in which it is expressed or realized is no instinct and no pure emotion. It is an outgrowth and culmination of instincts, a fusion of them into a new product.

It would be going too far afield to try to summarize here the psychology of moods or of the motive of power in the individual and in society, but the main fact needed for the moment seems plain. In this motive and its expression in feeling and conduct there is a very general tendency which is the source of many forms of interest and enthusiasm, of ambition, of the spirit of war, of various kinds of excitement, and to some extent of morbid and criminal tendencies. The spirit of war we think of as a summation of the same forces as those which in other ways appear as the energies behind various enterprises having quite different objectives. War is an anachronism, we may believe, a wrong direction taken by the forces of the social life, an archaic expression now, let us say, of the will to power which might and ought to have different objectives. In the life and the mood of the great city we see a very varied expression of the motive of power. The city life is still a crude life. It satisfies deep desires, but in it desires for we know not what are aroused. It is indeed as the seat of eager, unsatisfied desire that the city is best of all characterized. These desires readily take shape in the city as the spirit of war and as a craving for excitement of various kinds.

These same forces re-directed or finding different objects and working under different conditions appear in moral, religious, or aesthetic forms. In these higher experiences and more progressive moments in history or in the life of the individual, the forces which at other levels emerge in different forms and in search of different objects we may think of as transformed, or given new direction; but to suppose them annihilated or suppressed is to misunderstand, according to our view, the whole process of the development of spirit. Life is not a process in which instincts are balanced, or in which good motives stand in sharp contrast to bad motives, or in which an original selfishness is opposed and gradually overcome by an altruistic motive. We think rather of very complex processes in which many desires, gathered into moods, find many forms of expression. There are prevailing moods—of war and of peace—and these moods are deep forces, containing both the desires and the sources of energy, so to speak, out of which our future will be made. The ecstatic states of the social life, the moods of war and the enthusiasm of the periods of rapid change are conditions in which energies and purposes are deeply stirred. These are the moods of *intoxication,* if we wish to describe them by pointing out one of their chief common characteristics. Peace is a *reverie,* we may say, in which the purposes and the results expressed and attained in the more dramatic moments are elaborated and fulfilled, and in which new impulse is gathered of which the dramatic moment is itself the expression. But throughout the whole course of history and through all the life of the individual, the same motives are at work. Life in its fundamental movements and motives, we should argue, is both simple and continuous. It is fragmentary and complex only on its surface.

The whole problem of the nature of education of course resolves itself, from this point of view, into the question whether progress is something inherent in nature, or is something controlled by man. Or if we cannot make so sharp a contrast between nature and will, shall we say that progress is in the main and in all essential ways one or the other? Does conscious effort, the having of ideals, exert any profound effect upon the history of spirit? Does it accelerate, give direction, provide energy? Is the course of history inevitable or is the making of it in our hands? We can see what, in a general way, so far as regards the transformation of the fundamental motives of life, the order of development has been—how the original and basic desires or instincts have become merged and confused in the more general desires and moods, how the motive of power has emerged, finding so varied expression as we see in the whole movement of art and play in the world, how out of these motives of art and play more controlled enthusiasms have arisen. But the part in this movement played by conscious direction does not thus far appear to have been great. A movement of and within consciousness it has been, and no mere biological or physical development, but when we speak of conscious will or any ideals controlling the course of spirit in essential ways, we find as yet only a beginning. And yet, this does not indicate that in the future conscious direction may not be even the greatest factor in evolution. It is difficult to see how we can *know* with certainty that we have such powers; but to refrain from acting as though we had is also difficult, and indeed impossible.

As a working hypothesis, at least, we seem to be allowed to assume that much will depend, in the future, upon the extent to which conscious factors are brought to bear upon the world's progress as a whole, upon the form in which the world-idea shapes itself, and the power which is put behind that world idea by the educational forces of the world. The world appears now to stand balanced at a critical moment, its future depending upon whether old ideals and primitive emotions shall prevail, or whether a new spirit which is perhaps after all but a sense of direction growing out of the old order shall become the dominating influences. Whether the consciousness of nations shall be creative and progressive seems to depend now upon the extent to which the whole life of feeling is influenced by ideas which, although they are products, as we say, of the primitive biological processes that underlie history, are also outside these processes, as definite purposes, desires, visions, ideals. At least we seem to depend now upon these superior influences for many things that we regard as good—for the rate at which we shall make progress, and for the certainty of making progress at all. Upon these conscious factors directing and shaping the plastic forces represented in the moods of our time, we shall assume, the course of history will depend.

We are no longer to be satisfied with *natural progress*. We have gone too far and too long, let us say, upon a rising tide of biological forces, and we have not yet realized what conscious evolution might mean. We have been too well satisfied with the physical resources and the psychic energies that seemed sufficient for the need of the day. A world in which democracy is going to prevail can no longer live in this way. It will not grow of itself in a state of nature. Its principle, on the other hand, forbids program-making after the manner of autocratic societies. Democracy, as the form in which the youthful and exuberant spirit of the world now makes ready for creating the next stage of civilization, will advance, we may suppose, neither by nature nor by force. It is the main work of our day to find for ourselves a new and better mode of shaping history, by bringing to bear upon all the social motives of the day the best and strongest influences. Our whole situation is from this point of view an educational problem. Probably there was never a greater need than that the democratic forces of the world now have great leadership. It is a practical world, a world of politics and of business, but it is also a world exceedingly sensitive to many influences, good and bad, a world in which, we may think, nothing great and permanent can be accomplished unless moral, religious and æsthetic influences prevail and give to our civilization its new dominant.

It will depend upon these conscious forces—upon our efforts to make progress and upon the clarity of our vision—it must depend upon these—whether in the future our great war shall be looked back upon as after all an upheaval of primitive forces and a debauch of instincts, or as the beginning of a new life. It is for us to create out of the war the foundation of a better order. We cannot go back to the old régime. Our enthusiasms will either be directed to better things, or the emotions aroused by the war will run riot and finally settle into habits on a low plane, and destroy, it may be, all that civilization has thus far gained. All things seem possible, in this critical time.

Stated in the broadest possible way, the educational problem of our times seems plain. We must lay hold upon and set to work for a higher civilization the motives and purposes that in the past have worked obstructively, and now destructively. A great work of our day is to understand these motives and forces that were the main factors in the cause of the war, and make them count for progress. That they are powerful forces we can have no doubt. They are not for that reason hard to direct, at least not necessarily so. We see that, whether in war or in peace, we need greater power in the social life. Life must be made to satisfy the longing for intensity and abundance of experience. But this abundant life that we now seek cannot be something merely subjective and emotional. To see this is indeed the crucial test. This subjective life cannot remain an ideal in a world determined to become democratic, to make progress, to be a practical and well-coördinated world. Abundant life must now be sought in the performance of functions which express themselves in practical aims and consequences. The prevailing mood and form of this life may still be dramatic, and indeed it must be dramatic. The possession of this quality is the test of its power.

Such views, of course, imply that our practical educational problem is something very different from that of finding an *outlet for emotions*. For example, to search for a substitute for war now is a superficial way of looking at the problem of the control and education of the social consciousness. We think of the motives that have caused the war, according to these older views, as bad instincts or evil emotions, as we are usually asked to think of the motives behind intemperance, and the habits of gambling and the like. By some form of katharsis we hope to drain off these emotions (unless we undertake merely to suppress them). This we say is a narrow view of the problem, merely because the motives that underlie the conduct we deplore are not *bad instincts,* or indeed instincts as such at all, but rather feelings or moods which are variable in their expression, complex, and educable. They have no definite object of which they are in search, so that we may think the only way to thwart them is to find some object closely resembling theirs which may surreptitiously be substituted for them. These motives are indeed broad and general. We must do with them what education must do all along the line, find the fundamental desires they contain and utilize the energies expressed in these desires in the performance of functions—these functions being the purposes most fundamentally at work in the social life or representing our social ideals.

Such an ideal of education invites us to work beneath the political and all formal, institutional and merely practical affairs and to lay our foundations in the depths of human nature. There we shall begin to establish or to lay hold upon continuity, and there bring together the fragments of purpose which we find in the life we seek to direct. This which one can so easily say in a sentence is, of course, the whole problem of education. These things are what we must work for in establishing and sustaining our democracy, for we must, to this end, make forces work together, instead of separately and antagonistically as they themselves tend to do. It is the same problem, at heart, in the education of the individual—to harmonize desires, and to create a higher synthesis of energies than nature itself will yield.

And in the new and wider field of international life that opens up before us, the problem is still educational. The educational forces of the world must begin now the gigantic task of national character building. The spirit of the nations, the divergent motives of power, of glory, of comfort and pleasure-seeking that are said to dominate nations, the justice, and loyalty, and steadfastness and truth which at least they put upon their banners and into their songs must be made to work together in a practical and progressive world, or to make such a world possible.

The Germans like to interpret the tricolor of their flag as signifying *Durch Nacht und Blut zur Licht*. But plainly the night and bloodshed do not always lead to light, and of themselves they cannot. Nor, must we think, need the world continue always to seek its way toward light only through the blackness and guilt of wars and revolutions. In some distant day, let us think, justice and morality will have been bred into all the social life, and life will be lived more in the spirit of art and religion. Then they will see that, under the influence of these forces we call now educational, an old order will have given way to a new by imperceptible degrees, and it will be no longer through darkness and bloodshed that the world must make its way to light, but need only go through light to greater light.

BIBLIOGRAPHY

The following list contains the titles of a few books and articles that have contributed data or suggestions to this study. It is neither complete nor systematic. Numbers in the text refer to this list.

1. A.W. Small, General Sociology.
2. C. Andler, Frightfulness in Theory and Practice.
3. W.E. Walling, The Sociologists and the War.
4. H. Hauser, Germany's Commercial Grip of the World.
5. J.F. O'Ryan and W.D.A. Anderson, The Modern Army in Action.
6. R. Dunn, Five Fronts.
7. Mrs. Henry Hobhouse, I Appeal Unto Cæsar.
8. F.H. Giddings, The Western Hemisphere in the World of To-morrow.
9. O.H. Kahn, Prussianized Germany.
10. C. Mitchell, Evolution, and the War.
11. A. Wehrmann, Deutsche Aufsaetze Ueber den Weltkrieg, etc.
12. J.P. Bang, Hurrah and Hallelujah.
13. E. Boutroux, Philosophy and the War.
14. M.A. Morrison, Sidelights on Germany.
15. R. Lehmann, Was Ist Deutsch? (In Vom kommenden Frieden.)
16. Durkheim, Germany Over All.
17. H. Bergson, The Meaning of the War.
18. J. Burnet, Higher Education and the War.
19. C.L. Drawbridge, The War and Religious Ideals.
20. M. Dide, Les Emotions et la Guerre.
21. D.G. Brinton, The Basis of Social Relations.
22. Ernesta R. Bullitt, An Uncensored Diary from the Central Empires.
23. Hundert Briefe Aus dem Felde.
24. Mrs. Denis O'Sullivan, Harry Butters "An American Citizen."
25. W. Irwin, Men, Women and War.
26. G. Roethe, Von Deutscher Art and Kultur.

27. J.W. Gerard, My Four Years in Germany.
28. W.R. Roberts, Patriotic Poetry: Greek and English.
29. Schmitz, Das Wirkliche Deutschland.
30. Redier, Comrades in Courage.
31. Igglesden, Out There.
32. Madame Lucy Hoesch-Ernst, Patriotismus und Patriotitis.
33. W.E. Ritter, War, Science and Civilization.
34. Hobhouse, The World in Conflict.
35. G.S. Fullerton, Germany of To-day.
36. A. Pinchot, War and the King Trust.
37. J.T. MacCurdy, The Psychology of War.
38. E.L. Fox, Behind the Scenes in Warring Germany.
39. J. Chapman, Deutschland Ueber Alles.
40. G. Blondel, Les Embarras de l'Allemagne.
41. P. Bigelow, The German Emperor and His Eastern Neighbors.
42. G. Le Bon, The Psychology of the Great War.
43. T.A. Cook, Kultur and Catastrophe.
44. Cheradame, The German Plot Unmasked.
45. J.B. Booth, The Gentle Cultured German.
46. J. Claes, The German Mole.
47. T.F.A. Smith, The Soul of Germany.
48. W.N. Willis, What Germany Wants.
49. Hintze, The Meaning of the War. (Modern Germany.)
50. Zitelmann, The War and International Law. (Modern Germany.)
51. Schmoller, Origin and Nature of German Institutions. (Modern Germany.)
52. Hintze, Germany and the World Powers. (Modern Germany.)
53. F. Meinecke, Kultur Policy of Power and Militarism. (Modern Germany.)
54. O.G. Villard, Germany Embattled.
55. E.J. Dillon, Ourselves and Germany.
56. R. MacFall, Germany at Bay.
57. C. Tower, Changing Germany.
58. W.R. Thayer, Germany vs. Civilization.
59. Lamprecht, What Is History?
60. B.T. Curtin, The Land of Deepening Shadows.
61. P. Bigelow, Prussian Memories.
62. E. Troeltsch, The Spirit of German Kultur. (Modern Germany.)

63. A. Guilland, Modern Germany and Her Historians.
64. T.F.A. Smith, What Germany Thinks.
65. Von Bülow, Imperial Germany.
66. J.A. Cramb, Germany and England.
67. G. Bourdon, The German Enigma.
68. P. Collier, Germany and Germans.
69. H.B. Swope, Inside the German Empire.
70. Sumner, Folkways.
71. J. Novicow, Les Luttes Entre Sociétes Humaines en Leur Phases Successives.
72. H. Gibson, A Journal from Our Legation in Belgium.
73. A.M. Pooley, Japan at the Cross-Roads.
74. F.J. Adkins, The War.
75. H.E. Powers, The Things Men Fight For.
76. J. M'Cabe, The Soul of Europe.
77. Scheler, Der Genius des Krieges und der Deutsche Krieg.
78. S. Freud, Reflections on War and Death.
79. Nicolai, Die Biologie des Krieges.
80. P. Gibbs, The Soul of the War.
81. T. Roosevelt, America and the World War.
82. W. Trotter, Instincts of the Herd in Peace and War.
83. J. Novicow, Der Krieg und Seine Angeblichen Wohltaten.
84. G.R.S. Taylor, The Psychology of the Great War.
85. W. Wundt, Die Nationen und Ihre Philosophie.
86. Nusbaum, Der Krieg im Lichte der Biologie.
87. Edith Wharton, Fighting France.
88. Crile, A Mechanistic View of War and Peace.
89. Eleanor M. Sidgwick, The Morality of Strife in Relation to the War. (The International Crisis.)
90. G. Murray, Herd Instinct and the War. (The International Crisis.)
91. Bosanquet, Patriotism in the Perfect State. (The International Crisis.)
92. A.G. Bradley, International Morality. (The International Crisis.)
93. L.P. Jacks, The Changing Mind of a Nation at War. (The International Crisis.)
94. G.F. Stout, War and Hatred. (The International Crisis.)
95. E. Mach, What Germany Wants.

96. F. Peil, Der Weltkrieg.
97. T. Veblen, The Nature of Peace.
98. Hirschfeld, Kriegsbiologisches.
99. H.A. Gibbons, The New Map of Europe.
100. F.C. Howe, Why War?

INDEX

Symbols

A

B

C

H

I

J

L

M

N

O

P

R

S

T

U

V

W

9 789361 389566

Printed by Libri Plureos GmbH in Hamburg,
Germany